Lex Orandi Series

The Sacrament of the Eucharist

Lex Orandi Series

John D. Laurance, S.J.
Editor

The Sacrament of the Eucharist

John D. Laurance, S.J.

LITURGICAL PRESS
Collegeville, Minnesota

www.litpress.org

Cover design by Greg Becker.

Cover illustration: Alberto Arnoldi (fl. 1351–64). Eucharist, Museo dell'Opera del Duomo, Florence, Italy. Scala/Art Resource, New York. Used with permission.

Excerpts from the English translation of *The Roman Missal* © 2010, International Commission on English in the Liturgy Corporation. All rights reserved.

Excerpts from documents of the Second Vatican Council are from *Vatican Council II: Volume 1, The Conciliar and Post Conciliar Documents*, by Austin Flannery, OP © 1996 (Costello Publishing Company, Inc.). Used with permission.

Scripture texts in this work are from the Revised Standard Version of the Bible, Catholic Edition, Copyright © 1965, 1966, Division of Christian Education of the National Council of the Churches of Christ in the United States of America; Ignatius Edition, Copyright © 2006, Division of Christian Education of the National Council of the Churches of Christ in the United States of America. Used by permission. All rights reserved.

1   2   3   4   5   6   7   8   9

Library of Congress Cataloging-in-Publication Data

Laurance, John D., 1938–
    The sacrament of the Eucharist / John D. Laurance.
      p.   cm. — (Lex orandi series)
    Includes bibliographical references and index.
    ISBN 978-0-8146-2518-7 — ISBN 978-0-8146-3530-8 (e-book)
      1. Lord's Supper—Catholic Church. I. Title.

  BX2215.3.L38   2012
  234'.163—dc23

                           2012024866

Contents

Preface to the *Lex Orandi* Series

T he theology of the seven sacraments prevalent in the Catholic Church through most of the second millennium interpreted those rites more as sacred objects to be *passively* received than as *active* participations in Christ's paschal mystery. And their meaning was to be derived, not from the shape of their liturgical celebration, but from the Church's official teaching, teaching typically occasioned by historical challenges to her faith. Whereas in patristic times Church writers expounded the theology of the sacraments from the rites themselves, with the later expansion of Christianity into central Europe, confidence waned that the form and enactment of the liturgy in any way *manifested* the Mystery it contained. As the *Adoro Te Devote*, a medieval hymn on the Church's use of bread in the Eucharistic Liturgy, puts it, "Seeing, tasting, touching are in Thee deceived."

In recent times, however, there has been a kind of "Copernican revolution" in sacramental theology. Not only have sacraments come to be understood as actions of God *and* the Church, the truth of the ancient adage, *lex orandi, lex credendi* (how the Church prays expresses what she believes), has also been seen in a new light. Theologians have come to realize that if all Church dogma is rooted ultimately in her faith-experience of God, so too must her understanding of the sacraments derive from her experience of their liturgical celebration. Sacraments, too, must *manifest* the Mystery they contain. Consequently, in the tradition of ancient mystagogies, "liturgical theology"—that is, God's word ("first theology") to the Church through her worship—has come to be understood, along with official Church teaching, as an indispensable source for sacramental theology. And sacramental theology itself has returned to its proper place within a larger "theology of liturgy." The works of theologians such as Guardini, Casel, Rahner, Schmemann, Kilmartin, and Chauvet mark various stages in this historical development.

Although much has been written on the role of the celebrating Church, up until now no set of studies on all seven sacraments that we know of has attempted to exegete their meaning primarily from their typical celebrations. The aim of this present series, then, is precisely to investigate the sacraments as liturgical events in order to discover in them the faith understanding of Christian life of which they are both the source and the summit (SC 10).

However, since the theology of liturgy is but one part of the whole of systematic theology, liturgical events can be adequately interpreted as witnesses to the Church's faith only in light of the other ways she experiences God's word. Accordingly, individual volumes in this series analyze typical experiences of the rites they cover against the background of the rest of the Church's traditional life and teaching, and they do so guided by the unique synthesis of that tradition that each author, as theologian, brings to the work. To do anything less would be to fail in the task of theology. On occasion, then, authors will offer their own critique, whether of the rites themselves or of how they have experienced their celebration, doing so on the basis of other theological sources as well (including, for example, the official instructions introducing each rite).

Sacraments as liturgical *events* are not understood by most theologians today as they once were, that is, as so-called moments of consecration (the "This is my Body"; the pouring of water "in the name of the Father . . ."; etc.). Rather, similar to how Aristotle's *Poetics* envisions Greek tragedies, sacraments are seen as events extended through time, having beginnings, middles, and ends. True, as protracted events they include indispensable high points, but separated off from the whole liturgical celebration, those key moments, at least in the short run, lose much of their intelligibility and intensity and, therefore, their efficacy as well (see SC 14). Accordingly, volumes in this series attempt to study each sacrament as it unfolds through its total performance, discerning especially its basic structure and how various elements contribute to its overall faith meaning.

The motivating purpose of this new series on the sacraments is ultimately a pastoral one: to help foster the fuller liturgical participation called for by Vatican II, and not necessarily to "break new ground" in sacramental theology. The readership envisioned by the series, therefore, is a broad one, not confined just to liturgical experts. Individual volumes presuppose only a beginner's familiarity with Christian theology, such as that possessed by university upper-level undergraduate or master's level students.

Finally, the rites studied in this series are those of the Roman Rite of the Catholic Church in use today. As valuable as a comparison of various Christian liturgies would be, no one series can do everything. At the same time, it is hoped that efforts made here toward understanding the Roman Rite might help inspire other, more explicitly ecumenical studies of Christian liturgy.

John D. Laurance, s.j.
Marquette University

Abbreviations

CCSL   Corpus Christianorum, Series Latina. Turnhout, Belgium: Brepols, 1953–.

CSEL   Corpus Scriptorum Ecclesiasticorum Latinorum. Vienna, 1866–.

DS   Heinrich Denzinger and Adolf Schönmetzer, SJ, eds., *Enchiridion Symbolorum Definitionum et Declarationum de Rebus Fidei et Morum.* Freiburg im Breisgau: Herder, 1963.

LA   Congregation for Divine Worship and the Discipline of the Sacraments, *Liturgiam Authenticam* (Fifth Instruction for the Right Implementation of the Constitution on the Sacred Liturgy of the Second Vatican Council), March 28, 2001.

PG   J. P. Migne, ed., Patrologia Graeca. Paris, 1857–66.

PL   J. P. Migne, ed., Patrologia Latina. Paris, 1978–90.

SC   Vatican II, *Sacrosanctum Concilium* (The Constitution on the Sacred Liturgy), December 4, 1963.

Introduction

It is not surprising that the Eucharist, as the church's ritual participation in Christ's saving life, death, and resurrection, has been a major topic of theological reflection throughout the centuries. So great a mystery could never be fully fathomed in this world where the objects of faith are seen only "through a glass darkly" (1 Cor 13:12; KJV) and where, as embodied, temporal creatures, we human beings live in ever-changing cultures that condition and contextualize eucharistic celebrations and their meanings.

At the same time, because the Eucharist is an intramundane phenomenon as well as the action of a transcendent God, its various aspects are open to study from a variety of disciplines, including the human sciences, and so data from these sources do make possible a better understanding of its mystery. Historical studies of the Eucharist's origins and development are of special importance since in order to understand any reality one must know why and how it originated, what choices along the way affected its present shape, and therefore what it is intended to be and achieve.[1] Nevertheless, the primary purpose of this book is neither to provide a fresh historical look at the Eucharist nor to analyze it against any kind of social science background, as valuable as either endeavor might be. It is rather to investigate how the *lex orandi* of a typical Sunday celebration of the Eucharist manifests the professed faith of the church, her *lex credendi*.

That the Catholic faith is the focus of this work arises not only from the fact that only one historical Christian rite of the Eucharist can be studied at a time, but also from the purpose of the *Lex Orandi* series as a whole—that is, to study the Roman Rite celebrations of all seven sacraments of the Catholic Church. So the particular rite under study here will be the most recent English-language translation of the *Novus Ordo* of Pope Paul VI.

1

As already noted in the preface to this *Lex Orandi* series, each analysis provided by individual volumes is guided by the unique synthesis of the Catholic tradition that its author as theologian brings to the work. The three initial chapters of this book, therefore, will present those theological understandings that the present author has found most helpful both for fully entering into the celebration of the Eucharist and for understanding the faith of the church it reveals. The second part of the book with its four chapters will then attempt to draw out, in light of that theological background, the faith meaning of the Roman Rite Sunday Eucharist from its typical celebration in a modern-day American parish.

With deep gratitude, I dedicate this volume to three beloved, wise, and extremely generous scholars who first guided me into the field of liturgical studies: Fr. Everett A. Diederich, SJ (1920–2011), Fr. Edward J. Kilmartin, SJ (1923–94), and Fr. Archimandrite Robert F. Taft, SJ. I wish also to acknowledge the debt I owe to my graduate students at Marquette University whose scholarly interaction has helped refine my theological thinking. My very special thanks go to Fr. David Coffey of Sydney, Australia, and Fr. Jeremy Driscoll, OSB, of Mount Angel, Oregon, and San Anselmo in Rome for their careful and painstaking reading of the manuscript in draft form and for offering extremely valuable suggestions along the way. I am also very grateful for the encouragement of my Jesuit brothers at Marquette University and at St. Louis University where I spent the fall of 2011 in order to complete this work. And last, but not least, my thanks go to my family for their unfailing love and support through the years.

Notes, Introduction

[1] "To know yourself means to know what you can do; and since no one knows what he can do before he has tried it, the only key to what the human being can do is what he has already done. Thus the value of history consists of the fact that it teaches us what the human being has done and with that what the human being is." My translation of a quotation of R. G. Collingwood made by Angelus A. Häussling, OSB, in "Die kritische Funktion der Liturgiewissenschaft," in *Liturgie und Gesellschaft*, ed. Hans-Bernhard Meyer, SJ (Innsbruck-Wien-München: Tyrolia Verlag, 1970), 109.

Part One

Theological Background

Chapter One

A Sacrament of Christ

The ancient Greek poet Homer begins both of his epic classics, *The Iliad* and *The Odyssey*, by asking the divine muse for help in recalling the trials of their respective heroes. In regard to Odysseus, king of Ithaca, who underwent a long, treacherous journey home after the destruction of Troy, the poet writes: "Speak to me, Muse, of a tossed-about hero beset by many evils when he burned the sacred stronghold of Troy. He saw the cities and knew the minds of many peoples; many, too, were the heartaches he suffered at sea as he sought to secure his own life and the safe return home of his comrades. Yet save them he did not, in spite of his yearning to do so."[1]

Although much of Homer's fame as a poet is undoubtedly due to the majesty of his dactylic hexameter and the fascinating adventures he relates, it is rooted also in how skillfully he celebrates the great beauty of being human, a beauty only heightened by the specter of death looming always in the background, the end to all human life both in this world and in the next. Thus, throughout the work humans are referred to as *brotoi*: mortals. Though famed for his resourcefulness, the great hero Odysseus is totally powerless against the inevitability of death: "Yet save them [his comrades] he did not, in spite of his strong desire to do so." As a result, Homer's readers, after accompanying Odysseus through all his travels, are left with the hollow realization that without someone to save humans from their own mortality, the deepest desires of their hearts for unending goodness, truth, beauty, and permanent loving relationships

5

will never be fulfilled. Without such a savior, humans are mere passing illusions, without lasting meaning or value, destined to flit about eternally in a shadowy underworld.

If the *lex orandi* of the Eucharist, then, has any real significance for the human heart, it will be necessary to show how through the church's eucharistic celebrations Jesus Christ as long-awaited Savior provides, both to ecclesial participants and through them to the rest of the human family, the eternal life and salvation that all "mortals" hunger for to the very core of their being.

In one of his sermons St. Leo the Great (440–61) makes a remarkable assertion that unearths the very foundations of liturgical theology: "What . . . was visible [in the life] of the Redeemer has passed over into the sacraments."[2] In this simple sentence he establishes the claim that what occurred almost two thousand years ago—universal salvation in Christ—continues to be present and active in every successive celebration of the church's Eucharist throughout history. Yet what in God's construction of a time-and-space world could make such a leap across history even possible? And if spatial and temporal barriers could be overcome as Leo seems to suggest, in what way might the *lived events* of Christ's historical life on earth continue on now in the form of the church's *ritual celebration* of the liturgy? Indeed, unless we deal with the underlying philosophical issues raised by Leo's assertion, it will be impossible to understand how the *lex orandi* of the church's Roman Rite Eucharist manifests her *lex credendi*, that is, how Christ's salvation as the object of the church's faith is both evident and at work in the church's liturgy.

The first three chapters of our study, then, deal with three background questions. Chapter 1: How is it even possible in the first place for Jesus within the course of a single lifetime to bring about universal salvation? Chapter 2: How is this salvation made available to us now through the church as Christ's Body in this world? Chapter 3: How, according to the traditional adage, is the church's pattern of praying, the *lex orandi*, related to her pattern of believing, the *lex credendi*? If these questions can be answered satisfactorily, it should be possible to discern how Christ in his saving mysteries is present and acting in a typical Sunday celebration of the Roman Rite Eucharist (chaps. 4–7).

In this first chapter, then, we address the question of how Jesus of Nazareth through the course of a single lifetime on earth was able to bring about the salvation of the whole human race. What is it about the nature he has in common with the rest of humanity that makes this work of salvation possible?

A Theology of Symbol

For the twentieth-century theologian Karl Rahner (1904–84), everything in this world exists only by expressing and manifesting itself in what it does.[3] In Rahner's theological vision all created, material beings are multiple in their constitution precisely in order to be single, to be what each is individually meant to be. That is to say, all created beings exist only to the degree that they *express themselves*, say themselves in the actions they perform—or, as Rahner puts it, in their "real symbols"—even if only in their seemingly static physical attributes, as rocks in their hardness, shape, and color, or the periodic elements in their specific weights and behaviors. In the words of the nineteenth-century poet Gerard Manley Hopkins, "Each mortal thing does one thing and the same: / Deals out that being indoors each one dwells; / Selves—goes itself; *myself* it speaks and spells, / Crying What I do is me: for that I came."[4]

In addition, human beings as spiritual realities grow in their specifically *human* nature to the degree they discover and possess themselves in their self-expressions. Although each one's unique personal identity is rooted, prior to all activities, in God's own love for him or her from all eternity (cf. Jer 1:5; Sir 49:7; Ps 139:13-15),[5] it is only in one's self-symbolizing activities that each becomes self-aware and thereby able to exist as a person in this world by giving oneself away both to God and to others in love and freedom.

At the same time, humans realize themselves in their actions not only through their own bodies but through other things as well. For example, Barbra Streisand sang to Neil Diamond some years ago that he doesn't bring her flowers or sing love songs to her anymore. Anyone who would ask why these wealthy celebrities do not simply buy their own flowers would of course be missing the whole point of the song. For what each persona in the song looks for from the other are neither flowers nor love songs *in themselves*, but only as self-gifts of each to the other in love. Saying that he does not bring her flowers or sing love songs to her anymore therefore means that he no longer gives himself to her *in and through* such things as flowers and love songs. The fact is that human beings are doing this same kind of thing in myriad ways throughout their lives. They are constantly employing the various resources of the world around them to communicate themselves both to God and to one another.

Jesus of Nazareth as human was no exception. Not only did he give himself back to the Father through his bodily self-offering on the cross, but at the Last Supper he also offered his full self to his disciples through the bread and wine of the paschal meal. And he instructed Christians throughout the centuries to do the same, to offer and share themselves with one another in memory of him through the bread and wine of the church's Eucharist (cf. 1 Cor 11:29). (Obviously, more will be said on this point later on in this study.) To be human, then, means to be constantly appropriating things of the earth as further extensions of the body as the fundamental symbol of the self.

Although the whole world exists as God's self-expression (cf. Wis 13:1-9; Rom 1:19-20), human beings share in a special way in God's self-symbolizing activity (cf. Gen 1:28; 2:19-20; John 15:15-16). In the words of Edward Kilmartin (1923–94), "Creatures have more to say than what they are in themselves. They also announce that they are from God. . . . The rational creature does not simply speak from, and out of, oneself, but also from God."[6]

Relational Ontology

According to the French theologian Louis-Marie Chauvet, the fact that the whole of created reality is sacramentally symbolic in this way means that its very existence is ultimately relational. Instead of being composed of so many "objects" set out before us human beings that we then can possess as "subjects" in some absolute way as a kind of self-aggrandizement, or use as bartering tools in our relationships with one another, there is nothing in this world that is not essentially already part of God's self-offer in Christ to the human race. Everything exists only within an interpersonal, relational world, that is, within God's overall personal "word" to humankind in Jesus Christ (John 1:1-14). Therefore, to disassociate created things from their fundamental identity as gift— that is, as grace from God—is tantamount to dwelling in a completely impersonal world where love itself, the fulfillment of human nature, becomes simply a blind passion, a biological drive, or a psychological need that clamors to be fulfilled and is no longer a realization of human interrelationality, rooted in each one's fundamental relationship to God in Jesus Christ.[7]

Chauvet points to how the biblical story of manna in the desert illustrates this basic relational nature of the world. In Exodus 16 God feeds the Israelites with "bread from heaven" (16:4) that settles in fine flakes like hoarfrost on the ground. The fact that its very name is a question, "*Man hu?*" (What is this?), signifies for Chauvet that although in itself it was nothing, as God's relational self-gift to his people in love it was true bread from heaven. Neither was its essence measurable, as if it were some *purely* objective, disconnected reality, since those who gathered much did not have too much, and those who gathered little were still satisfied (16:18). And if anyone tried to hoard it as some kind of marketable value in itself, it became wormy and inedible, losing its very reality as bread. Only in its sacramental relationality as God's self-gift to his people—manifesting and instancing his life-giving presence and love—did it have any true existence in this world.[8]

Human Unity in Christ

This story of the manna in Exodus 16 is meant, therefore, as a symbol for all of creation, how the whole universe is created *for* human beings as a relational mode of God's self-giving to them. According to biblical faith, nothing in this world is merely what it seems from a purely naturalistic or scientistic point of view[9] in which things and persons are first set forth as self-contained realities before they enter into any of their relationships. Rather, since "in [Jesus Christ] all things were created" (Col 1:16), precisely in each creature's being uniquely itself is it also a participation in, and manifestation of, the infinite grace of Jesus Christ that God offers to humanity as a whole and to each individual personally within it. The church herself is a sacrament, therefore, and carries out her sacramental activities, such as the Eucharist, within this overall sacramentality of the whole world as created and redeemed in Christ.

"The Liturgy of the World"

Furthermore, says Rahner, human beings are able to know the world in the first place only because of its finite nature, for it is the limits of any created thing, defining and distinguishing it from the rest of reality, setting it apart on its own, that make it knowable. And yet, what are actually experienced in individual creatures are transcendental qualities that of themselves are unlimited: truth, beauty, love, and goodness. As the source of all being, God alone is the infinite source of all truth, beauty, and goodness in this world, so that in knowing anything at all in this created world human beings necessarily also have an encounter with God present within them. Thus, although this experience of God is *mediated*, since it occurs only in and through the experience of finite beings, it is nevertheless also *direct*, because God is neither reasoned to nor hinted at, but directly met as those infinite qualities shining through the finitude of all created reality. As St. Irenaeus has observed, "There is nothing that does not signify God."[10]

Given, then, that God who is absolute truth, beauty, and goodness is constantly offering himself to human persons in and through their experiences of the created world, and given that humans as knowing and loving beings were made for absolute truth and goodness, for anyone then to refuse to love God wholly in return is actually, according to Scripture, to live a lie (cf. Wis 13:1-9; Rom 1:18-21; 1 John 2:22-3). As St. Augustine puts it, "Thou hast made us for Thyself and our hearts are restless till they rest in Thee."[11] That is why when Jesus in the gospel, after being abandoned by the crowds, asks his disciples whether they will also leave him, St. Peter, encountering in him the very fullness of God, answers as he does: "To whom shall we go? You have the words of eternal life" (John 6:67-68).

Furthermore, it is in human beings as the culmination of all creation and evolution that the universe as a whole becomes aware of itself and so is able to attain its purpose by acknowledging itself as God's self-gift.[12] Rahner accordingly terms this return self-offering to God "the liturgy of the world,"[13] an offering through which God gives God's Self to the world as grace:

> This grace [self-gift of God] is not a particular phenomenon occurring parallel to the rest of human life but simply the ultimate depth of everything the spiritual creature does when he realizes himself—when he laughs and cries, accepts responsibility, loves, lives and dies, stands up for truth, breaks out of preoccupation with self to help the neighbor, hopes against hope, cheerfully refuses to be embittered by the stupidity of daily life, keeps silent not so that evil festers in his heart but so that it dies there—when in a word, [a human being] lives as he [or she] would like to live, in opposition to selfishness and to the despair that always assails him. This is where grace occurs, because all this leads [a person] into the infinity and victory that is God.[14]

Now, if such reflections apply to human nature in general, they must also be true of Jesus of Nazareth in the course of his own human life on earth. And so it must have been precisely through his love of the Father as the Father was manifested to him throughout creation—in the birds of the air and flowers of the field, in the rain that falls on the just and unjust alike, and in his fellow human beings as well as his own self—that Jesus, the Son of God, fulfilled his humanity as the Father's full self-expression in the world, the incarnate Word, thereby bringing about the absolute salvation from sin and death needed by the human race.

In addition, according to the New Testament, not only was the world saved through the theandric love of Jesus, but it was through that same enacted love that it came into existence in the first place (cf. Col 1:16; Heb 1:2; and John 1:3), all taking place through his humanity. In the words of Karl Rahner, "[Jesus] alone, in an ultimate loneliness and freedom of which we are not capable, out of a depth within his human nature to which we can never completely reach, abandoned his whole being, in love and obedience, to the bottomless abyss which is silence and mystery, and in the act of doing so, called that Incomprehensible by the name of 'Father.' That single unique act is our redemption; it makes the Church, as the community of those in grace."[15]

Rahner then concludes that "the innermost dynamism of the normal 'secular' life of [humanity] as it exists always and everywhere has found in Jesus of Nazareth its clearest manifestation, and in him has proved itself as real, victorious and attaining to God." The reason why this grace expressing itself in the world is none other than Jesus Christ is the fact that when "the eternal *Logos* of the Father communicates and wants to communicate himself to the non-divine, there comes to be precisely what we call [Christ's] humanity."[16] That is to say, given the fundamental nature of the universe as God's self-expression, the humanity of Christ—to be shared by all the members of the human race—is what *necessarily* results when God speaks himself out fully into the created world: "Indeed, the Logos made man has been called the abbreviated Word of God. This abbreviation, this code-word for God is man, that is, the Son of Man and [human beings], who exist ultimately because the Son of Man was to exist."[17]

Rahner obviously comes to these theological conclusions out of the church's traditional teaching that Christians are saved by believing not only in the *fact* of salvation but also in the *form* of the one in whom salvation took place: the life, death, and resurrection of Jesus of Nazareth. In other words, true Christian faith attains to God precisely by participating in the *shape* (*morphē*: Phil 2:4) of him in whose saving events it believes (cf. 1 Cor 15:1-11). Hence, St. Paul tells the Corinthians, "Be imitators of me as I am of Christ" (1 Cor 11:1), and St. Leo asserts in regard to the liturgy, "What . . . was visible [in the life] of the Redeemer has passed over into the sacraments." To be Christian, then, is to be a type of Christ, and to celebrate Christian liturgy is to be taken up typologically into the transforming events of his salvation.

In his self-offering even unto death to the Father through patient love for sinful humanity, Jesus has become "the source of eternal salvation to all who obey him" (Heb 5:9), to all who allow him to continue his same self-offering in and through their own lives in this world. This "liturgy of the world," as Rahner calls it, is possible only through the power of Christ's love and his paschal mystery at work now throughout salvation history as its inner dynamism and meaning. It is this same "liturgy" that St. Paul has in mind when exhorting the Romans "to present your bodies as a living sacrifice, holy and acceptable to God, which is your spiritual worship" (Rom 12:1), an exhortation echoed in 1 Peter's urging Christians to be "like living stones . . . built into a spiritual house, a holy priesthood, to offer spiritual sacrifices acceptable to God through Jesus Christ" (4:5).

At the same time, precisely because Jesus is divine, salvation is ultimately a pure gift from God. As St. Paul teaches, "It is all God's work. It was God who reconciled us to himself and gave us the work of handing on this reconciliation" (2 Cor 5:18). But, we can ask, how is this possible? For if to be human means to realize oneself in one's own free choices, then salvation must somehow also be freely chosen by those who are saved. How then can salvation both be wholly *given* to human beings and yet also be something they themselves *do* along the way?

Symbolic Exchange

In answer to this question, Louis-Marie Chauvet builds upon anthropologist Marcel Mauss's theory of gift giving.[18] According to Chauvet, in any gift it is the giver himself or herself that is ultimately received. Otherwise, what is given would amount to nothing more than a kind of windfall, a disconnected happening in one's life without any apparent purpose or meaning. In addition, no gift can be received except through some kind of gift in return, that is, without its being part of a "symbolic exchange."[19] For in order to receive anything as a gift, the receiver must open himself or herself to the *person* of the giver present within the gift, to that person's whole way of seeing and being in the world. Thus, by explicitly accepting the gift, the receiver actually bestows a gift in return: "making room for the other," that is, giving a kind of personal existence within the original receiver's own personal "world."[20]

On the basis of a similar reflection, Karl Rahner draws a very important conclusion—because we are God's creation, we human beings exist precisely as God's own self-gift to ourselves in grace: "Our whole existence [consists in] *the acceptance or rejection of the mystery which we are.*"[21] We become what we are created to be—God's self-gift—only by opening ourselves to God in all the actions of our lives, by fully accepting ourselves as God's self-gift. Yet to accept ourselves as God's self-gift means to accept ourselves in all our human limitations, as we are and not simply as we would like to be: "To be in harmony with what now in fact belongs to this nature, with its corporality, its sexuality, its constriction, its death-trend, with its pain, its shared existence with others, its earthly origin, with its incorporation into the history of nature and the rest of [hu]man-kind."[22] Here Rahner concludes that because the fullness of God was expressed precisely in Jesus' grateful recognition throughout his life that all that he was and possessed was in fact the Father's self-gift to him, the "incarnation of God is . . . the unique, *supreme*, case of the total actualization of human reality, which consists of the fact that man *is* in so far as he gives up himself."[23] Thus, in John's gospel when the apostle Philip asks Jesus to show them the Father, Jesus responds, "Have I been with you so long and yet you do not know me, Philip? He who has seen me has seen the Father. . . . Do you not believe that I am in the Father and the Father is in me?" (John 14: 9-10).

By accepting himself as the Father's self-gift, incarnated within the historical and material limits of his humanity, Jesus also accepted, and therefore realized, his oneness with the rest of the human race, people who, however, unlike him and without him, were helplessly imprisoned in their sinful conditions, thereby causing him the especially painful death he had to undergo. Our common humanity therefore is not some kind of philosophical concept formed by abstraction from the individualities of all the human beings who have ever lived. No. It is rather our actual participation in the one humanity of Christ enacted fully in the sacred events of his life. Jesus does not simply *reveal* God's love for us from all eternity; he *accomplishes* it in his own person. As a result, says Rahner, "In each [human being] all of [humanity] is contained and made uniquely manifest."[24] Thus, like Jesus and in Jesus, the more we love all of God's children in all their limitations without exception, even in their being wounded by sin, the more we are authentically human and truly become *somebodies* in the world, realized as fully unique individual persons in our own right.

Jesus of Nazareth, then, was not one out of many possible saviors God had to choose from in order to express his divine nature fully into a created world. Jesus' historical existence is the very pattern according to which the whole world is created in the first place. As the letter to the Colossians tells us, "In him all things were created, in heaven and on earth. . . . In him all the fullness of God was pleased to dwell, and through him to reconcile to himself all things, whether on earth or in heaven, making peace through the blood of his cross" (Col 1:16, 19-20). Thus, in Romans St. Paul writes, "For those whom he foreknew he also predestined to be *conformed to the image of his Son*, in order that he might be the first-born among many brethren" (8:29; emphasis added). That is also why, says Rahner,

> we meditate on the life of Christ, why we say we will imitate Christ in his poverty, why we say that our life is a participation in the death and in the cross of Christ. All these things have a certain contingency in the life of Jesus; they need not be so, they are again concrete expressions of a free attitude of the *Logos*, who wanted to reveal himself just in this way. But it is just this actual shape of the life of Jesus which then becomes the law of our life. . . . The Lord is the ultimate standard; there is none higher than he, since the ultimate standard of necessity is revealed to us just in this actual person. For it is just here that the *Logos* became man and not simply any man, but this man.[25]

According to Rahner, then, Jesus in his humanity does not simply *reveal* God's love for us from all eternity, as if Jesus were a cosmic human bumper sticker announcing, "Smile, God loves you!" Rather, in Jesus of Nazareth as a particular Jewish man of the first century and in his loving interactions with all others in his life—especially in his passion and death as his totally obedient love of the Father in return—God has in fact *enacted* God's saving love for all of humanity. And so, in order to be formed and shaped by that love, we need to be conformed to the selfsame saving *acts* that in Christ's life on earth shaped his human heart into total conformity to his Father's will in the first place. That is why through the centuries meditation on Christ's passion has been so esteemed for its power to transform believers into his image. Dwelling on the unfathomable mystery that the eternal Lord of the universe has entered human history and undergone such suffering and death out of an infinite love for humanity as a whole, and for each individual human being, can only serve to overthrow all merely human estimations of the meaning of human existence and to open one's mind and heart to the incalculable value God's love has given to every human person who has ever lived. The further realization that Christ's suffering and death are never separated from his resurrection, that God's will in Christ throughout all the joys and sufferings of this world is our peace and sanctification,[26] is ultimately what also motivates the church's celebration of the Eucharist as her sacrifice of thanksgiving.

On the one hand, then, the reason the New Testament and the patristic writers read the meaning of all human history typologically—finding in Christ the origin and full realization of all the other ways that God acts and has acted throughout history—is the faith conviction that the world is not only redeemed but even created in the first place precisely in those saving events of Christ's life. And so Christ in his life, death, and resurrection was already somehow proleptically present and active at the very first moment of creation. That is also why the liturgy of the Catholic Church from the beginning has been structured typologically, symbolizing in its enactment how all of reality exists only to the extent that it is a manifestation of Christ in his paschal mystery.

On the other hand, since in Jesus Christ God spoke himself out completely in the lifelong self-offering of a Palestinian Jewish man of the first century, and in a way that was intrinsically both spatial and temporal, the phenomena of time and space themselves exist and have meaning only insofar as they, too, are participations in this reality of Jesus Christ. And so, in the liturgy both the *temporal* unfolding of its rites and the *spatial* use of movement and actions in blessed buildings specifically set aside for that purpose (churches and cathedrals) themselves become sacramental symbols of Christ's paschal mystery. In her celebration through time and space the church in the liturgy effectively symbolizes how all times and places are intended by God to manifest and realize the mystery of his love in Jesus Christ.[27]

The Faith of Jesus

The Second Vatican Council's Constitution on the Sacred Liturgy (*Sacrosanctum Concilium*) begins its teaching on the fundamental nature of the church's sacred liturgy by recalling how God fully enacts his eternal plan of salvation through his Son, Jesus Christ. According to the council, God brings it about by "speaking" God's Self in the humanity of Jesus:

> God who "wills that all men be saved and come to the knowledge of the truth" (1 Tim 2:4), "who in many times and various ways spoke of old to the fathers through the prophets" (Heb 1:1), when the fullness of time had come sent his Son, the Word made flesh, anointed by the Holy Spirit, to preach the Gospel to the poor, to heal the contrite of heart, to be a bodily and spiritual medicine: the Mediator between God and man. For his humanity united with the Person of the Word was the instrument of our salvation. Therefore, "in Christ the perfect achievement of reconciliation came forth and the fullness of divine worship was given to us."[28]

The full sentence from which the Hebrews quote here was taken reads, "In many and various ways God spoke of old to our fathers by the prophets; but in these last days he has spoken to us by a Son, whom he appointed the heir of all things, through whom also he created the world" (Heb 1:1-2). The letter then goes on to explain *how* God spoke through Jesus so as to make him both (a) the origin of creation and the Lord of all things and (b) the one in whose person all Old Testament realities are fulfilled and find their ultimate meaning. It begins by presenting Jesus as typologically fulfilling the Old Testament priesthood of Melchizedek. Just as the priest Melchizedek offered but a single sacrifice consisting of bread and wine (Gen 14:18), so too has Jesus the eternal Son through his suffering and death offered a once-and-for-all sacrifice (10:10). As a result, he has entered into the heavenly sanctuary where now through his flesh, as the source of *all* of God's blessings throughout history both before and after his historical life on earth, human beings have full access to God (10:20).

Hebrews also explains *how* Jesus' bloody death wins forgiveness of sins and full access to God: "Consequently, when Christ came into the world, he said, 'Sacrifices and offerings you have not desired, / but a body have you prepared for me; / in burnt offerings and sin offerings you have taken no pleasure. / Then I said, 'Behold, *I have come to do your will*, O God,' / as it is written of me in the roll of the book'" (Heb 10:5-7, citing Ps 40:6-8; emphasis added). Jesus' death is the means of universal human salvation not by fulfilling prescribed rules for a proper sacrifice, or as the result of any mystic power the shedding of blood might have of itself to save (cf. 9:22), but rather because Jesus in his voluntary bloody death completed the total offering of his whole life as a single act of *obedience* to the Father's will.[29]

Although the English word "obedience" is most often understood as an external compliance with some imposed duty irrespective of personal preference, etymologically the word has a much richer meaning. It originates from two Latin words, *audire* and *ob*, meaning "to listen to," just as its Greek equivalent found in Hebrews 5:8, *hypakoē*, is formed from *akouein* and *hypo* to convey the same meaning. Thus, instead of enforced conformity, "obedience" in Hebrews suggests that through gratitude and love Jesus in his humanity willingly conformed himself, not so much to the Father's demands as to the Father himself, to the Father's whole way of seeing and loving (cf. John 14: 9-11). Thus, by his obedience Jesus became in his human nature what he is as the Second Person of the Trinity from all eternity: "the image of the invisible God" (Col 1:15). However, Hebrews also recognizes that to be obedient in this way is not always a pleasant or easy task: "Although he was a son, he learned obedience *through what he suffered*; and being made perfect he became the source of eternal salvation to all who *obey him*, being designated by God a high priest after the order of Melchizedek" (Heb 5:7-10; emphasis added).

According to Hebrews, then, through his obedience unto death Jesus' eternal divinity became fully realized in the total enactment of his human nature unto death[30] so that, even though he is fully Son of God from the very first moment of his incarnation, his relationship to his Father had to be realized in his humanity in and through all the choices he made throughout the course of his life on earth, a life lived fully in faith—a complete handing over of himself to his Father ("the assurance of things hoped for, the conviction of things not seen" [11:1]).[31] Obedience, then, is actually another word for faith, as we see in Hebrew's reference to Psalm 95:[32] "And to whom did he swear that they should never enter his rest, but to those who were *disobedient*? So we see that they were unable to enter because of *unbelief* " (3:18-19; emphasis added).

Salvation by Faith

In Hebrews 5:7-10, quoted above, we see also that by his obedient faith not only was Jesus himself fully united in his humanity to God the Father, but the whole of the human race was also included in him in his death on the cross, so that now "he is the source of salvation to all who obey him." Accordingly, through the saving power of Christ's death,

Moses, by virtue of his obedience to God's will, shared in the reality of Jesus himself, the "faithful one" (*pistos*; 3:2), as did many other holy men and women throughout the Old Testament, from Abel through David and the prophets, who participated in Christ by living lives of faithful obedience to God's will (cf. Heb 11). In fact, by the power of Jesus' faith working within them they were able to "know" him even in advance of his historical life on earth. Hebrews tells us that because Moses somehow realized in his own humanity that his troubles in leading the chosen people out of Egypt were his share already in "the abuse of the Christ,"[33] he accounted them as "greater wealth than the treasures of Egypt" (11:26).

Having laid out all the necessary elements for doing so, Hebrews explains how "in these last days [God] has *spoken* to us by a Son" (1:2): "By faith Abel offered to God a more acceptable sacrifice than Cain" so that, although he died, "*through his faith he is still speaking*" (11:4; emphasis added). Thus, it is precisely through humanity's own share in the saving faith of Jesus that God "speaks" himself fully to the human race. Jesus has become, through his life on earth, both the origin and the goal of saving faith at work in human beings throughout all ages: "Therefore, since we are surrounded by so great a cloud of witnesses, let us . . . [look] . . . to Jesus the originator [*archēgon*] and fulfiller [*teleiōtēn*] of *our* faith" (12:1-2; emphasis added). Note, however, that whereas the Revised Standard Version renders *archēgon* as "pioneer" and *teleiōtēn* as "perfecter," Jesus was not *historically* the first to believe in God—the "pioneer" in doing so—nor was he simply the "perfecter" of something that existed both prior to and independently of him. Rather, it was in his already entrusting himself to the Father *within* those Old Testament figures that they found salvation through their lives of faith, just as he himself continues to be present as the source of the faith of all who please God and give him fitting worship.

The Spirit of Christ as Entelechy

As we have seen, Vatican II begins its theology of the liturgy by citing 1 Timothy 2:4: "God who 'wills that all men be saved and come to the knowledge of the truth'. . ." (SC 5). Now, since "there is no other name under heaven given among men by which we must be saved" (Acts 4:12),

Christ in his saving humanity must always have been somehow available to all human beings, even to those who lived *historically prior* to the time of his incarnation and death on the cross. How this is true remains part of Christ's mystery, as St. Augustine recognizes: "It is still beyond our understanding that [Christ] was begotten from the Father before the day star, . . . that his name existed before the sun" (cf. Ps 71:17).[34] And yet, through theological reflection an ever-fuller understanding of this mystery, and its ramifications both for liturgy and for the rest of Christian life, may still be possible.

In an article entitled "Jesus Christ in the Non-Christian Religions,"[35] Karl Rahner addresses the question of how Jesus Christ was savingly present to those who lived and died even before his incarnation, cross, and resurrection. Arguing from Scripture, Rahner concludes that the Holy Spirit from the very beginning is the "entelechy,"[36] the determining principle, of the history of both creation and salvation. David Coffey, following a lead provided by Peter Phan, defines Rahner's use of "entelechy" here as "a (or the) guiding principle of a process, which not only moves it forward to its *telos* or end, but as it operates actively seeks out this end."[37] According to Rahner, humanity's salvation did not take place because God the Father reversed a judgment of damnation on our sinful humanity on the basis of Christ's faithful obedience unto death. Rather, God's purpose from all eternity has always been the same: Jesus Christ and the salvation of all human beings in him. Even before his historical life on earth, in the operation of the Holy Spirit as entelechy, Christ was already savingly present in the world. "Since the efficacious cause of incarnation and cross (i.e., the Spirit) has its goal within itself, as inner entelechy, and fulfills its own being (as communicated to the world) only in the incarnation and cross, the Spirit is from the outset the Spirit of Jesus Christ."[38]

But how does this "Spirit of Jesus Christ" act as entelechy to make Christ present to human beings even prior to the incarnation and his death on the cross? Rahner concludes that the Spirit is present to all human beings in their own spirits as "the seeking *memoria* (memory) of the absolute bringer of salvation, who is by definition the God-man who arrives at his consummation through death and resurrection."[39] This "memory," like Plato's *anamnesis*, is not simply a recalling of things gone by but a memory that also searches in human experience for something particular yet to be discovered. For one "can only find and retain what he encounters in history if there is an *a priori* principle of expectation, seeking, and hope in [his or her] finding and retaining subjectivity."[40]

Thus, the Spirit as the seeking *memoria* is already a *possession by anticipa-tion* of the God-man who is "the absolute bringer of salvation," Jesus Christ. Human spirits mysteriously seek this absolute bringer of salvation and are on the watch for him because the Spirit operating within them knows and intends Christ as the goal of creation—not as the abolition of history, but in that particular "event in history in which the free deci-sion for a saving end of all history is made and is within our grasp; and where this decision is made in the light of the liberty of God and man alike, and for the one history of mankind as a whole."[41] That is why Christ in his saving life, death, and resurrection is not only normative for all truly human life and activity in this world but also constitutive of it.[42]

David Coffey finds in 1 Peter scriptural ratification of Rahner's notion of the presence of Christ through the Holy Spirit as entelechy, both before Christ's incarnation and throughout the world in all human per-sons, including those who have never heard of him: "Concerning this salvation, the prophets who prophesied of the grace that was to be yours made careful search and inquiry, inquiring about the person or time that the Spirit of Christ within them indicated when it testified in advance to the sufferings destined for Christ and the subsequent glory" (1 Pet 1:10-11; NRSV).[43] Here as in other places[44] the New Testament teaches that Old Testament prophets were guided by the "Spirit of Christ" to foretell the Christ even in the details of his suffering and glory (e.g., Isa 53). Since the Spirit referred to here could not have been the Spirit unit-ing believers to Christ in his risen humanity, which the risen Lord sends from the Father only *after* his glorification,[45] it must have been the Spirit of Christ as entelechy through whom the world was created in the first place (cf. Gen 1:2) and who guided humankind's expectation and longing for the Savior from its very beginnings. Indeed, it must have been this same Spirit as entelechy who, according to St. Cyril of Jerusalem (ca. 313–86), is at work in the experience of new catechumens desiring to enter the church, an experience Cyril refers to in his *First Instruction* in preparation for baptism: "Perhaps you did not know whither you were coming, nor in what kind of net you are taken. You have come within the nets of the church. Be taken alive and flee not. For Jesus is angling for you, not in order to kill, but by killing to make you alive. For you must die and rise again."[46] Like fish that are taken in nets unawares, Cyril's catechumens might have been puzzled why and how they were so drawn to the church, and to a gospel that runs so contrary to the wisdom of this world, as to offer their very lives to Christ whom they have never seen or known "according to the flesh" (2 Cor 5:16; cf. 1 Pet 1:8). It was the Spirit acting within their own created spirits inexorably seeking, as if by some knowing "memory," the God-given goal of all creation: Jesus Christ.

If the prophets of old were able to predict Christ in the particularities of his saving life by the guidance of the Spirit within them, Christ's first disciples were likewise taught by the Spirit as Paraclete to see signs of Christ's presence everywhere throughout history—first in obvious predictions of him in Scripture (e.g., Luke 24:13-35), but also in objects (e.g., John 2:19-21; 6:51; 1 Cor 10:4), in events (e.g., 1 Cor 5:7; 2 Cor 5:17), and particularly in those human beings who in some outstanding way manifest in their lives Christ's own obedient faith in God his Father, the saints of God (e.g., Heb 11:1–12:2; 1 Cor 11:1). Within this overall theological vision of the Letter to the Hebrews, then, the fuller meaning of its definition of faith becomes evident: "Faith . . . is the substance [*hypostasis*] of things hoped for, the proof [*elegkhos*] of events [*pragmatōn*] not seen (Heb 11:1).[47] That is to say, by their participation in the faith of Christ (*hypostasis*), believers are united to his saving events (*pragmatōn*), which in turn produces in them a conviction (*elegkhos*) of its truth. Hebrews 11 depicts just how Christ in his saving deeds of faith was already present and active (through the Spirit) in Old Testament figures, "speaking" through them by their lives of faith, leading to the conclusion in 12:1-2 that Jesus is "the originator [*archēgon*] and fulfiller [*teleiōtēn*] of our faith." Consequently, just as Christ exercised his saving work by the Holy Spirit as entelechy in the faith of Old Testament prophets and saints, so "in these last days" (1:2) his work of salvation continues, now by the Spirit of the risen Christ, through the "sacrifices" (13:16) and common worship of his church (10:25) offering to God "a sacrifice of praise" (13:15).

In summary, then, if Jesus Christ has become, through faith realized in suffering and death, "the source of eternal salvation to all who *obey him*" (5:9; emphasis added), then his sacrificial faith is the "fullness of divine worship" given to the church. Through the gift of the Holy Spirit, Jesus himself is now both the *content* and the *sharing source* of Christian faith. As the fullness of God's Word, spoken out into the world, Jesus is *what* Christians believe when they offer themselves in and with and through him. He is also the One *who believes* (that is, entrusts himself to the Father) in them, and through whose faith they believe as they offer their lives in his own once-for-all, eternal self-offering to the Father. Hence, as the ancient euchology prays and Vatican II's Constitution on the Sacred Liturgy confirms, "in Christ the perfect achievement of reconciliation came forth and the fullness of divine worship was given to us" (SC 5).

Conclusions

In answer to our first question, how Jesus of Nazareth through the events of his single lifetime accomplished universal salvation, we can conclude that

1. since a human being realizes himself or herself in the world only in outward bodily self-expressions and in using other things for the same purpose as extensions of the body,

2. Jesus of Nazareth, God incarnate, accomplished the salvation of the whole human race by lovingly accepting the oneness of his humanity as God's self-gift with that of all other human beings in all their limitations, doing so in and through the saving events of his life; and

3. because of Christ's saving events, then, any human being who, through the gift of the Spirit, now lives true to his or her own humanity as God's self-gift in Christ also manifests and so realizes his or her share in the one humanity of Christ and his salvation.

Notes, Chapter One

[1] My own translation of the Greek here transliterated: "Andra moi ennepe, mousa, polutropon, hos mala polla / planchthê, epei Troiês hieron ptoliethron epersen: / pollôn d' anthrôpôn iden astea kai noon egnô, / polla d' ho g' en pontôi pathen algea hon kata thumon. / arnumenos hên te psuchên kai noston hetairôn. / All' oud' hôs hetarous errusato, hiemenos per."

[2] Leo the Great, *Sermo* 74, 2 (PL 54:398a): "Quod Redemptoris conspicuum fuit in sacramenta transivit." Unless otherwise indicated, translations throughout this work of material taken directly from foreign-language publications are my own.

[3] Karl Rahner, "The Theology of Symbol," in *Theological Investigations*, vol. 4, trans. Kevin Smyth (Baltimore: Helicon, 1966), 221–52.

[4] An excerpt from Sonnet 57.

[5] Note how children, from their earliest engagements with the world, seem set with unique "personalities" prior to any shaping through interaction with others.

[6] Edward J. Kilmartin, *Christian Liturgy I: Theology and Practice* (Kansas City, MO: Sheed and Ward, 1988), 56–57.

[7] Louis-Marie Chauvet, *Symbol and Sacrament: The Sacramental Reinterpretation of Christian Existence*, trans. Patrick Madigan, SJ, and Madeleine Beaumont (Collegeville, MN: Liturgical Press, 1995), 7–154.

[8] Ibid., 44–45.

[9] For an analysis of how modern technological culture inhibits awareness of the essentially symbolic nature of human existence, see Neil Postman, *Technopoly: The Surrender of Culture to Technology* (New York: Vintage Books, 1993).

[10] Irenaeus, *Adversus haereses* IV, 18, 2.

[11] Augustine, *The Confessions of St. Augustine*, trans. F. J. Sheed (New York: Sheed & Ward, 1943), 3.

[12] Ps 19:1: "The heavens are telling the glory of God; / and the firmament proclaims his handiwork." According to Leontius of Neapolis (ca. 590–650), quoted in Norman H. Baynes, "The Icons before Iconoclasm," *Harvard Theological Review* 44, no. 2 (1951): 101–2 (= PG 93:1603B), "Creation does not venerate the Maker directly and by itself, but it is through me that the heavens declare the glory of God, through me the moon worships God, through me the waters and showers of rain, the dew and all creation, venerate God and give him glory." Edward Kilmartin writes, "As embodied spirits, human beings are a kind of symbol of the world; for in them traits of the various levels of created being are found. As beings of the cosmos, they can respond in thanksgiving for the gift of creation on behalf of all created reality" (*Christian Liturgy I*, 57).

[13] Karl Rahner, "Considerations on the Active Role of the Person in the Sacramental Event," in *Theological Investigations*, vol. 14, trans. David Bourke (New York: Seabury, 1976), 166, digested in *Theology Digest* 19, no. 3 (Autumn 1971): 227–34. For a particularly lucid explanation of Rahner's notion of "the liturgy of the world," see Michael Skelley, *The Liturgy of the World: Karl Rahner's Theology of Worship* (Collegeville, MN: Liturgical Press, 1991).

[14] Karl Rahner, "How to Receive a Sacrament and Mean It," *Theology Digest* 19, no. 3 (1971): 228.

[15] Karl Rahner, "The Significance in Redemptive History of the Individual Member of the Church," in *The Christian Commitment: Essays in Pastoral Theology*, trans. Cecily Hastings (New York: Sheed & Ward, 1963), 91.

[16] Karl Rahner, *The Priesthood*, trans. Edward Quinn (New York: Seabury, 1973), 76.

[17] Karl Rahner, "On the Theology of the Incarnation," in *Theological Investigations*, vol. 4, trans. Kevin Smyth (Baltimore: Helicon Press, 1966), 116.

[18] Marcel Mauss (1872–1950), "Essai sur le don" (1924), in *Sociologie et anthropologie* (Paris: Presses Universitaires de France, 1950), 143–279.

[19] Chauvet, *Symbol and Sacrament*, 99–109.

[20] Kilmartin notes, "The movement by which the person goes out to the other as other begins the completion of the circle of presence-to-self and presence-to-other. . . . The beloved is made aware of his or her otherness and unique value. . . . On the other hand, the lover uncovers his or her own mystery in the discovery of the ability to bestow meaning on the beloved" (*Christian Liturgy I*, 64–65).

[21] Rahner, "On the Theology of the Incarnation," 108 (emphasis added).

[22] Rahner, *Priesthood*, 79.

[23] Rahner, "On the Theology of the Incarnation," 110.

[24] Karl Rahner, "Marriage as a Sacrament," *Theology Digest* 17, no. 1 (Spring 1969): 6.

[25] Rahner, *Priesthood*, 81.

[26] "For he is our peace . . . through the cross, thereby bringing the hostility to an end" (Eph 2:14, 16); "For this is the will of God, your sanctification" (1 Thess 4:3).

[27] Fixing wax nails into the Easter candle during the Easter Vigil of the Roman Rite, the presider declares, "Christ yesterday and today, / the Beginning and the End, / the Alpha / and the Omega / *All time belongs to him / and all the ages . . .*" (emphasis added). Within this understanding there is, among the traditional four-fold meanings of Scripture, ultimately no difference between the literal sense and the three spiritual senses: typological, tropological, and anagogical. For fuller discussions of scriptural interpretation, see Enrico Mazza, *Mystagogy* (New York: Pueblo, 1989), 7–13; and Chauvet, *Symbol and Sacrament*, 65–69, 215–16.

[28] The Constitution on the Sacred Liturgy (*Sacrosanctum Concilium* = SC), no. 5, in *Vatican Council II: Volume 1, The Conciliar and Post Conciliar Documents*, ed. Austin Flannery, new rev. ed. (Collegeville, MN: Liturgical Press, 1992), 3. Henceforth, all references to Vatican II documents will come from the work just cited.

[29] As Cor Traets writes in "Sacrificial Event, Meal Rite, Presence: Some Considerations about the Eucharist," *Questions liturgiques* 88 (2007): 272, "Jesus has saved humankind, not by performing a ritual sacrifice nor by offering 'something' to God, but, rather, by giving up himself. So he made the sacrifice of his self-giving, and this self-giving was not reduced to his passion and death. Those were the confirmation of his whole existence that he had lived given to the Father and to humankind: a sacrifice thus in its entirety." For a classic theological reflection on defining the role of death for one's human life, see Karl Rahner, *On the Theology of Death* (New York: Herder and Herder, 1965).

[30] "In him the whole fulness of deity dwells bodily" (Col 2:9).

[31] Gerald O'Collins, SJ, and Daniel Kendall, SJ, in "The Faith of Jesus," *Theological Studies* 53 (1992): 416, note that when Jesus encourages his disciples to have faith the size of a mustard seed, which would move mountains (Luke 17:6), he is actually making a statement about his own faith that allowed him to do miracles (*credere in Deum*).

[32] Cf. Luke Timothy Johnson, "Rom 3:21-26 and the Faith of Jesus," *Catholic Biblical Quarterly* 44 (1982): 77–90, esp. 86: "Paul invites us, in effect, to understand faith as a response of obedience to God, and obedience as a response of faith (cf. Rom 10:16-17)."

[33] Here I have preferred to translate *ton oneidismon tou Christou* as "*the* abuse *of* the Christ," substituting it for the RSV rendition, "abuse *for* the Christ," as more in line both with the existence of the first definite article and the genitive case of *Christou* and with the overall theology of Hebrews. For in the context of the whole letter, the author, by this textual allusion to Ps 89:51, a psalm of David, clearly implies that Moses, by identifying himself with the sufferings of a people later represented in the Davidic kingship (*Christos* = Anointed One), was in fact taking on the sufferings, and therefore the faith, of Jesus Christ (*tou Christou*).

[34] Augustine, *Sermo* 94, *In natali Domini* 11, 4 (PL 38:1017): "Nondum contemplari possumus quod genitus est ante luciferum a Patre, . . . quod ante solem permanet nomen ejus."

[35] Karl Rahner, "Jesus Christ in the Non-Christian Religions," in *Theological Investigations*, vol. 17, trans. Margaret Kohl (New York: Crossroad, 1981), 39–50.

[36] Ibid., 46.

[37] David Coffey, "The Spirit of Christ as Entelechy," *Philosophy and Theology* 13 (2001): 364.

[38] Rahner, "Jesus Christ in the Non-Christian Religions," 46.

[39] Ibid., 46–47.

[40] Ibid., 47. Note the similarity of Rahner's reasoning here to that of St. Augustine in his reflection on Romans 8:25-27: "[The Spirit of God] makes the saints intercede with unutterable groanings, inspiring in them a desire for so great a Reality though still unknown, which we look for through patience. For how, in its being desired, could what is unknown be put into words? Still, were it altogether unknown, it would not be desired; yet neither would it be desired or sought for with groanings if it could be seen." *Ep.* 130:15, 28 (CSEL 44:73).

[41] Rahner, "Jesus Christ in the Non-Christian Religions," 48.

[42] For a fuller explanation of the distinction between "normative" and "constitutive," see Joseph H. Wong, OSB Cam, "Anonymous Christians: Karl Rahner's Pneuma-Christocentrism and an East-West Dialogue," *Theological Studies* 55 (1994): 620–22.

[43] Coffey, "The Spirit of Christ as Entelechy," 386.

[44] E.g., Luke 24:27; Acts 2:25; 3:24; Heb 11:26.

[45] Cf. David Coffey, "The 'Incarnation' of the Holy Spirit in Christ," *Theological Studies* 45 (1984): 466–80.

[46] Cyril of Jerusalem, *Procatechesis* 5:3–4, in F. L. Cross, ed., *St. Cyril of Jerusalem's Lectures on the Christian Sacraments: The Procatechesis and the Five Mystagogical Catecheses* (Crestwood, NY: St. Vladimir's Seminary Press, 1977). Cf. John 21:11b: "Although there were so many [fish], the net was not torn."

[47] Here the RSV reads, "Now faith is the assurance of things hoped for, the conviction of things unseen."

Chapter Two

A Sacrament of the Church

After losing the National League pennant by one game in 1978, manager Chuck Tanner's Pittsburgh Pirates took on the mission of winning it all the following year. In the course of the next season this closely knit team, featuring such greats as Hall of Famer Willie Stargell, Dave Parker, Kent Tekulve, Phil Garner, Bill Madlock, and Omar Moreno, adopted as their anthem the then-popular disco song "We Are Family." Their group spirit was so infectious that the chant "Fam-a-lee," echoing from the stands back then, is still for baseball fans even today synonymous with the 1979 World Champion Pirates.

After having investigated in our previous chapter how Jesus within a single lifetime brought about the universal salvation that comes to us in the Eucharist, because the Eucharist is a sacrament of the church, a new question arises: How is that salvation realized now through a community? In other words, in what way are Christians also part of a "family," individuals whose core identity includes that of a whole group of people?

The Second Vatican Council's Constitution on the Sacred Liturgy (*Sacrosanctum Concilium*) presents a patristic image[1] that expresses the Lord's relationship to his church: "'In Christ . . . the fullness of divine worship was given to us,'" and "it was from the side of Christ as he slept the sleep of death upon the cross that there came forth 'the wondrous sacrament of the whole Church'" (SC 5). Just as Eve emerged from the side of Adam while he was "dead to the world" in a deep sleep, so too did the church come forth from the heart, that is, the love of Christ realized in his death on the cross. And just as Eve shared in Adam's humanity as bone of his bones and flesh of his flesh (Gen 2:23), so does the church now share in the risen humanity of Christ. And so if, according to Colossians, "all the *fullness* of God was pleased to dwell" in Jesus (1:19; emphasis added), similarly is the church, as Ephesians tells us, "his body, the *fullness* of him who fills all in all" (1:23; emphasis added).

Language as the Matrix of Being

The church in this metaphor is also depicted as an *individual* reality: the new Eve. And yet in everyday life the church is always experienced as a *community* of persons, a plural subject, a "we." How, then, can she at the same time be both plural and individual, both a multiplicity of persons and a single agent in the world? According to Louis-Marie Chauvet, "Linguists tell us that the pronoun 'we' does not designate the sum of the 'I' and 'you' but is 'a complex person' from the start."[2] Using the philosophy of Martin Heidegger, he then goes on to explain what is meant here by "complex person."

Chauvet points first to the fact that human beings function as persons only in and through the language of the communities to which they belong: the spoken and enacted words that incarnate the whole human world of a given community, its shared set of meanings and values, its common way of seeing and acting in the world. For example, imagine our being deep in the Amazon Rainforest far from civilization, our ears filled with myriad sounds of birds and other exotic animals. Then suddenly out of the dense vegetation come the words, "Ah, baloney!" Our first thought would not be about the dictionary meaning of "baloney," something one might cook on a stove. Rather, we would be struck by the realization that we were not, after all, the only human beings in all that wilderness—that those are human sounds. And in the words "Ah, baloney," we would also be confronted with the whole world of American culture, its exuberance, casual brashness, and disdain for any pretensions—"Ah, baloney!"—qualities shared to some degree by almost all Americans.

One way of understanding the cultural nature of language is in terms of the figure of speech called "metonymy," where the whole of some reality becomes strikingly evident in one of its parts. For example, say we were touring England, and our English host, pointing to the countryside in front of us, said, "All these lands belong to the crown." We would intuit immediately how "crown" in this context contains almost everything that has to do with the queen. As a metonym, then, the word "crown" refers not only to the object a monarch wears on her head, but to the monarch herself who wears it as a sign of authority and even, in a more extended way, to the whole nation over which the monarch presides as her kingdom.

Examined more closely, all human language is by nature metonymic. Any individual word has meaning only within the complete context of language of which it is a part, that is, in relation to the whole aggregate of words and their meanings to which it belongs. Besides "Ah, baloney," another example of the metonymic characteristic of language is the one-word response General Tony McAuliffe gave to the Germans when they demanded surrender at the Battle of the Bulge in the Second World War: "Nuts!" Because this slang expression was unique to American culture at the time, only the general's fellow Americans could have grasped its full import in that situation. In it they would also have experienced in a way *the whole* of America, along with their own identity as Americans and their solidarity with compatriots all over the world.

Although the language of the church— embodying her shared way of seeing, loving, and acting in the world—is also metonymic in this way, it originates not as the result of some mutual agreement among members but as a pure gift of Christ dwelling within them: their unity in the saving events of his life, death, and resurrection into which they were baptized. As St. Paul says, "I have been crucified with Christ; it is no longer I who live, but Christ who lives in me" (Gal 2:20), and, "Who shall separate us from the love of Christ? . . . I am sure that neither death nor life . . . nor anything else in all creation will be able to separate us from the love of God in Christ Jesus our Lord" (Rom 8:35, 38-39). If, therefore, to be a "person" is to be a center of consciousness, the church can be called a "complex person" in Christ because, through the Spirit, it is the one Christ who expresses himself in and through the faith of all of her members, unifying them as his Body in this world in a common vision of reality—his mind and heart—and embodying that vision especially in Scripture and in the liturgy as the common language of the church. As St. Paul tells the Corinthians, "For who has known the mind of the Lord so as to instruct him? But we have the mind of Christ" (1 Cor 2:16).

In order for individuals to function as "persons" in any human community, they first need "to be spoken" into existence by that community, to be given their names and thus their identities within its common cultural world.[3] For Christians, this is precisely what happens in baptism.

In the current Roman rite of infant baptism, when the priest or deacon asks the parents what they seek for their child, they can respond either "Faith" or "Baptism," since the two are fundamentally the same. By being baptized into the faith of the church, the child is actually baptized into Christ himself, into his way of seeing, loving, and acting in the world realized in him by the saving events of his life, death, and resurrection.

If, then, an individual comes into his or her personal existence as a Christian only in and through the shared language of the church, the church herself exists only in and through her members as sharers in that common language. And so, when individuals gather to do the liturgy, by using the symbols of the church to express their *personal* faith, they also realize the "we" of the church in themselves and in one another. In the church, individual and community are two sides of the same coin. In the words of Karl Rahner, "The whole of mankind is in principle already accepted for salvation in this member and head of mankind (Jesus Christ) who is irrevocably united with God in unity of person,"[4] so that the grace of Christ, in bearing "something of the distinctive trait of him who as God-*Man* has introduced it in a definite manner into the world, . . . has an incarnational tendency."[5] Rahner explains: "By the will of Christ her founder, [the church] is the organized community of the people of God, established through the incarnation in the unity of the one human race. Even if such a society is represented by individual human beings, it still remains a community. Such a collectivity may in a true sense continue in being even when all its members are asleep and the common business or activity for the moment has completely ceased."[6] And so the Christian is in the church, but the church is also in the Christian. "Hence the abiding truth," says Rahner, that "the Church lives by the acts of individuals done within that act by which she was founded,"[7] that is, Christ's self-offering on the cross, which fully embodied in him the Father's own way of seeing and loving.

Fundamental Sacrament of Christ

If all of created reality is sacramentally symbolic of God's love for humanity in Christ in the way described in the previous chapter, then why does Vatican II here seem to ascribe the title "sacrament" to the church in a special way ("It was from the side of Christ . . . that there came forth 'the wondrous sacrament of the whole Church'" [SC 5])? And why are the Eucharist and the other major rites of the church traditionally named "sacraments" as if to differentiate them, too, from the rest of creation in this way?

According to Rahner, although it is true that God's self-offer occurs within every human experience in this world, yet because of (a) the superficiality and self-centeredness of human beings that results from sin, (b) the somewhat ambiguous character of the physical world (e.g., water connoting life *and* death), and (c) the unfathomable mystery of God's goodness and grace in Christ, the grand "liturgy of the world" in which Christ continually offers himself in love and self-sacrifice to the Father in the depths of people's hearts must be clarified and brought into reflex awareness in the church and in what is ordinarily called "liturgy."[8] If this is not done, not only is it more difficult for human beings to recognize God's continual self-offers in their lives (cf. Wis 13:6-7), but it is impossible to appreciate and respond to the fullness of God's Word to the world, Jesus Christ in his paschal mystery.

Christ's salvific love for *all* humankind forged in his own humanity through his life, death, and resurrection has been "incarnated" in the church through the gift of the Holy Spirit,[9] thereby establishing her also as "catholic," or universal. The historical Catholic Church thus consists in a concrete communion of local churches throughout the world, each sacramentally manifested in the person of its bishop[10] as a member of a universal episcopate in union with the pope, the Bishop of Rome, at its head. As universal, the love of Christ incarnated in the church and manifested in her structures "compels" (1 Cor 5:14) her into the world to gather all of God's children into God's kingdom by means of liturgy, witness, and service.

In order for God's historically tangible and irreversible self-offer in Christ to continue on in history, the institutional church must also be indefectible. That is to say, God must preserve the church—in her teaching, liturgy, and life—in the truth of her witness to the original apostolic faith (cf. Matt 16:18; 28:20). Otherwise universal salvation in Christ would be defective in principle, inevitably doomed to defeat over the course of history through human distortion and confusion.[11]

Although according to Vatican II only in the Catholic Church are embodied *all* the substantial elements of this faith witness and the necessary guarantee of concrete continuance in its essential integrity until the end of time, to the degree that other Christian faith communities manifest in their structures and common life the salvation won by Christ, and individuals outside of the Catholic Church do so in their personal lives, they, too, share in her sacramental nature as part of what Vatican II calls "the church of Christ" (*Lumen Gentium* 8).[12] In the words of St. Irenaeus, "Where the church is, there too is the Spirit of God; and where the Spirit of God is, there is the church and every grace."[13] Indeed, today "among the churches that participate in the ecumenical process there is a consensus about the fact that unity [among the churches] cannot simply be an invisible unity";[14] it must take some enduring, embodied form, although understandings still differ among various denominations regarding in what precisely such substantial unity must consist. Toward the end of his life, reflecting on the then-current ecumenical situation among the various Christian denominations, Rahner remarked:

> Attempts at ecumenical rapprochement have made it much more difficult in practice, at least for Catholic Christians, to still allow their church the unique status which, even at the Second Vatican Council, it claimed for itself as opposed to all the other Christian churches. . . .
>
> On the other hand, . . . the average Catholic will answer yes to a double question and thus legitimize his or her relationship in faith to the Roman Catholic Church. A Catholic will ask whether he or she can find in this church the liberating spirit of Jesus, his truth, without at the same time encountering obstacles in the shape of the church itself or its doctrine or an absolutely binding practice. A Catholic will ask whether he or she, despite and through all historical and unavoidable change, can find in this church the clearest and strongest possible connection in historical continuity with the beginnings of the church and so with Jesus.
>
> An affirmative answer to this double question seems to me, a born Catholic, to give me the right and duty to maintain an unqualified relationship with my church, a relationship which naturally, by its nature, includes a critical attitude to it as the locus of evangelical freedom.[15]

The Public Nature of Grace

The liturgy constitution goes on next to give a fuller account of the church's beginnings and of the indispensable work she is sent to do: "Just as Christ was sent by the Father, so also he sent the apostles, filled with the Holy Spirit. This he did so that they might preach the Gospel to every creature [cf. Mark 16:15] and proclaim that the Son of God by his death and resurrection had freed us from the power of Satan [cf. Acts

26:18] and from death, and brought us into the Kingdom of his Father. But he also willed that the work of salvation which they preached should be set in train through the sacrifice and sacraments, around which the entire liturgical life revolves" (SC 6).

Here the council teaches that the church first took shape as a visible institution and continues in that existence through the mission that Jesus Christ gave to his apostles: to preach the "Good News," the word of faith in him as God's salvation for the whole human race. For it is through this preached and sacramentalized apostolic word of faith that Christians explicitly participate in Christ's own saving events, his "paschal mystery," as the culmination and summation of his own life of faith: "Thus by Baptism [human beings] are grafted into the paschal mystery of Christ; they die with him, are buried with him, and rise with him [cf. Rom 6:4; Eph 2:6; Col 3:1; 2 Tim 2:11]. They receive the spirit of adoption as sons 'in which we cry, Abba, Father' (Rom 8:15) and thus become true adorers such as the Father seeks [cf. John 4:23]. In like manner as often as they eat the Supper of the Lord they proclaim the death of the Lord until he comes" (SC 6).

Hence the apostolic word is not intended to remain just a spoken or written word, a verbal message conveyed only to human intelligence. It is to become embodied through sacramental liturgy in the persons who receive it: "That was why on the very day of Pentecost when the church appeared before the world those 'who received the word' of Peter 'were baptized'" (SC 6). Therefore, any strict dichotomy between "word" and "sacrament" is theologically groundless.[16] As was evident in our study of the Letter to the Hebrews, a word is truly heard only when it is incarnated in a person's whole attitude and way of being in the world, their way of embodying the word.[17] More than just a philosophical or religious set of beliefs, Christianity is a whole new mode of human existence, inaugurated in a person through the ritual promises and bath of baptism, but progressively lived out as he or she is more and more conformed in faith to the heart and mind of Christ. If the church, then, is a participation in the faith of Jesus, and if the church's liturgy is truly "the summit toward which the activity of the Church is directed [and] the fount from which all its power flows" (SC 10), the liturgy must so "proclaim the death of the Lord until he comes" that participants, taken up by it into the faith of Christ (cf. 1 Cor 11:20-21), are made ready to bear each another's burdens and those of all humankind, living already their own "eternal salvation" (Heb 5:9).

The liturgy constitution describes next what results from this proclamation and celebration of the faith of Christ:

And 'they continued steadfastly in the teaching of the apostles and in the communion of the breaking of bread and in prayers . . . praising God and being in favor with all the people' (Acts 2:41-47). From that time onward the Church has never failed to come together to celebrate the paschal mystery, reading those things 'which were in all the scriptures concerning him' (Luke 24:27), celebrating the Eucharist in which 'the victory and triumph of his death are again made present,'[18] and at the same time 'giving thanks to God for his inexpressible gift' (2 Cor 9:15) in Christ Jesus, 'in praise of his glory' (Eph 1:12) through the power of the Holy Spirit. (SC 6)

Thus, because the saving events of Christ's life, death, and resurrection—through which the human race was both created and redeemed (Col 1:15-20)—were, as St. Leo the Great puts it, "visible" and therefore public, when "on the very day of Pentecost" the church as the fruit of those events first "appeared before the world" (SC, 6), she did so also as a publicly visible *community of persons* in and through the *public liturgy* of baptism.

As we saw earlier, in coming forth from the side of Christ, the church issues ultimately from his heart, his infinite and universal love. True love, as we know, is received only to the degree that it is given away, and given away *bodily*, corresponding to its original embodiment in Christ's historical life, death, and resurrection. Hence the structures, rites, disciplines, and outreach of the church. To the degree, then, that anyone lives by Christ's grace, through their faith and love they are also to the core of their being one, not only with the concrete institutional church throughout the world, but also with all human beings everywhere who hear and struggle to live faithful to God's word in a public, bodily way in their everyday lives. As Rahner notes,

> The grace of Christ is intended for humanity as a whole; it reaches the individual in so far as he is a member of the one community . . . which represents the human race as a unity. . . . 'Individual' and 'community' in this sense . . . are two sides of the one reality . . . which can only increase or decrease together and to the same degree. But in accordance with the characteristics of human nature . . . God wills [this communion of persons] as a communion which as such creates its own expression for itself in the visible and spatio-temporal dimension of history, or rather receives this expression in its institution by Christ.[19]

In the society of the church, therefore, the individual and the community are two sides of one reality because, through his theandric love for the

Father and all humankind, Christ in his life, death, and resurrection actualized in himself, an individual, the true humanity in which all human beings are created and redeemed as a single mystery.

Arguing from Christ's universal salvation on the one hand and from the interdependent nature of redeemed human existence in the one Christ on the other, Rahner concludes, "The more basic and significant an act is for the individual and the community, the greater must be the public explicitness demanded by this act."[20] The *public* event of the Eucharist on every Sunday and day of obligation throughout the year, therefore, can never become merely one option among others for members of the church in their busy lives. Given the progressive, developmental nature of human existence and the changing nature of social life, constantly presenting new perspectives and raising new questions, this regular public exercise of the fullness of the faith is absolutely necessary for continued Christian life in the world.

The Letter to the Hebrews (10:25) and the Didache[21] in the first century, St. Ignatius of Antioch's second-century *Letter to the Magnesians*,[22] and the third-century *Didascalia apostolorum* all emphasize the need for all Christians to come together to celebrate the Sunday Eucharist. As the *Didascalia* puts it, "You should also command and exhort the people to be constant in the assembly of the church. . . . Otherwise, what excuse before God have those who do not assemble on the Lord's day to hear the word of life and to be nourished with the divine food which abides forever?"[23] Emeritus, a fourth-century Christian martyr of Abitina, North Africa, even gave his life for this principle. When the Roman proconsul asked him why he broke the law in holding public eucharistic assemblies in his house, he answered, "Without the *dominicum* [Sunday Eucharist], we cannot exist."[24] His fellow martyr, Felix, explained: "The Christian is constituted in the *dominicum* and the *dominicum* in the Christian, so that neither can exist without the other."[25] It is likewise true, then, that "without the Eucharist there is no church, [and] without the action of the church there is also no Eucharist."[26]

Human Solidarity in Christ

Such is the nature of being human that deep in their bones, as it were, all human beings realize that somehow they are part of one another (e.g., Luke 16:19-31). The many limited familial, religious, or national unities to which every human being belongs in the particularity of his or her life on earth actually function as so many symbolic expressions of that one universal human solidarity which transcends all such categories.[27] The eulogy of Prime Minister P. J. Keating on November 11, 1993, dedicating the tomb of the Australian Unknown Soldier, evidences how powerful the sense of the solidarity is even among citizens of the same country:

> We do not know this Australian's name and we never will. . . . Yet he has always been among those whom we have honored. We know that he was one of the 45,000 Australians who died on the western front. One of the 416,000 Australians who volunteered for service in the first world war. One of the 324,000 Australians who served overseas in that war and one of the 60,000 Australians who died on foreign soil. One of the 100,000 Australians who have died in wars this century.
>
> He is all of them. And he is one of us. . . .
>
> His tomb is a reminder of what we have lost in war and what we have gained. We have lost more than 100,000 lives, and with them all their love of this country and their hope and energy. We have gained a legend: a story of bravery and sacrifice . . . and a deeper understanding of what it means to be Australian.

Because all human beings were created and redeemed in Christ, according to St. Paul, "There is neither Jew nor Greek, there is neither slave nor free, there is neither male nor female; for you are all one in Christ Jesus" (Gal 3:28). Elsewhere Paul contrasts our true humanity realized in Jesus Christ, the "new man" (*kainos anthropos*), with what he terms the "old man" (*palaios anthropos*), our inherited complicity from birth in the sin of Adam.[28] Jesus made Gentiles and Jews one "*in his own flesh* . . ., that he might create *in himself one new man* in place of the two, . . . and might reconcile us both to God in one body through the cross" (Eph 3:14-16; emphasis added).

The supreme realization of the oneness of humanity in Christ, according to Catholic faith, is the Blessed Virgin Mary,[29] the "Mother of God."[30] David Coffey has demonstrated on the basis of Vatican II's Dogmatic Constitution on the Church (*Lumen Gentium*) that because "God chose to make his great saving intervention in Christ dependent on the free assent of Mary" (cf. Luke 1:38), she plays "a key role in the great saving event of Christ, namely the reception of this event on the part of believing Israel, which passes over into the NT Church." And so "the role of Mary is inseparable from that of Christ, though not to be confused with it. . . . The NT presents Christ not on his own, but in union with those who receive him (as distinct from those who 'received him not'), viz. the Church, and indeed the Church symbolized in the person of Mary."[31]

In the First Letter of John we are told that "God is love" (1 John 4:16), so that God's very nature is self-giving. The life of grace is therefore a life of sharing. And so Mary, living wholly out of love of God and neighbor, is also one with the total holiness of the church, the "communion of saints," the common patrimony of God's love in Christ shared by *all* human beings to the degree that they are open in believing obedience to God's will.[32] Because of Christ, as we have seen already, in the words of Karl Rahner, "In each [human being] all of [humanity] is contained and made uniquely manifest."[33] Consequently, Mary does not possess her extraordinary gifts in any other way than as totally available to all others according to their capacities to live out of that same grace. Just as Jesus "emptied himself, taking the form of a servant" (Phil 2:7), so too is Mary given away completely in Christ's transformative love for *all* of God's children. And so she is not only the "Mother of the Church"; as an actualization of the fullness of the church in a single human being,[34] Mary is the "New Eve"[35] as well, the mother of the whole human race in the order of grace, identifying herself completely with even the least of Christ's brethren. Hence the fittingness of depicting Mary in iconography as belonging now to one, now to another of the many races and human cultures across the ages, thereby signifying the universality and commonality of Christ's grace at once both hers and all humankind's.[36]

This communal nature of grace as our participation in God's inner life of self-giving not only throws light on the relationship of the Blessed Virgin to the rest of the church, but also grounds the church's response to the Donatists, who claimed that in order for the sacraments to take place at all, those ordained sacramental ministers (bishops, priests, and deacons) who lead sacramental celebrations must themselves be personally in the state of grace. Sacramental celebrations enact the life of grace possessed by the whole church, so that the total life of grace won by Christ and offered to humanity through the gift of the Holy Spirit becomes available to each recipient of the sacrament, again only in proportion to his or her grace-given willingness and capacity to receive it at any given time in his or her life.

As a "sacrament," therefore, the historically tangible community of the church is an actualization of that inner unity all human beings have with one another,[37] whether they know it or not, receiving their own mystery as God's self-offer in the grace of Christ. In the words of St. Augustine, "For there is no other mystery of God, except Christ."[38]

Liturgy as Ritual

The church acts as the fundamental sacrament of Christ in three basic ways: faith witness (*martyria*), service (*diakonia*), and ritual worship (*leitourgia*).

Catherine Bell begins her major work, *Ritual Theory, Ritual Practice*,[39] by asking how human activity differs from all other actions in the world. For only by knowing what characterizes human activity in general can one begin to understand ritual as one of its types. For an answer to this question, Bell turns to Pierre Bourdieu and his theory of human practice.[40]

According to Bourdieu, (a) human beings exist fundamentally as embodied *dynamisms*, beings who, from the very first moment of their existence, are set in motion to make their mark on the world in one way or another; and (b) all of their conscious activity has a direct effect upon the way they exist *bodily* in the world. Upon entering the world, as humans begin to grow in consciousness, their dynamism takes the form of wanting to shape the world according to their own personal vision of what is right and good. Bell terms this first characteristic of all human action (1) "redemptive hegemony." Human action is also (2) "situational." That is to say, as embodied and therefore finite beings, humans are able to act in this world only from within their own particular time and place in history. In addition, human action is (3) "strategic" as well, in the sense that it invariably requires and embodies forethought and planning, using means to an end, in order to bring about the desired change. And finally, all human action is marked to some degree by (4) "misrecognition," for even when the strategies employed more or less succeed, because people act only within a physical, historical world, their actions continue to have effects well beyond the immediate situations in which they are initiated. And so they invariably have some unforeseen and unintended consequences, the full extent of which the agent will never be aware.[41] As the old saying goes, "Be careful what you wish for!"

Since humans are embodied spirits, even spiritual activities such as praying or plotting, by contributing to a particular *habitus* of ingrained dispositions, intentions, and attitudes, restructure their whole bodily way of being in the world. And as social beings, living within highly structured environments of human cultures, they invariably appropriate to their own personal dispositions the various cultures in which they live. Thus, for example, all Italians to some extent manifest an identifiably Italian way of thinking and being (however one might characterize it). The common language, interactions, and practices of humans' respective cultures imprint individuals with bodily ways of being in the world that reflect the values of those cultures.

According to Bell, rituals differentiate themselves from all other human activity in two basic ways: they present themselves as both (1) *different from* and (2) *more important or more powerful*.[42] Christian liturgy does this by *stylizing* ordinary elements of human life (water, oil, bread, wine, clothes, movements, etc.), thereby making them metonyms of the deeper, somewhat hidden identity of all human life present within them: the mystery of God's self-gift in Jesus Christ. Thus, rituals like church sacraments are meant not so much to educate and inform participants intellectually but rather to reveal the deeper mysteries of existence by practicing them in conformity to Christ in his paschal mystery of dying and rising. St. Paul first tells the Corinthians, "Be imitators of me as I am of Christ" (1 Cor 11:1), and then he goes on to illustrate how in the Eucharist that is precisely what the church does, imitating through the breaking of the bread the sharing of Christ, who gave himself completely in all that he is and has: "Do this . . . in remembrance of me" (11:25).

The ritual act of kneeling, then, does not so much communicate a message *about* subordination as embody subordination (cf. Phil 2:10).[43] In the words of Chauvet, "One is in prayer as soon as one simply assumes the ritual position of kneeling."[44] Similarly, the handshake of peace near the end of the Eucharist takes place not so much in order to welcome those particular people who happen to be in the same area of the church, but to communicate Christ's own universal, unconditional love for all human beings of all times and places (cf. Phil 2:5), thereby fostering a *habitus* of showing unconditional reverence for everyone throughout the rest of one's life as well. Note, however, that the metonymic, stylizing nature of ritual, declaring itself both other and more important than ordinary human activities, does not require that one shake the hand of *everyone* in the assembly in order to communicate that love. Rather, it is precisely through metonymy, shaking the hands *only* of those who just happen to be nearby in a given celebration, that the *universal* nature of this acceptance is so powerfully conveyed and ingrained, as if to say, "Because of our oneness in Christ, I would be just as totally welcoming to anyone who happens my way in life" (cf. Luke 10:25-37).

In the same way, in regard to the ritual of footwashing in the Holy Thursday liturgy, were the presiding celebrant to wash the feet of everyone in the church, this ritual would lose most if not all of its formative power. Christ's command at the Last Supper was not that his disciples should *literally* wash everyone's feet and do so regularly (cf. John 13:14), but rather that they adopt the attitude *symbolically embodied* in his washing their feet of always living to serve others in their daily lives. Consequently, any attempt on Holy Thursday to do more than the truly real but symbolic washing called for by the rite would simply betray a fundamental misunderstanding not only of the footwashing rite itself but of ritual in general. In the reenactment of the Last Supper footwashing, we are invited to see how Christ laid down his life in service of his brothers and sisters, and therefore to conform ourselves bodily to him through celebrating this rite so that in our daily lives we will continue to do the same (cf. 1 John 3:16). Even if at a given Holy Thursday liturgy we are not among the few whose feet are washed, nevertheless we still participate in the ritual actively by witnessing it take place in our midst. Taking the action in with our eyes and by our physical presence and accompanying it by our singing are also ways of being bodily ritualized into a readier and more joyful Christian living for God and our neighbor.

Bourdieu's practice theory also throws new light on the adage "The church makes the Eucharist and the Eucharist makes the church." For since the church exists as Christ's Body precisely in her members, it is through the celebration of the sacraments, where Christians bodily appropriate Christ's own *habitus* most intentionally, that they, as members of the church, are most powerfully conformed to him as his sacraments to the world.

Conclusions

In answer, then, to our second question, how this salvation in Christ is made available to us through the church as his Body in this world, we can conclude that

1. the church originates from Christ's self-offering to the Father in and through the saving events of his life;

2. the church as a "complex person" is the unity of her members in the mind, heart, and saving activity of Christ dwelling within them, a unity manifesting and realizing itself in a common "language" symbolically embodying those same saving events; and

3. Christ conforms church members to himself in his saving events most especially through the church's symbolic self-offering in him to the Father (*leitourgia*), but also by faith witness (*martyria*) and service of the neighbor (*diakonia*) beyond the liturgy.

Notes, Chapter Two

[1] Irenaeus (ca. 185) writes, "As the Scripture has said, 'Out of his heart shall flow rivers of living water.' . . . The Church is the fountain of living water that flows to us from the heart of Christ." *Adversus haereses* III, 24, 1 (PG 7:966), quoted in Hugo Rahner, "The Beginnings of the Devotion in Patristic Times," in *Heart of the Saviour*, ed. Josef Stierli, trans. Paul Andrews, SJ (New York: Herder and Herder, 1958), 44. Tertullian (ca. 200) adds, "If Adam was a type of Christ, then the sleep of Adam was a type of the sleep of Christ, who slept in death, in order that through a similar cleaving of the side the true mother of the living might be formed, namely the Church." *De anima* 43 (CSEL 20:372, lines 1–5), quoted in Hugo Rahner, "The Beginnings," 54.

[2] Louis-Marie Chauvet, *The Sacraments: The Word of God at the Mercy of the Body* (Collegeville, MN: Liturgical Press, 2001), 32.

[3] Cf. Louis-Marie Chauvet, *Symbol and Sacraments: A Sacramental Reinterpretation of Christian Existence*, trans. Patrick Madigan, SJ, and Madeleine Beaumont (Collegeville, MN: Liturgical Press, 1995), 84–99.

[4] Karl Rahner, *The Church and the Sacraments*, trans. W. J. O'Hara, Questiones Disputatae 9 (New York: Herder and Herder, 1963), 14.

[5] Karl Rahner, "Personal and Sacramental Piety," in *Theological Investigations*, vol. 2, trans. Karl-H. Kruger (Baltimore: Helicon Press, 1963), 119.

[6] Rahner, *The Church and the Sacraments*, 20.

[7] Karl Rahner, "The Significance in Redemptive History of the Individual Member of the Church," in *The Christian Commitment* (New York: Sheed and Ward, 1963), 91.

[8] Karl Rahner, "How to Receive a Sacrament and Mean It," *Theology Digest* 19, no. 3 (August 1971): 229–30.

[9] Cf. David Coffey, "The 'Incarnation' of the Holy Spirit in Christ," *Theological Studies* 45 (1984): 466–80.

[10] Cyprian of Carthage, *Epistle* 66:8: "You ought to realize that the bishop is in the church and the church is in the bishop, and whoever is not with the bishop is not in the church" (*The Letters of St. Cyprian of Carthage*, vol. 3, trans. G. W. Clarke [New York: Newman Press, 1986], 121). Latin original: "Unde scire debes episcopum in ecclesia esse et ecclesiam in episcopo et si qui cum episcopo non sit in ecclesia

non esse" (*Saint Cyprien: Correspondence*, vol. 2, ed. Louis Bayard [Paris: Société D'Édition "Les Belles Lettres," 1925], 226).

[11] Cf. Karl Rahner, *Foundations of Christian Faith* (New York: Seabury, 1978), 329–30.

[12] For a particularly lucid exposition of the relationship of the Catholic Church to the rest of Christianity, see Francis A. Sullivan, SJ, *The Church We Believe In: One, Holy, Catholic, and Apostolic* (New York: Paulist, 1988).

[13] Irenaeus, *Adversus haereses* III, 24, 1 (PG 7:966). Cf. *Lumen Gentium* 8–16; Matt 25:34-39.

[14] Walter Kasper, "Unité ecclésiale dans une perspective catholique," *Revue des sciences religieuses* 75, no.1 (2001): 7. Some Christian denominations, however, do not concur. For example, some years ago the Southern Baptist Convention in the United States discontinued thirty years of bilateral talks with the Catholic Church because, in the spokesperson's words, "We're not ecumenists; we're evangelicals committed to sharing the Gospel" (ZENIT News Agency, March 23, 2001, www.zenit.org).

[15] Karl Rahner, "Why Am I a Christian Today?" in *The Practice of Faith: A Handbook of Contemporary Spirituality* (New York: Crossroad, 1983), 14, reprinted from *Our Christian Faith: Answers for the Future* (with Karl-Heinz Weger), trans. Francis McDonagh (London: Burns & Oates, 1981).

[16] Cf. Edward Kilmartin, *Christian Liturgy I: Theology and Practice* (Kansas City, MO: Sheed and Ward, 1988), 240–51; Chauvet, *Symbol and Sacrament*, 220–27.

[17] Cf. Fritz Tillmans, "The Sacraments as Symbolic Reality of Faith: A Theological Programme," in *Fides Sacramenti, Sacramentum Fidei*, ed. H. Auf der Maur et al. (Assen, The Netherlands: Van Gorcum, 1981), 265–67.

[18] Council of Trent, Session 13: Decree on the Holy Eucharist, chap. 5 (*Enchiridion Symbolotum, Definitionum, et Declarationum de Rebus Fidei et Morum*, 33rd ed., ed. Heinrich Denzinger and Adolf Schönmetzer, SJ [Freiburg im Breisgau and New York: Herder, 1965], no. 1644; this source is henceforth cited as DS).

[19] Rahner, "Personal and Sacramental Piety," 122.

[20] Ibid., 127.

[21] Hebrews 10:23, 25: "Let us hold fast the confession of our hope without wavering, for he who promised is faithful; . . . not neglecting to meet together, as is the habit of some." Didache 14:1: "Assembling on every Sunday of the Lord [*kata kuriakēn de kuriou*], break bread and give thanks" (Huub van de Sandt and David Flusser, eds., *The Didache: Its Jewish Sources and Its Place in Early Judaism and Christianity* [Minneapolis: Fortress, 2002], 15).

[22] Ignatius of Antioch, *To the Magnesians* 9: "Living in accordance with the Lord's day [*kata kuriaken zontes*] . . . in order that we might be found to be disciples of Jesus Christ" (Michael W. Holmes, ed., *The Apostolic Fathers* [Grand Rapids, MI: Baker Books, 1999], 154).

[23] *Didascalia* 13 (Sebastian Brock and Michael Vasey, eds., *The Liturgical Portions of the Didascalia* [Bramcote, Notts.: Grove Books, 1982], 17).

[24] Theodericus Ruinart, ed., *Acta martyrum Saturini, Dativi et aliorum plurimorum martyrum in Africa*, in PL 8:711A: "In domo mea, inquit, egimus dominicum . . . quoniam sine dominico non possumus."

[25] Ibid., PL 8:696B: "An nescis, Satanas, in dominico christianum et in christiano dominicum constitutum, ut nec alterum sine altero valeat esse?"

[26] Wolfgang Beinert, "Eucharistie wirkt Kirche—Kirche wirkt Eucharistie," *Stimmen der Zeit* 215 (1997): 665: "Ohne Eucharistie keine Kirche, aber ohne das Wirken der Kirche auch keine Eucharistie."

[27] Cf. Bastiaan van Iersel, SMM, "Some Biblical Roots of the Christian Sacrament," in *The Sacraments in General: A New Perspective*, ed. Edward Schillebeeckx and Boniface A. Willems, Concilium series (New York: Paulist, 1968), 5–20, esp. 15–20.

[28] Eph 2:15; 4:24. Cf. also Rom 5:12–6:11; 7:24; 1 Cor 2:14; 15:21–49; Col 3:9–10. Other texts depicting Christ as the source and embodiment of true humanity include John 1:3-5; 8:57-58; and Heb 1:2.

[29] For a magisterial account of the theological development through history of this veneration in both East and West, see Brian E. Daley, SJ, *Woman of Many Names: Mary in Orthodox and Catholic Theology* (Milwaukee: Marquette University Press, 2008).

[30] In Greek, *Theotokos* (Council of Ephesus, June 22, 431).

[31] David Coffey, "Mary, Prototype of Salvation," in "Idea of Salvation," supplement, *Prudentia* 20, no. S3, ed. D. W. Dockrill and R. G. Tanner (1988): 96–98 passim.

[32] Thomas Aquinas: "Since in their heavenly home the saints will possess God completely, . . . eternal life consists of the joyous community of all the blessed, a community of supreme delight, since everyone will share all that is good with all the blessed. Everyone will love everyone else as himself, and therefore will rejoice in another's good as in his own. So it follows that the happiness and joy of each grows in proportion to the joy of all." "Colloquium super credo in Deum," in *Opuscula theologica*, vol. 2, ed. Raymundo Spiazzi (Turin: Marietti, 1954), 217; ET: *The Liturgy of the Hours*, vol. 4 (New York: Catholic Book Publishing Co., 1975), 564.

[33] Karl Rahner, "Marriage as a Sacrament," *Theology Digest* 17, no. 1 (Spring 1969): 6.

[34] Cf. also Karl Rahner, "The Significance in Redemptive History," 75–113.

[35] Karl Rahner, "The Interpretation of the Dogma of the Assumption," in *Theological Investigations*, vol. 1, trans. Cornelius Ernst, OP (Baltimore: Helicon, 1961), 218.

[36] As one can witness in the vast array of Marian images in the National Shrine of the Immaculate Conception in Washington, DC.

[37] *Catechism of the Catholic Church*, no. 775: "The Church is . . . the sacrament of the unity of the human race."

[38] Augustine, *Ep.* 187:11, 34 (PL 33:846).

[39] Catherine Bell, *Ritual Theory, Ritual Practice* (New York: Oxford University Press, 1992). Cf. also Catherine Bell, *Ritual Perspectives and Dimensions* (New York: Oxford University Press, 1997). For an analysis of Bell's contribution to liturgical theology, see John D. Laurance, SJ, "Catherine Bell and Liturgical Theology," *Antiphon* 4, no. 2 (1999): 14–8.

[40] Pierre Bourdieu, *Outline of a Theory of Practice*, trans. Richard Nice (Cambridge: Cambridge University Press, 1977).

41 Ibid., 81–85.

42 Ibid., 74.

43 Ibid., 100.

44 Chauvet, *Symbol and Sacrament*, 327.

Chapter Three

Lex Orandi, Lex Credendi

A fter dealing with the questions on how Jesus during his life on earth brought about universal salvation, and how as risen Lord he continues that work through his Body, the church, we arrive at our third preliminary question: If Jesus' historical self-offering in faith is realized in a special way in the church's *liturgical* expression of faith, how are we to see it there? What relationship does her way of praying (*lex orandi*) have to the church's way of believing (*lex credendi*)?

"First Theology" and "Second Theology"

The liturgy of the church belongs to what scholastic theology referred to as "first theology." Along with other ecclesial "sources of theology," such as Sacred Scripture, official Catholic Church teachings, writings of the fathers of the church, lives of the saints, and consensuses of theologians,[1] the liturgy is an expression of the church's life of faith and so is part of God's self-manifestation to the world. Faith, as we know, is impossible apart from God's power at work in the believer: "No one can say 'Jesus is Lord' except by the Holy Spirit" (1 Cor 12:3). And, as we have seen, all true faith shares in the saving faith of Jesus. Thus it is a form of "theo-logy" (God-word).

"Second theology,"[2] on the other hand, is what is typically understood by the term "theology": the church's systematic study of "first theology" in order to understand her life of faith more deeply, so as to live it more fully and humanly. In recent years some theologians have named the "first theology" of the liturgy "liturgical theology," and the "second theology" of subsequent reflection on the liturgy "theology of the liturgy."[3]

The famous adage *lex orandi, lex credendi* (law of praying, law of believing) came into existence in the history of the church in relation to this same conviction, namely, that there is an intrinsic connection between how the Holy Spirit guides the church in her prayer and how he guides her in her beliefs.[4] Therefore, if the Eucharist is the fullest expression of the church's *lex orandi*, it is also the most concentrated manifestation of her *lex credendi*, and if in our succeeding chapters we are to read the faith of the church in her rites at all accurately, it will be important beforehand to investigate just how this adage arose in church history in the first place and precisely what the theological relationship between the *lex orandi* and the *lex credendi* is that it was meant to convey.

Lex Orandi, Lex Credendi

Most scholars agree that *lex orandi, lex credendi* owes its origin to a phrase found in the writings of Prosper of Aquitaine (+ ca. 455), a church writer of the fifth century. In his *Indiculus de gratia Dei* (ca. 435–42) Prosper gives arguments, first from papal and conciliar teachings and then from the liturgy itself, against the semi-Pelagian contention that human beings must take the first step toward God before God will grant them any grace for salvation. In chapter 8 of the *Indiculus* Prosper writes:

> In addition to the unchangeable directives of the most blessed and apostolic see, by which the most pious fathers [the popes] have taught us to reject the arrogance of harmful novelty and to attribute to Christ's grace the beginnings of good will and the growth in laudably good efforts and perseverance in them up to the end, let us also consider the sacraments of priestly intercessions, which, handed down by the apostles, are celebrated uniformly in the whole world and in every Catholic church, in order that the law of supplicating may establish the law of believing [*ut legem credendi lex statuat supplicandi*].[5]

Karl Federer, in a 1950 monograph about the relationship between liturgy and faith, notes that at the time of his writing no scholarly consensus existed regarding the meaning of *lex orandi, lex credendi.*[6] Pope Pius XII in his 1947 encyclical on the liturgy, *Mediator Dei*, taught that whatever faith authority the liturgy possesses it receives ultimately from the magisterium, the divinely established teaching office in the church shared by the pope with the bishops around the world in union with him. Consequently, according to Pius, the adage should actually be read in reverse: *lex credendi, lex orandi* ("the pattern of the church's believing determines the pattern of the church's praying").[7] Federer sets out therefore to investigate the writings of the fathers of the church in order to discover the original force of the phrase and, with it, whence ultimately the liturgy derives its authority as an expression of the church's faith and as a source of theology.

When Federer examines the text from Prosper quoted above, he notes that in speaking about "sacraments of the priestly prayers," Prosper has the following passage from 1 Timothy in mind:

> First of all, then, I urge that supplications, prayers, intercessions, and thanksgivings be made for all [human beings],[8] for kings and all who are in high positions, that we may lead a quiet and peaceable life, godly and respectful in every way. This is good, and it is acceptable in the sight of God our Savior, who desires all [human beings] to be saved and to come to the knowledge of the truth. For there is one God, and there is one mediator between God and [human beings], the man Christ Jesus, who gave himself as a ransom for all, the testimony to which was borne at the proper time. For this I was appointed a preacher and apostle (I am telling the truth, I am not lying), a teacher of the Gentiles in faith and truth.
>
> I desire then that in every place the men [*andras*] should pray, lifting holy hands without anger or quarreling. (2:1-8)

On the basis of this biblical text Federer argues that Prosper's *lex supplicandi* (= *lex orandi*) refers not to the liturgy or liturgical prayer in general, but only to the particular bidding prayers (= "the universal prayer" of the Roman Rite) that have become the custom in Catholic churches throughout the world. More particularly, the word *lex* in the phrase designates the apostolic recommendation in 1 Timothy 2:1, now given the force of law (*lex*) and taken up by the whole church, that has become a universal pattern (*lex*) of praying.[9] In Prosper's thinking, the church's praying universally that nonbelievers receive the gift of faith constitutes her reception of the apostolic directive, thereby witnessing to a *sensus ecclesiae* (a Spirit-guided faith consciousness of the whole church)[10] that, without grace from God, not even the first step toward conversion is possible.[11] As evidence of the *sensus ecclesiae*, then, the liturgy in the case of the bidding prayers and their contents possesses an authority all its own as a norm for faith: *legem credendi lex statuat supplicandi* (let the law of praying establish the law of believing).[12] Federer then demonstrates Prosper's dependence in regard to this conviction on St. Augustine (354–430), who was, according to Federer, the first to argue from the liturgy in order to settle questions about the faith.

In a 1978 article Paul De Clerck revisits the historical roots of the adage *lex orandi, lex credendi* and agrees with the basic findings of Federer.[13] De Clerck later on develops a "heuristic principle" on the basis of Prosper's argument to aid theologians in deciding when and where *lex orandi, lex credendi* applies and to what degree a particular liturgical practice can be used as a source for theology.[14] De Clerck's principle is derived from his analysis of Prosper of Aquitaine and is constituted by three logical steps:

1. 1 Timothy 2:1 constitutes *a scriptural law* that the church should pray for all human beings.

2. The church's obedience to this law results in *a liturgical practice*, which in turn becomes a *liturgical law*.

3. (Since all practice involves a particular form,) to the degree that the formulation of the prayers implements this scriptural law, they are *lex orandi* expressions of the *sensus ecclesiae*, the church's faith.[15]

For De Clerck, therefore, any legitimate appeal to *lex orandi, lex credendi* must ultimately be grounded on the 1 Timothy 2:1 scriptural injunction that the church pray for all human beings. Consequently, one cannot argue independently of this "scriptural law"—as is often done—that just because the church in a particular liturgy or liturgies in the course of history performed some action or prayed some prayer, all aspects of that action or that prayer are necessarily expressions of the church's faith. (On this point Federer agrees, noting how even St. Augustine seems to have fallen into this trap where he claims that Jesus must in fact have been born on December 25 because it is on that day of the year that the church in its liturgy celebrates his birth.[16] Obviously, the chronological date of Christ's birth is not of the same order of truth as the church's belief that he is truly human and was born of the Virgin Mary at some point in history.) According to De Clerck, then, it is only to the degree that the church in its liturgical prayer obediently witnesses to the *biblical* command to pray for all human beings that the liturgy itself can, as expression of the church's faith, be used as a source for theology.

More recently, however, Daniel Van Slyke has convincingly demonstrated that in claiming this much De Clerck has gone somewhat beyond the clear meaning of Prosper's writings.[17] From a larger body of Prosper's textual evidence, Van Slyke concludes that "Prosper believes that the church's prayer and liturgy are sources of doctrine insofar as they are sanctioned and practiced by the Roman see."[18] Whether or not the theological principle understood by the traditional adage *lex orandi, lex credendi* had roots in and is reflected by Prosper's *legem credendi lex statuat supplicandi*, the questions remain, however: Does it have sufficient grounding in the tradition of the church? And, if so, what is the source of its validity? How does the liturgy *by its very nature as liturgy* become a source of the church's faith?

In a tightly reasoned article on the relationship between the church's liturgy and the so-called hierarchy of truths of Catholic teaching, Hans-Joachim Schulz provides a penetrating, and to my mind convincing, method for analyzing the liturgy as a source of theology. From his article the following points can be distilled in response to the questions just posed.[19]

1. The Second Vatican Council's Decree on Ecumenism (*Unitatis Redintegratio*) teaches that "in Catholic doctrine there exists an order or 'hierarchy' of truths, since [those truths] vary in their relation to the foundation of the Christian faith" (UR 11). As an indication of what that "foundation" is on which all other truths of the faith are based and from which they derive their ultimate meaning, the decree refers to the letter to the Ephesians 3:8-12:

> To me, though I am the very least of all the saints, this grace was given, to preach to the Gentiles the unsearchable riches of Christ, and to make all men see what is the plan of the mystery hidden for ages in God who created all things; that through the Church the manifold wisdom of God might now be made known to the principalities and powers in the heavenly places. This was according to the eternal purpose which he has realized in Christ Jesus our Lord, in whom we have boldness and confidence of access through our faith in him.

According to Ephesians, then, "the foundation of the Christian faith" is God's will from all eternity to unite all human beings to himself in Christ and to do so "through the Church."

2. Indeed, it is on the basis of this same ultimate foundation of the faith—namely, that God wills in Christ for "*all* [humans] to be saved and to come to the knowledge of the truth" (1 Tim 2:4; emphasis added)—that the author of 1 Timothy, cited by Prosper, recommends "that supplications, prayers, intercessions, and thanksgivings be made for *all* [humans]" (1 Tim 2:1; emphasis added).

3. The Ephesians 3 appeal to the Christ mystery concludes with a prayer that exhibits a fundamentally anamnetic, epicletic, and doxological structure characteristic of the whole apostolic faith experience:

> For this reason I bow my knees before the Father, from whom every family in heaven and on earth is named, that according to the riches of his glory he may grant you to be strengthened with might through his Spirit in the inner man,[20] and that Christ may dwell in your hearts through faith; that you, being rooted and grounded in love, may have power to comprehend with all the saints what is the breadth and length and height and depth, and to know the love of Christ which surpasses knowledge, that you may be filled with all the fullness of God. Now to him who by the power at work within us is able to do far more abundantly than all that we ask or think, to him be glory in the Church and in Christ Jesus to all generations, for ever and ever. Amen. (Eph 3:14-20)

In recalling God's saving action in Christ (anamnesis) and asking that it have effect in the present (epiclesis), the author of Ephesians actually *experiences in faith* God's acting through his prayer in accord with what God has already fully accomplished in principle in the person, words, and actions of Jesus Christ, leading the author of Ephesians to praise and glorify God (doxology).[21] With this observation Schulz in effect confirms the "symbolic exchange" explanation given above of how universal salvation is realized in Jesus of Nazareth and how that salvation is made available now to the members of his church especially through *the grateful faith offering of themselves in memory of him* in the sacred liturgy.

4. The *lex orandi* helps form the *lex credendi*, therefore, not primarily because the liturgy obeys a "scriptural law" by consciously complying with 1 Timothy 2:1, but to the degree that it directly participates in the apostolic faith itself in the Christ mystery as God's realization of universal salvation *by expressing Christ's unconditional love for all humanity*, a faith that is recorded and proclaimed in Scripture.[22] Consequently, the more original, historically continuous, and widespread (universal) a given liturgical practice, the more it manifests itself as the authentic *lex orandi*.

5. Furthermore, in comparison with other sources of theology, the liturgy as the church's prayer most explicitly embodies in its own existential categories those of the original apostolic faith experience itself: anamnesis, epiclesis, and doxology. Thus, in the liturgy, dogma exists as a lived witness of faith (*martyria*) and of truth as a conscious participation in Christ, "the way, and the truth, and the life" (John 14:6). Among authentic witnesses to the relative importance of any truth within the hierarchy of truths of the faith, apart from Scripture itself, preference should therefore be given to the liturgy over all others, including conciliar and papal teaching.

6. Because they most explicitly embody the anamnetic, epicletic, and doxological structure of the original apostolic faith experience, eucharistic prayers, especially early ones celebrated widely in the undivided church of the first millennium, are the most authoritative witnesses of the church's faith.[23]

7. In realizing God's plan for universal salvation, the Christ mystery includes in itself the whole of creation. The fullness of that mystery enters into the whole of human history in the person of Jesus Christ as the source and goal of salvation, doing so within the historical context of God's relationship with ancient Israel. The original apostolic faith experience of that mystery, therefore, occurs in terms of the church as the fulfillment in Christ of God's chosen people, that is, as the "new Israel." Accordingly, as is evidenced in the New Testament itself, the apostolic faith witness consists necessarily in reading Old Testament realities and events *typologically*, finding the Christ mystery both as already proleptically active within them and as their ultimate fulfillment. It is on this same faith basis that all other realities and events throughout history are also to be understood, especially those occurring within the church's liturgical worship itself.

8. Continuing the apostolic witness found in Scripture, therefore, the church's liturgy expresses the *lex credendi* also in a fundamentally typological way. ("Christ, our paschal lamb, has been sacrificed. Let us, therefore, celebrate the festival" [1 Cor 5:7-8].) Thus, the central liturgical event in the church year, the paschal Triduum, is also the most highly typological in its readings and rites: washing of the feet, adoration of the cross, accounts of creation and exodus, blessings of new fire and baptismal water, not to mention the Eucharist itself with its enacted remembrance of Christ's Passover.[24]

From this detailed analysis and appropriation of the argument of Hans-Joachim Schulz we can derive four principles. The liturgy is an authentic manifestation of the church's faith and therefore a source of theology

1. to the extent that it expresses and thereby makes available the life, death, and resurrection of Jesus Christ as the primordial realization of God's plan for universal salvation (principle 1: universal salvation in Christ);

2. to the extent that it presents Old Testament realities and events typologically, that is, as imaging, making present, and being fulfilled in the life, death, and resurrection of Christ (principle 2: typological forms);

3. to the extent that in its prayer witness it expresses, articulates, and activates the Christ mystery in the anamnetic, epicletic, and doxological structure of the original apostolic faith experience (principle 3: anamnetic, epicletic, and doxological structure);

4. to the relative extent that a particular liturgical element, *in its manifesting the prior three principles*, has been practiced from ancient times, throughout the centuries, across the world, and by the whole church (principle 4: universal witness).[25]

Universality

It comes as no surprise that, according to Schulz, "the foundation of Christian faith" is God's salvation in Jesus Christ. But why is it that *universality* is the most important indicator of the authentic *lex orandi*: "I urge that supplications, prayers, intercessions, and thanksgivings be made for *all* [humans]" (1 Tim 2:1; emphasis added)?

Federer notes that Cyprian of Carthage (ca. 210–58), writing about two hundred years prior to Prosper of Aquitaine, was very influential for Augustine's understanding of the faith authority of the liturgy.[26] In his treatise on the Lord's Prayer, *De dominica oratione*, Cyprian writes:

> Before all else [Christ as] the teacher of peace and instructor of unity did not wish the prayer to be made individually and in private in a way that when someone prays he would do so only for himself. We do not say, "My Father, who art in heaven" nor "give me my daily bread." . . . Our prayer is public and common, and when we pray, we pray not for

one, but for the whole people, because as a whole people we are one. The God of peace and the teacher of concord who taught unity wished each to pray for all just as he himself bore everyone in [his] one [self] [*in uno omnes ipse portavit*]. The three boys closed up in the fiery furnace observed this law of prayer [*legem orationis*], praying aloud and of one accord in the agreement of the Spirit. . . . They spoke out as if from one mouth, even though Christ had not yet taught them to pray. For that reason was the speech heard and beneficial for those praying; for the peace-filled, honest, and spiritual prayer was deserving of the Lord.[27]

In this passage Cyprian uses the phrase *legem orationis* (the law of prayer), the wording of which is very similar to the *lex orandi* (the law of praying) we have been studying. In commenting on this and other texts of Cyprian, Federer concludes that *legem orationis* refers to the obligation Christians have to pray in the words of the Lord's Prayer since those words come from Christ himself.[28] However, the context here seems to suggest otherwise: that Cyprian actually has a much more comprehensive "law" in mind. True, he begins by noting how, because the Lord taught his followers to pray "Our Father" and not "My Father," all Christian prayer should be made with everyone in mind and not just for oneself alone. However, he then goes on to demonstrate how even when people in the Old Testament—those who like the three young men in the furnace (Dan 3:51) lived before the words of the Lord's Prayer were formulated— pray in this all-inclusive way, it too is heard by the Lord and so is effective. The power of such prayer, then, lies not in the prayer's repeating words that Jesus taught during his lifetime, but rather in its being rooted in the reality of Christ himself, who "bore everyone in [his] one [self]" (*in uno omnes ipse portavit*).

Cyprian's use of *portare* (to bear) here to characterize Christ's relationship to humanity is further developed in his *Epistle* 63 where he writes: "For because Christ who bore [*portabat*] us all bore [*portabat*] even our sins . . ."[29] Cyprian's *portare* thus appears to be an allusion to Deutero-Isaiah's Suffering Servant: "Surely he has *borne* our griefs. . . . He shall *bear* their iniquities" (Isa 53:4, 11; emphasis added). Here, then, Cyprian is making an implicit argument: If Christ "bore" in his own body the sufferings due to our sins, then he must have borne us *completely*, that is, all that is in us and all of us as well, all human beings everywhere and of all times. For if he were willing to identify himself with us in our worst ("he shall bear their iniquities"), then what remains in us that could separate us from his love (cf. Rom 5:8-9) so that no one in fact is excluded from Christ's universal, all-encompassing love?

Centuries later, in a Lenten sermon, the Cistercian abbot St. Isaac of Stella (ca. 1100–73) characterized humanity's relationship to Christ in the same way, using the same verb, *portare*, and in doing so also linked it to a biblical law: "Why are we so unconcerned, brothers, to find occasions to aid one another, so that when we see a greater need we might be of greater help to each other and carry one another's fraternal burdens? For this is what the blessed Apostle admonishes, saying, "Bear [*portate*] one another's burdens, and in this way you will fulfill the law of Christ [*legem Christi*]" [Gal 6:2] . . . who truly 'bore [*tulit*] our weaknesses' in the Passion and 'carried [*portavit*] sorrows' [Isa 53:4] with compassion, loving those he carried [*portavit*], carrying [*portans*] those he loved."[30] Salvation, then, comes to us human beings through our solidarity in Christ's humanity accomplished through his total and unconditional love for us. Furthermore, in our being united to Christ we are all also united *in the reality of Christ* to all who have been made one in him in his universal love.

According to Cyprian, then, the sanctifying power of the Our Father, in which we pray not for ourselves exclusively but as one with all others, does not lie simply in the fact that it repeats the Lord's words. Rather, because in his own life, death, and resurrection Christ "carried everyone" in himself, he now continues to do so through prayer that participates in, and therefore imitates, the universality of God's own saving love in Christ. Consequently, anyone throughout human history who truly opens his or her heart to include others in his or her prayer operates out of the selfsame love of Christ that won our salvation in the first place. That is why the church too, *precisely as church* and as one with the original apostolic faith experience, must be universal both in her love—her identification with all humanity—and in her prayer.

Furthermore, since the liturgy is the prayer of the church as church, and so a fundamental manifestation of Christian faith, the *lex orationis* of Cyprian is identical with both Prosper's *lex supplicandi* and tradition's *lex orandi*. For to the degree that the liturgy *through its forms and structure* allows the church to imitate Jesus Christ in identifying herself with all human beings everywhere, sinners as well as saints, it expresses and activates the church's fundamental nature as true humanity created in and redeemed by the one Christ,[31] in accordance with God's unconditional and *all-inclusive* salvation offered to the world in the Christ mystery of

Ephesians 3 and recommended to be embodied in the church's prayer by 1 Timothy 2:1. Once again, then, *lex orandi, lex credendi*.

The Liturgy as God's Embodied Love

If God's love in Christ for all humanity were not universal, if there were even one human person in the course of history whom God did not love infinitely and unconditionally, then the absolute assurance of the Gospel that God in Christ loves any human in particular would actually be suspect. There would be no basis for the kind of complete faith in God's love called for by the Gospel, and neither would there be any basis for the obligation that we love him completely in return (cf. Matt 22:36-38 and parallels). Put in another way, were Jesus to die on the cross only for the majority of the human race but not for all, his witness to the love of God would lose all of its effectiveness. His then would be a love that measures out only to the degree it receives; thus, it would not be love at all, but only calculating self-interest. True love by definition must be universal. As William Shakespeare writes in Sonnet 116, "Love is not love / which alters when it alteration finds, / or bends with the remover to remove."[32] And so the First Letter of John teaches, "In this is love, not that we have loved God, but that he loved us and sent his Son to be the expiation for our sins" (1 John 4:10).

On the other hand, the love that animates *God's universal salvation* does not arise from some innate moral imperative or blind force operating throughout the world (e.g., an attraction of opposites). It is God's *personal* love incarnated[33] in Jesus Christ by his total gift of self unto death for each and every human person taken both singly and in union with all others. "The heart of the Messiah, around which God formed a human body, is the innermost sanctum of the temple. There stands the altar of the sacrifice which redeemed the world."[34]

Since the saving events of Christ's life were truly historical events, as the Scripture teaches (e.g., 1 Cor 15:1-19; 1 John 1:3; 4:2-3), Jesus brought about universal salvation precisely in and through his absolute love for those particular people whom he encountered during his life on earth, including those around him who hated him most at the time of his death. By his "carrying" them fully in his heart, he in effect "carried" all the members of the human race, as Cyprian teaches, including all who lived both prior to and after his own human lifetime. Christ's salvation, then, consists not in his appeasing some kind of exacting, vengeful God by submitting to extreme suffering as infinite *payment* for sins,[35] but rather in that all-forgiving theandric love which is, and has always been, as concrete in this world as giving someone a cup of water (cf. Mark 9:41) or surrendering one's last coin to the temple treasury (Mark 12:42). Thus, too, the Good Samaritan parable: "Which of these three, do you think, proved neighbor to the man . . . ? . . . Go and do likewise" (Luke 10:36-37).[36]

Authentic Liturgy

It is clear from the history of the church that although the *universality* with which a particular liturgical element has been practiced is one indication of its being an authentic manifestation of the church's faith, it is not the case that no liturgical text or practice can ever be changed. How, then, should this norm of universality be understood and applied?

The question of universality has gained special urgency since the recent appearance of the fifth instruction issued by the Vatican Congregation for Divine Worship and the Discipline of the Sacraments (CDWDS) "for the right implementation of the Constitution on the Sacred Liturgy of the Second Vatican Council," entitled *Liturgiam Authenticam* (Authentic Liturgy).[37]

Promulgated on March 1, 2001, the aim of *Liturgiam Authenticam* (LA) is to provide official guidelines for translating the Latin *editio typica* of the Roman Rite into the various vernacular languages used throughout the world, in order to ensure that the resulting translations be truly *authentic* to the language and spirit of the Latin original. Thus, the object of our present study, the new English translation of the Roman Missal, attempts to embody the translation principles articulated in this Vatican document. As is well known, LA has been criticized by many liturgical scholars[38] and others especially for its call for greater adherence to the lengthy, periodic Latin sentence structure of presidential prayers and for its rendering of all Latin words by their English cognates if possible.

Some years ago the venerable Italian liturgist Salvatore Marsili, OSB, argued that what is actually needed for an authentic renewal of the liturgy is "a new liturgical language":

If a *new* liturgical language is not created, the liturgy will remain always and uniquely a "festive garment" which, as we know, can have exotic forms and colors that glitter but fail to express what lies within them. Above all, this would be the sign that our theology has not rethought revelation as something new, as the announcement of presence (kerygma), and that the "eternal" reality of the "history of salvation" has not been "temporalized" in a language which "incarnates" it in our time, and that therefore it has ceased to be a "history" and remained only the "account" of a history made in terms and accents of other times.[39]

Liturgical theologian Jeremy Driscoll, OSB, agrees that "in liturgy . . . one is translating a text to be used in contemporary worship, and to some extent history and difference create a gap that needs to be bridged."[40] In his view, however, it is also important that those elements in the original language of an established tradition like the Roman Rite should be retained which carry the faith wisdom accumulated by the church over the centuries:

> With the Roman Missal a whole world is being entered, and it is different from—or at least more than—my own mundane and everyday world. It is bigger than my own understanding of the Christian faith or of my particular community's understanding of that faith, even of my own culture's understanding. . . .
>
>   What [the church] believes is happening in the actual celebration of the liturgy . . . is ultimately nothing less than communion in divine trinitarian life. Insofar as this is expressed in language, it is a very delicate interplay of scriptural, liturgical, and doctrinal language. In short, the language of the Roman Missal represents the synthesis of key ideas of biblical faith. This language is a *lex orandi* upon which a *lex credendi* is formulated.[41]

Winfried Haunerland takes the occasion of the promulgation of *Liturgiam Authenticam* to reflect on the larger question of what in general constitutes authentic liturgy.[42] He observes first that liturgy is encountered only in live celebrations of concrete communities. However, because many people report that they cannot discover expressed in the fixed texts of the liturgy—passed on from ancient and medieval times—their own contemporary questions and concerns, their own joys and faith experiences,[43] mere conformity to the prescribed ritual can make authentic liturgy actually difficult, if not impossible, for them. On the other hand, this same desire for relevance oftentimes leads them to privilege their own experiences, theological criteria, or faith situations as the ultimate criteria for judging what truly authentic liturgy is. Although it is true that meaningful personal involvement is essential to authentic liturgy, creating ever-new forms for each new celebration only ends up destroying the basic identity of liturgy itself.[44] And so, in order to avoid individualism, Haunerland suggests that participants be advised to enter into their liturgical participation in much the same way as actors engage in their craft, that is, by completely immersing themselves into their roles: "Whoever engages in the work of the liturgy has taken on a role and is no longer a private person."[45] Participation in the liturgy is meant to be not each person's unique self-expression but rather his or her service to the whole community. Authentic liturgy therefore demands that everyone enter into, and personally identify with, the particular role they are called on to play.

In a later article Haunerland elaborates on this communal dimension of the liturgy:

> Every Christian worship is a celebration in community. It is only successful if there is a culture of community. That demands basic personal capabilities. A person must be ready and capable of denying his or her own ego and ordering himself or herself to the greater good. It puts too much responsibility on the worship celebration of the church itself to demand that it be the first and only place where this is learned. The family and circle of friends, kindergarten and school are places in which these are and must be practiced. Thus, upbringing and self-discipline belong to a liturgical propaedeutic.
>
> The capacity for liturgy can be defined even more concretely. The person who wants to act in a communal way also needs to be able *to be silent* and *to listen*. Whoever is always speaking and making noise, unable to be peaceful, is concerned only with himself or herself and is not open to others. Without openness to other cocelebrants, the liturgy is impossible. But not only is openness necessary on a horizontal level. If liturgy must necessarily be stamped by the Word of God, then only those persons are capable of liturgy who are able to hear the Word, silently present themselves to the Word of God, and be open to what they do not already know.
>
> Community activity places a premium above all on regarding other people as precious. This is demonstrated not only in listening to others but also in a readiness to share and to thank. Whoever wants to regard everything in terms of himself or herself (What am I getting out of this?) is not capable of either community or liturgy. Also, anyone who believes that he or she is indebted to no one and has only himself or

herself to thank for his or her life will never really be connected to a community. Communities live out of giving and receiving.[46]

Haunerland notes how, from the very beginnings of church history, Sunday as the "Day of the Lord," has always been recognized as the unquestioned day of the week to gather for the celebration of the Eucharist. "Whether the Eucharist is celebrated on Sunday is not dependent on agreements or needs of individuals or particular groups. It has much more to do with the mandate of the Lord to come together in his memory, to pronounce the thanksgiving over bread and wine and thus be united with him."[47] From this example of the Sunday Eucharist he concludes,

> The Christian community does not do what it wants, but what it should. Going even further, it celebrates the Eucharist precisely because it understands itself not as an autonomously acting group, but because it experiences itself there in communion with its Lord. It knows that it is not the independent subject of the liturgy, but that Jesus Christ himself is the real agent and thereby the primary subject. Accordingly, a eucharistic celebration is authentic to the degree that its form coincides with this basic faith understanding. . . . The previously described regulations protect the celebration of the Eucharist from arbitrariness and personal preference. At the same time the celebrating community signals its connectedness with the whole church of Jesus Christ.[48]

These reflections prompt Haunerland to ask next whether the individuality of each participant and that of the locally gathered community play no role at all in authentic liturgy. After all, Vatican II calls for a "full, conscious, and active participation" of the faithful (*Sacrosanctum Concilium* 14). By use of examples drawn from areas of the church's liturgy other than just the Sunday Eucharist, he concludes that in a truly authentic celebration of the liturgy another element is required: *the active faith involvement* of each individual and of each local assembly as a whole in the liturgical event. As one example of the extraordinary importance that the official church itself places on the role of active faith, he points to how, because of the Lord's command to all Christians to "pray always," the church allows the official rites of the Liturgy of the Hours to be shortened or modified in any way necessary to allow groups of Christians to fulfill this injunction. The fixity of liturgical forms is therefore not always sacrosanct, nor is it the *only* requirement for authentic liturgy even if in some cases it is inviolable (e.g., the trinitarian baptismal formula).[49]

Reflecting on the church's funeral liturgy, Haunerland notes that it takes place not in response to Christian death in general, but only in service to a particular brother or sister who has died. By its very nature, then, a funeral Eucharist actually *requires* a personalization of the faith to a degree that would not at all be appropriate for a Sunday Eucharist. Nevertheless, it stands as another example that conformity to fixed rites must also serve the uniquely incarnated, here-and-now character of any liturgical celebration, including the Sunday Eucharist, so that participants are able to make honest, wholehearted offerings of their individual and corporate lives to God as they presently exist at this time in salvation history.

From these examples Haunerland concludes that celebrations of the church's liturgy are authentic to the extent *both* (a) that they embody in word and action the faith of the universal church *and* (b) that through them participants are enabled to express their share in the common faith of the church. "For it is not formal conformity that guarantees unity and cohesiveness with the universal church, but rather *the agreement in the expression of faith that different forms of expression make possible.*"[50]

Edward Kilmartin some years ago held for much the same thing:

> The variety of rich liturgical traditions, through which the life of faith is manifested and realized, are only relatively appropriate to express what is proper to the event signified: a saving encounter between God and his people. The Church knows this instinctively and, therefore, does not award any liturgical tradition absolute value, or even pride of place. Rather, the Church is conscious of the fact that the Spirit, who is the ultimate architect of all authentic liturgical tradition, works with what is at hand. In new situations, it can be expected that the Spirit will inspire changes in forms of celebration in order that culturally and historically conditioned believers may be enabled to respond more fully to God's invitation to personal communion, and the consequences it implies for the daily life of faith.[51]

Joseph Gelineau concurs:

> Purely ritualistic repetition, which is a constant and pervasive danger of all symbolic behavior, is doubly illusory. By repeating at the physical level something whose essence is symbolic, there is a risk of forgetting that the cultural context is in continual evolution and never ceases taking different forms. In other words, if one is not attentive to this element of change, something which was once considered fresh will not now be seen as inappropriate; that what was regarded in one place

as familiar will not be recognized in another as foreign. A refusal to modify the form of the rite may distort its meaning. On the other hand, purely repetitive ritualism takes no account of the people who are celebrating nor of the events which influence them. It forgets that the "sacraments are for people" and that the liturgy is our history.

Total improvisation, which is attractive in times of renewal and adaptation like our own, is also doubly illusory. Firstly, by cutting itself off from memory and experience, it remains at the surface of the event it wishes to celebrate. In addition, by avoiding the means of communication that people recognize and have already made sufficiently part of themselves, it only achieves a participation in the most impoverished forms and in an enthusiasm without roots.[52]

Conclusions

An analysis of biblical and patristic texts, official church documents, and the writings of theologians reveals that any given liturgy or liturgical element (*lex orandi*) manifests the church's faith (*lex credendi*) to the degree that it (1) expresses the *universality of God's salvation* accomplished in Jesus Christ; (2) presents Old Testament realities and events *typologically*, that is, as imaging, making present, and being fulfilled in the life, death, and resurrection of Christ; (3) expresses the Christ mystery in the *anamnetic, epicletic, and doxological* (symbolic exchange) *structure* of the original apostolic faith experience; and (4), while manifesting the first three principles, has been practiced from the earliest times and throughout the church. Conversely, in any particular celebration of the church's liturgy the manifestation of the church's faith likewise depends on the relative ability that any given individual or community has both spiritually and culturally to enter into, or to make their own by any necessary adaptation, the objective faith content of her official rites. Like the Word of God itself, the liturgy must be "living and active" (cf. Heb 4:12).

Notes, Chapter Three

[1] Theologians as early as St. John Damascene (675–749) identified the basic expressions of the church's faith as topics or sources for theological study, thereby

imitating Aristotle in his dividing the physical world into so many study topics (Greek: *topoi*; Latin: *loci*; English: "places"). An indication of how little theologians traditionally understood the liturgy as God's self-manifestation in the church's faith, and therefore as one of these "topics" or sources of theology as a study of that faith, is the *Locorum Theologicorum Libri Duodecem* of Melchior Cano, OP (1509–60). The author omits the liturgy altogether from his list of ten such sources. Francis A. Zaccaria, SJ (1714–95) was one of the first in modern times to recognize the liturgy among the "topics" or "places" for systematic theological reflection ("De Usu Librorum Liturgicorum in Rebus Theologicis" (1767), in *Theologiae Cursus Completus* . . ., ed. J. P. Migne [Paris, 1841], 208–310).

[2] This distinction between "first theology" and "second theology" arises from the word "theology" itself, composed as it is out of the Greek *theou*, "of God," and *logos*, "word" or "explanation." As the genitive form of *theos*, *theou* can be taken in either a subjective or an objective sense. As subjective, "of God" refers to the "word" that God as subject "speaks," his self-revelation to human beings in the works of both creation ("general revelation") and salvation in Christ ("special revelation") as received in and through the church's faith. The "of God" as objective refers to academic theology, or "second theology," the systematic investigation into the "first theology" of God's self-revelation taken now as object, providing the church with a fuller explanation (*logos*) and appropriation of the content of that faith. Cf. Karl Rahner et al., eds., *Sacramentum Mundi*, vol. 6 (New York: Herder and Herder, 1970), 236–37; Aidan Kavanagh, *On Liturgical Theology* (New York: Pueblo, 1984), 74–75, 89; and Gordon W. Lathrop, *Holy Things: A Liturgical Theology* (Minneapolis: Fortress, 1993), 4–8 passim.

[3] Cf. Edward J. Kilmartin, SJ, *Christian Liturgy I: Theology and Practice* (Kansas City, MO: Sheed and Ward, 1988), 93. At the same time, other authors have employed different terms; see Kevin Irwin, "Liturgical Theology," in *The New Dictionary of Sacramental Worship*, ed. Peter E. Fink, SJ (Collegeville, MN: Liturgical Press, 1990), 721–33. For a particularly fine analysis of some major differences among authors in understanding this relationship and their broader ramifications, see Maxwell Johnson, "Liturgy and Theology," in *Liturgy in Dialogue*, eds. Paul Bradshaw and Bryan Spinks (Collegeville, MN: Liturgical Press, 1993), 203–27.

[4] Enrico Mazza, in "*Lex Orandi* et *Lex Credendi*: Que dire d'une *Lex Agendi* ou *Lex Vivendi?*" *La Maison-Dieu* 250 (2007): 111–33, argues convincingly that recent scholarly efforts to establish a *lex agendi* or a *lex vivendi* in addition to and on equal footing with the *lex orandi* and *lex credendi* fall short ultimately because both neologisms actually do no more than help explicate the fuller meaning of the *lex orandi*.

[5] "Praeter beatissimae et apostolicae sedis inviolabiles sanctiones, quibus nos piissimi patres, pestiferae novitatis elatione deiecta, et bonae voluntatis exordia et incrementa probablilium studiorum et in eis usque in finem perseverantiam ad Christi gratiam referre docuerunt, obsecrationum quoque sacerdotalium sacramenta respiciamus, quae ab apostolis tradita, in toto mundo atque in omni catholica Ecclesia uniformiter celebrantur, ut legem credendi lex statuat supplicandi." Prosper of Aquitaine, *Indiculus de gratia Dei* 8 (PL 51:209C).

[6] Karl Federer, *Liturgie und Glaube: "Legem credendi lex statuat supplicandi"* (Freiburg in der Schweiz: Paulusverlag, 1950), 5.

[7] Pius XII teaches in *Mediator Dei* (Nov. 20, 1947), no. 48, "But if one desires to differentiate and describe the relationship between faith and the sacred liturgy in absolute and general terms, it is perfectly correct to say, *'Lex credendi legem statuat supplicandi'*—let the rule of belief determine the rule of prayer." *Acta Apostolicae Sedis* 39 (1947): 540. Cf. also Federer, *Liturgie und Glaube*, 4.

[8] The RSV rendition of *anthropous* by "men" has been changed here to "human beings" in order to preserve the gender-neutral character of the Greek.

[9] Federer in *Liturgie und Glaube*, 13, confirms his interpretation of the meaning of *lex* by appealing to another text of Prosper's: *Aut quod Ecclesia quotidie pro inimicis suis orat* . . . (Or the fact that the church daily prays for its enemies . . .) (*Contra collatorem* 12:35).

[10] Cf. Avery Dulles, *"Sensus Fidelium," America* (November 1, 1986), 240–43, 263–4.

[11] Federer, *Liturgie und Glaube*, 14.

[12] *Pace* Paul V. Marshall, "Reconsidering 'Liturgical Theology': Is There a *Lex Orandi* for All Christians?" *Studia Liturgica* 25 (1995): 140.

[13] Paul De Clerck, " 'Lex orandi, lex credendi:' Sens originel et avatars historiques d'un adage équivoque," *Questions liturgiques* 59/4 (1978): 193–212. ET: "'Lex orandi, lex credendi': The Original Sense and Historical Avatars of an Equivocal Adage," *Studia Liturgica* 24 (1994): 178–200.

[14] Paul De Clerck, "Lex orandi, lex credendi: Un principe heuristique," *La Maison-Dieu* 222 (2000): 61–78.

[15] Ibid., 69.

[16] Augustine, *Sermo* 203:1, 1 (PL 38:1035). There are instances, however, where the church's festal calendar does provide unambiguous witness to its faith. The fact that the solemnity of the Annunciation as a feast of the Lord (March 25) occurs nine months to the day before the solemnity of Christmas (December 25), as well as the Solemnity of the Immaculate Conception's (December 8) taking place exactly nine months before the feast of the Birth of Mary (September 8), is clearly intentional. They are a combined, unmistakable testimony to the church's universal faith through the centuries that all human life begins *even as personal* with conception in the womb.

[17] Daniel Van Slyke, *"Lex Orandi Lex Credendi*: Liturgy as *Locus Theologicus* in the Fifth Century?" *Josephinum Journal of Theology* 11/2 (2004): 130–51.

[18] Ibid., 148.

[19] Hans-Joachim Schulz, "Der Grundsatz 'Lex Orandi—Lex Credendi' und die Liturgische Dimension der 'Hierarchie der Wahrheiten,'" *Liturgisches Jahrbuch* 49 (1999): 171–81.

[20] *Ton eso anthrôpon*, i.e., "the man/humanity inside"—Christ dwelling within the believer as a new humanity, replacing the old humanity originating in Adam.

[21] Edward Kilmartin in *Christian Liturgy I* independently makes the same observation in regard to the church's liturgy: "Through the experience of the liturgy, believers are led to the conclusion that the fixed forms of expression of faith, as well as the personal faith expressed by the assembly, are supported by Christ himself: the High Priest of the worship of the church" (46).

[22] It is in this comprehensive sense that De Clerck uses the phrase *lex scriptuaire* ("'Lex orandi, lex credendi': Sens originel," 212). And it is on this same basis that Prosper argues that the liturgy is a witness to the church's faith inasmuch as the prayers are "celebrated uniformly in the whole world and in every Catholic church" (*Indiculus de gratia Dei* 8).

For a differing interpretation of Prosper's reliance on Scripture, see Frieder Schultz, "Evangelische Rezeption der Formel 'Lex Orandi—Lex Credendi,'" *Liturgisches Jahrbuch* 49 (1999): 183: "Evangelium legem statuat credendi et orandi."

Jeremy Driscoll, OSB, observes how there is "a more primitive *lex*" at work behind both the *lex orandi* and the *lex credendi*: the *regula fidei*, "a useful catch phrase which identifies the dynamic by which the early communities identified the faith that came to them from the apostles" (*Theology at the Eucharistic Table: Master Themes in the Theological Tradition*, Studia Anselmiana series [Rome: Centro Studi S. Anselmo; Leominster, UK: Gracewing, 2003], 47–48).

[23] Schulz, "Der Grundsatz," 181.

[24] For an appreciation of the extent to which the liturgy is typological, see Jean Danielou, SJ, *The Bible and the Liturgy* (Notre Dame, IN: University of Notre Dame Press, 1956); and Enrico Mazza, *Mystagogy* (New York: Pueblo, 1989). Noted Methodist liturgical scholar Geoffrey Wainwright, in "'Bible et Liturgie': Daniélou's Work Revisited," *Studia Liturgica* 22 (1992): 159, writes, "One valuable service which Daniélou's works can perform is to recall weary ecumenists to the task of seeking an ecclesial unity grounded upon substantial agreement in the scriptural and patristic faith as this comes to expression in the classic liturgies of the early Church. . . . A contribution which liturgical theologians might offer is close examination of the relations between anamnetic, epicletic, and *proleptic* dimensions that mark Christian worship as part of salvation history" (emphasis added).

[25] "Celebrated uniformly in the whole world and in every Catholic church" (Prosper of Aquitaine, *Indiculus de gratia Dei* 8). Note also Vincent of Lérins's classic criteria for judging true doctrine: "In ipsa item catholica ecclesia magnopere curandum est ut id teneamus quod ubique, quod semper, quod ab omnibus creditum est. Hoc est etenim vere proprieque catholicum, quod ipsa vis nominis ratioque declarat, quae omnia fere universaliter comprehendit" (*Commonitorium* 2:3 [PL 50:640]).

De Clerck notes further that because present-day liturgical documentation is based heavily on traditional data recovered and reintroduced into living liturgies under the impulse of the liturgical movement, it too enjoys great authority, as do contemporary liturgical books since, as duly approved by the official church, they enjoy a kind of external confirmation of their *internal* authority ("Lex orandi, lex credendi: Un principe heuristique," 73).

[26] Federer, *Liturgie und Glaube*, 59.

[27] Cyprian of Carthage, *De dominica oratione* 8 (CSEL 3, 1, 271). Cf. Dan 3:51ff.: "Then these three in the furnace with one voice sang . . ."

[28] Federer, *Liturgie und Glaube*, 60.

[29] Cyprian of Carthage, *Epistle* 63:13: "Nam quia nos omnes portabat Christus qui et peccata nostra portabat . . ."

[30] Isaac of Stella, *Sermo* 31 (PL 194:1793).

[31] "The chorus of Christ [the church] is now the whole world." Augustine, *In psalm.* 149, no. 7 (PL 37:1953): "Chorus Christi jam totus mundus est."

[32] It could be argued further that the basis for the call of conscience to do good and avoid evil that is universal to every human being born into the world—what is known as "natural law"—is the inborn conviction in each human being that one is wholly known and loved as an individual by the personal Source (God) of one's being and of all reality and therefore owes that Source a total response of obedient love in return. Precisely because it goes against this fundamental human awareness, any denial of God as one's supreme and sovereign good is, according to Scripture, a lie (cf. Pss. 14:1; 53:2; 1 John 2:22).

[33] Cf. David Coffey, "The 'Incarnation' of the Holy Spirit in Christ," *Theological Studies* 45 (1984): 466–80.

[34] Hugo Rahner, "On the Biblical Basis of the Devotion," in *Heart of the Savior*, ed. Josef Stierli (Freiburg, Germany: Herder, 1957), 23.

[35] It is true that the NT refers to Christ's work of salvation as a "ransom" for sin (Mark 10:45) and a paschal sacrifice (1 Cor 5:7-8), but the overall context of its teaching (e.g., Rom 5:1-11) gives clear indication that these and other such images (e.g., Heb 10:12) are intended only as metaphors to assure readers that salvation has already been fully realized in Christ, needing only our acceptance in faith.

[36] Note the medieval "Good Samaritan" stained glass window in Chartres Cathedral in France intuiting the concrete way in which Jesus saved the human race and continues to do so through those who "do likewise."

[37] Congregation for Divine Worship and the Discipline of the Sacraments, *Liturgiam Authenticam*: On the Use of Vernacular Language in the Publication of the Books of the Roman Liturgy, Fifth Instruction on the Implementation of the Constitution on the Sacred Liturgy (Washington, DC: USCCB, 2002) (= LA).

[38] E.g., Peter Jeffery, *Translating Tradition: A Chant Historian Reads* Liturgiam Authenticam (Collegeville, MN: Liturgical Press, 2005) = *Worship* 78 (2004): 2–24, 139–64, 236–65, 309–41; Bishop Donald Trautman, "The Relationship of the Active Participation of the Assembly to Liturgical Translations," *Worship* 80 (2006): 290–309; Mark R. Francis, "The Call for Eucharistic Renewal in a Multicultural World," *Ecclesia Orans* 24 (2007): 99–118, esp. 111–18; and John F. Baldovin, SJ, *Reforming the Liturgy: A Response to the Critics* (Collegeville, MN: Liturgical Press, 2008), 119–24. Jeffery objects especially to the document's presupposition that there exists a unitary Latin tradition across history to be reclaimed in a new translation.

[39] Salvatore Marsili, OSB, "Liturgical Texts for Modern Man," in *The Crisis of Liturgical Reform*, Concilium 42 (New York: Paulist Press, 1969), 63, quoted in Keith F. Pecklers, SJ, *Dynamic Equivalence: The Living Language of Christian Worship* (Collegeville, MN: Liturgical Press, 2003), 226–27.

[40] Jeremy Driscoll, OSB, "Conceiving the Translating Task: The Roman Missal and the Vernacular," in *The Voice of the Church: A Forum on Liturgical Translation* (Washington, DC: United States Catholic Conference, 2001), 53.

[41] Ibid., 53–54, 60.

[42] Winfried Haunerland, "Authentische Liturgie," *Liturgisches Jahrbuch* 52 (2002): 135–57.

[43] Ibid., 138–39.

[44] Ibid., 143.

[45] Ibid., 140

[46] Winfried Haunerland, "Gottesdienst als 'Kulturleistung,'" *Liturgisches Jahrbuch* 56 (2005): 70.

[47] Haunerland, "Authentische Liturgie," 142, quoting Robert Taft, SJ, "The Frequency of the Celebration of the Eucharist Throughout History," in *Between Memory and Hope: Readings on the Liturgical Year*, ed. Maxwell E. Johnson (Collegeville, MN: Liturgical Press, 2000), 78.

[48] Ibid., 143.

[49] Haunerland, "Authentische Liturgie," 144–46.

[50] Ibid., 150. Emphasis added.

[51] Kilmartin, *Christian Liturgy I*, 61.

[52] Joseph Gelineau, SJ, "Conclusions," in *Growing in Church Music: Proceedings of a Meeting on "Why Church Music?"* Strawberry Hill, London, England (Washington, DC: Universa Laus, 1979), 56.

Part Two

The Eucharistic Rite

Chapter Four

Liturgical Assembly: Its Time and Place

On the basis of the theology of liturgy set forth in part 1, we begin our study of how a typical Sunday Eucharist of the Roman Rite participates in Christ's paschal mystery, the saving events of his life, death, and resurrection.

Every Sunday Eucharist throughout the year is assigned its own scriptural readings and presidential prayers, that is, its own "propers." The Mass formulary chosen for this study is that of the Ninth Sunday in Ordinary Time, Year A, because its scriptural readings are fairly brief and yet provide a clear instance of liturgical typology, of how all of human life and meaning is fulfilled in Christ's paschal mystery.

Since the eucharistic liturgy from beginning to end constitutes a single self-offering in faith, the liturgy as a whole, and not just key portions of it, is a vehicle for God's saving activity in the life of the church. "The various rites of the Eucharistic celebration are not simply juxtaposed haphazardly; they fit together according to a coherent architectonics, thereby forming a vast structured ensemble which itself must be considered as one great symbol, *a single sacramental whole*. Each element can be understood as symbolizing with the others, linked together within this whole."[1] As with any literary work such as a poem or a play, even those more important moments in the rite that may be indispensable for its valid celebration attain their fullest faith meaning—and therefore their full sacramental effectiveness—only within the whole complex of significant rites surrounding them. Any distinction, then, between ritual elements that are sacramentally effective and those that are *merely* ceremonial or adiaphoral is no longer theologically tenable.[2] In our efforts to recognize more fully God's self-manifestation in the church's Eucharist, we therefore need to study each of its ritual elements in light of the whole liturgical act as it unfolds from beginning to end.

It is obviously impossible to gather all members of the church throughout the world together in one place for a single Eucharist. How then can the Eucharist be a true celebration of the full unity of the church, and not simply of the unity of each local eucharistic assembly? As part of our investigation of a typical Sunday Eucharist, then, we examine first the basic nature of the liturgical assembly, how it is a realization of the whole church. And because within the full *lex orandi* of a typical Sunday Eucharist are included both the day itself of the celebration (Sunday) and its typical locale (the church building), prior to our consideration of the introductory rites of the Mass we will also investigate what these temporal and spatial parameters reveal about the church's faith, her *lex credendi*.

Liturgical Assembly

The term "introductory rites" refers here to all that takes place from the entrance procession up to and including the opening prayer just before the readings. However, for anything at all to take place, there must first be a gathering of worshipers.

According to the 1978 United States Bishops' Committee on the Liturgy (BCL) document, Environment and Art in Catholic Worship, "Among the symbols with which the liturgy deals, none is more important than [the] assembly of believers."[3] The liturgical assembly includes in its mystery more than just the gathered members of a local church. It is a sacramental realization of the whole church throughout history and across the world, with Christ as her head, as well as the whole human race created and redeemed in him. But how does it do this? To the naked eye, one particular gathering of people *as such* hardly appears to be much different from any other—be it a mob watching a fire, an audience at Speakers' Corner in Hyde Park, London, or a cheering crowd at a grade school soccer match. Therefore, we first need to ask in what way the assembly of believers is itself a liturgical, eucharistic symbol.

Thierry Maetens, in his 1964 work *Assembly for Christ*, notes that Christian assemblies have their roots in the Old Testament *qahal*, "the assembly of all the tribes," sometimes translated into Greek by *synagōgē* or *ekklēsia*.[4] The *qahal,* called together by God through prophets or kings as God's representatives, came to be seen as a repetition of the Sinai assembly through which God first established Israel as his people.[5] The fact that the *qahal* was initiated by God also signified its preeminence over all other activities of the people. In it the people gathered (a) to hear God's Word and (b) to respond by a profession of faith, most typically in the form of a sacrifice as an act of thanksgiving for God's wonderful deeds of salvation, often made through a prayer by the president of the assembly.[6] Fifth- and fourth-century BC prophetic texts begin to recognize the fundamentally universal nature of Israel's assemblies, how God intends through them to gather to himself all the peoples of the earth.[7]

According to Maertens, every liturgical assembly throughout the Bible (a) is called together by God through a representative (b) to hear the Word of God, (c) to then commit itself in faith to that Word, and finally (d) to be sent forth by a dismissal rite to live true to that Word. "The function of the dismissal corresponds to that of the invitation. Each is reserved to the president of the assembly in order to keep intact its official character. . . . [The] dismissal is an acknowledgment that the assembly is not the whole people. . . . [It] establishes a continuity between the work of the assembly inspired by the Word of God, and the work of daily life based on fidelity to the pact sealed in the assembly, in obedience to the Word proclaimed and ratified."[8]

Turning to New Testament evidence, Maertens observes, "The first Christians had a better understanding of the fact that the liturgical assembly is an act by which God has already gathered [humankind] together. They saw the close connection between the mission that seeks to bring about the assembly of all [humankind] in the Church and the mystery contained in the liturgical assembly."[9] He continues, "The most profound of all signs of the Lord's presence in the midst of the assembly is the Eucharist. It was during a eucharistic meal that the disciples at Emmaus recognized him."[10]

According to Pierre Grelot, for St. Paul "the coming together in common (*synerkomai epi to auto*; 1 Cor 11:20) constitutes [Christians'] reunion 'as church' (*synerkomai en ekklēsia*; 1 Cor 11:18)."[11] Grelot adds,

> In Acts Luke approvingly presents believers as assembling "in common" or "in the same place." . . . The word to name these reunions is *ekklēsia*. . . . Its biblical background evokes the assembly of Israel (*qahal*), convoked for the worship and service of God. Luke is not ignorant of this meaning: in the desert Israel already constitutes an

ekklēsia (Acts 7:38). That is why, when he reprises the word to apply it to the Christian community, he characterizes [this community] generally as one that gathers in assembly, as a new Israel convoked by God around the risen Christ. . . . From this comes the first conclusion: . . . *The church without assembly would be a contradiction.* . . .

In order to fulfill her purpose, [the church, then,] must let [the faithful] experience their unity in Christ. . . . It is important that every assembly maintain awareness of its being "the church of God" found in a particular place—not a group of believers coming together out of like sympathies or human allegiances, but a cell of the Body of Christ, therefore a group *open* to the totality of the Body, where there is "neither Greek nor Jew, nor slave nor free person, nor man nor woman" (Gal 3:28; cf. 1 Cor 12:13; Col 3:11). . . . A group that of its own free will wants to be restricted to one particular people, race, class, cultural background, etc., would be a negation of church, even if it intends for its part to celebrate the Day of the Lord with fervor, for that fervor would rest mostly on shared outlooks or sensibilities in the group. The same would be true of any group that constructs within itself barriers that separate people from each other—for example, if it uncritically espouses any kind of social hierarchy with partitions and abuses of power. . . . The church exists there—and there only—where the *community*, correctly understood, is *reunited* around the resurrected Christ and in his name.[12]

Grelot reflects next on how according to the New Testament the liturgical assembly necessarily images the structure of the church: "If the church, in virtue of her very name (*ekklēsia*), is the assembly convoked by God around the resurrected Christ to offer herself in him in spiritual homage (*tēn logikēn latreian*; Rom 12:1) and to receive from him the grace that saves human beings, the common prayer of her members constitutes the manifestation of her very being. The structure of the group that makes this prayer espouses (*épouse*) the structure of the local church. The function of presidency is then also essential to it as to the community that maintains with it a visible form received from the apostolic founders."[13]

David Coffey gives a helpful explanation of this structure and the essential relationship the ordained presider has to the rest of the liturgical assembly as liturgical symbol:

The priest does not represent Christ and the Church in exactly the same way. He represents Christ in that he sacramentally makes visible and active in the Church an invisible reality, Christ in his headship. This is not the case with his representation of the Church, for in a real sense the Church is visible already. But in this case he adds headship, apostolate, or leadership to the action of this group of believers, in order to constitute them as Church in the full sense. Apart from his presence and ministry they are only a group of believers, unable of themselves to represent the Church. But at the same time, the fact that he represents them by no means renders their presence and action superfluous, for just as their faith is positive and active, so too is their priesthood. Thus it can be seen that, even though the priest represents a reality that is already at least partially visible, . . . what he adds is drawn not from them, but from Christ. And it is precisely this contribution that, along with theirs, truly constitutes the Church, and therefore the Church at prayer, i.e. the priesthood of the Church.[14]

The priest-presider's typology of Christ's headship actually forms part of that overall typological structure of the liturgy discussed in chapter 3, how the church partakes in Christ's paschal mystery through liturgical imitation of those saving events. The Western church's discipline of priestly celibacy, through a kind of "presence of the absence,"[15] serves to intensify this same typological function. That priest-presiders are graced to choose to live without spouses "for the sake of the kingdom of heaven" (Matt 19:12), in imitation of Jesus' own celibacy, highlights how humanity's absolute hunger for love and companionship ("It is not good that the man should be alone" [Gen 2:18]), although experienced as the absence of God who is love, paradoxically manifests his *presence* as of the One who alone can fulfill the infinite desires of the human heart. The celibacy of presiders, therefore, also contributes to the Eucharist's overall manifestation of the church's faith: her complete self-gift in Christ to the Father.

For Maertens, the fact that the first Christian assembly was gathered around the apostles, sent by the Lord to be witnesses of his resurrection, has great significance.

> The first primitive assembly met round this group of witnesses and at once two principles emerged from its conduct: First of all, the assembly, even for the liturgy, gathered round these "witnesses." It did not gather round a hierarchy of administrators as in the synagogue, nor of those who offered sacrifices as in the Temple, but round a missionary hierarchy of those who had been sent. . . . This analysis of the means employed by the Jerusalem community to bring [people] together teaches us the essential lesson that an assembly can call all nations together only if it is gathered around those who have received a mandate from the Lord. . . . [Thus, to] the extent that an assembly sees its president as a minister of worship, or one who offers sacrifice, rather

than a missionary, the essential meaning of the assembly—a sign of a universal gathering—is impaired.[16]

In other words, just as Jesus' whole life and ministry were directed toward gathering all into the kingdom of God (e.g., Luke 19:41-4; John 17:18-26), so is the Eucharist the continuation of his work of assembly, by means of his representatives, sharing his own mind and heart with the members of his Body, the church, sending them forth to continue that same work of gathering all into his one humanity fully united in God.

By referring to the assembly as a liturgical symbol, the BCL document Environment and Art in Catholic Worship signals also that it is through the fixed forms of the church's liturgy, manifesting her common faith across the centuries, that each local assembly acts as a symbol of the whole church as sacrament of Christ. At the same time, in order for an assembly to be a true *symbolic embodiment* of the church, it has to incarnate its use of those rites within its own historical situation in the world, the particular needs and concerns of its own community and the world in which it lives.

In summary, the assembly of worshipers for the Sunday Eucharist is an essential expression of their identity as Christians: humanity called together by God in Christ. They gather in the church's ritual to hear and embody God's Word in Christ, to be sent out as his apostles into the world to continue his salvation of assembling all of God's children to himself. The act of assembling thus marks the beginning already of the Sunday Eucharist, revealing the saving power of Christ's death on the cross (typological) through which he united in himself all of humanity (universal).

Sunday

As noted already, since in Jesus Christ God spoke himself out completely in the lifelong self-offering of a Palestinian Jewish man of the first century, that is, in a way that was intrinsically both spatial and temporal, time and space themselves exist and have their ultimate meaning only as participations in the reality of Jesus Christ. Because in her eucharistic memorial of that salvation the church as a divine/human society is also confined to particular times and places, our next task will be to discover how the temporal and spatial parameters of the Sunday Eucharist are also manifestations of the church's faith, her *lex credendi.*

Although Acts 2:46 may indicate that Luke's ideal Christian community celebrated Eucharist daily,[17] our present study focuses on a typical Sunday Eucharist because from the very beginning the church saw herself obligated to a weekly gathering for the Eucharist.[18] Whether that took place originally on Friday or Saturday evenings is uncertain.[19] If the former, since the Jewish day begins at sundown, it would have been as a Jewish-Christian replacement for the opening Sabbath meal; if the latter, it would have been as an inauguration of Sunday as the new Day of the Lord, that of Christ's resurrection. In any event the question arises, "Why this seven-day frequency, and why on the same day of the week, Sunday?"

The roots of the seven-day week go back to time immemorial. An "astrological week of Chaldean origin . . . seems to have become popular, at first in Asia Minor and Egypt in the second century BC, then in the Empire generally. It is what was called the 'planetary' week, and began with the day of Saturn, corresponding with the sabbath, the last day of the Jewish week. The second day was that of the Sun, then came that of the Moon, of Mars, of Mercury, of Jupiter and of Venus."[20] In fact, the seven-day week was standard in the Near East thousands of years before Christianity, apparently having developed out of religious observance of the cycle of the moon. The 29½ days of the lunar cycle are visibly divisible into roughly four seven-day periods: (1) "new moon" (dark), (2) "first quarter," with the moon's semicircle lighting, (3) "full moon," and (4) "third quarter," with an opposite semicircle of light.[21] Ancient Babylonians called the new moon *sapattu* (stop; = Sabbath?), for the moon appears to rest. And the Assyrians offered sacrifices to different gods on the days beginning each of the four phases, days observed religiously by the Sumero-Akkadians and Hindus as well.[22] Inheriting this Mideastern practice of a seventh-day rest, ancient Israel then came to regard it as divine in its origins, as an essential characteristic of the created world (cf. Gen 1).

By celebrating weekly Eucharist on Sunday, the church recalls how Christ in his life, death, and resurrection is the source and goal of all creation (cf. Col 1:15-20), and that Sunday, like Easter, encompasses in its eucharistic celebration not only Christ's resurrection but also his suffering and death along with his future coming in glory.[23] Accordingly, in the Roman Rite calendar, every Sunday of the year holds the same supreme feast-day rank of "solemnity" as does Easter itself.

> By a tradition handed down from the apostles, which took its origin
> from the very day of Christ's resurrection, the Church celebrates the
> paschal mystery every seventh day, which day is appropriately called
> the Lord's Day or Sunday. For on this day Christ's faithful are bound
> to come together into one place. They should listen to the word of God
> and take part in the Eucharist, thus calling to mind the passion, resur-
> rection, and glory of the Lord Jesus, and giving thanks to God who
> "has begotten them again, through the resurrection of Christ from the
> dead, unto a living hope" (1 Pet 1:3). The Lord's Day is the original
> feast day, and it should be proposed to the faithful and taught to them
> so that it may become in fact a day of joy and of freedom from work.
> Other celebrations, unless they be truly of the greatest importance,
> shall not have precedence over Sunday, which is the foundation and
> kernel of the whole liturgical year. (*Sacrosanctum Concilium* 106)

Only with the Constantinian peace of the fourth century were Christians freed from having to work on Sundays, and it was not until the
sixth century that the church began legislating against "servile work" on
the Lord's Day.[24] The Sabbath rest of the Old Testament freed God's
people as spiritual beings from being dominated totally by the rhythms
and necessities of physical life.[25] J. M. R. Tillard notes how the ancient
Israelites by their Sabbath worship actually partook in God's own Sabbath rest among his people, a rest in which they both experienced his
friendship and tasted already that future Day of the Lord when God
would come with a full, definitive salvation for his people (cf. Deut 12:9-
12; Pss 95:11; 132:13-4).[26] And so it may be that already in New Testament times, because Christ by his rising from the dead on a Sunday
realized the promised Day of the Lord, the day of the Eucharist became
known as "the Lord's Day" (Rev 1:10).

In the phrase "the Lord's Day" the Greek adjective *kuriakos* (the Lord's)
occurs for the second of only two times in the New Testament, the other
appearing in 1 Corinthians 11:20: "the Lord's supper." According to
Adolf Adam, Sunday is holy not only as the day of the week on which
Christ rose from the dead, but even more so because it is the day when
Christians continue to encounter their risen Lord in a special way in
their celebration of the Eucharist.[27] In other words, Sunday would not
be the Lord's *Day* without the Lord's *Supper*, just as according to the
martyrs of Abitina one could not be Christian without the Eucharist
("We cannot live without the *dominicum*").[28] In the poetic language of
Psalm 19:2, "Day to day pours forth speech, / and night to night declares
knowledge." Established by God in Christ's death and resurrection as

the day of salvation, Sunday in Christian consciousness thus "proclaims" to the other days of the week, as it were, that only that which gives praise and glory to God throughout the week has any lasting value and meaning (cf. Col 3:17).

Yet how does not only the Sunday Eucharist but even the day itself proclaim the church's faith? In a poem entitled "Bereft," the twentieth-century American poet Robert Frost presents a unique experience of nature had by someone who has just been abandoned in life by the death of a spouse or someone very dear. The world about him seems suddenly to have become foreign, unsettled, and even "sinister." The poem is so effective because we have all known times when the world around us echoes in sights and sounds our own inner experiences, as well as the feelings of elation or fear that may come with them. Indeed, with the dawning of Sunday and its call to the Eucharist, the whole world for faithful Christians seems somehow renewed, instilled with joy at the rising of Jesus Christ on Easter Sunday morning, the "sun of justice" (Mal 3:20), the great eighth day of the "new creation" that will never end (cf. 2 Cor 5:17; Rev 21:23).

Thus, for believers the day itself carries with it a kind of sacred, other-worldly reality and aura. This awareness is further strengthened for Catholics by the consciousness that on every Sunday the whole Catholic Church throughout the world gathers to celebrate the one same Eucharist. It is this worldwide solidarity in the faith—the realization that on every Sunday each local assembly is part of a universal assembling of Catholics everywhere—that above all makes the day itself such a palpable and powerful sacramental manifestation of Christ, who *unites all* in the Eucharist to himself and to each other with the bonds of his paschal love.

In summary, Sunday, as one of the days of a seven-day week, witnesses to how human beings as temporal creatures, confronted each day with an ever-changing world and themselves ever changing and growing in response, must renew their eucharistic self-offering in Christ at least weekly if they are to continue to be given over fully to God in all the moments of their lives. Established by God in the death and resurrection of Christ as a special day of salvation, Sunday as one particular day in the week proclaims to all the others that only that which gives praise and glory to God throughout the week can have lasting value and meaning in God's eternal kingdom (cf. Col 3:17). In the church's having set Sunday aside from the very beginning for her common celebration of the Eucharist, therefore, Christians experience the day itself as part of the *lex orandi*, a powerful witness of the church's faith, calling everyone each week to dress up in their "Sunday best" and celebrate together the immensity of God's love, to offer their endeavors and all human endeavors to the Father through the once-for-all self-offering of Christ. The obligation for doing so—offering themselves fully to God in return—lies in how the infinite goodness and holiness of the gift itself, Christ the Lord, demand this recognition. Once again, it is only in such complete self-offering in return that Christians receive the immensity of God's self-gift in Jesus Christ and in the world created in him in the first place: "*the Christian mode of appropriation is through disappropriation.*"[29]

The Church Building and Its Furnishings

The assembly acts as a liturgical symbol, as we have seen, not simply in its performance of the texts and actions of the eucharistic ritual, but also by the specific day set aside for its gathering: Sunday, the Day of the Lord. The same holds true for the place of its worship: the church building dedicated for that purpose. Although it is true that human beings are able anywhere to meet and worship God "in spirit and in truth" (John 4:23-24), and, as St. Stephen in Acts tells us, "the Most High does not dwell in houses made with hands" (7:48), nevertheless, in order to continue as sacrament of Christ in the world, the church as a public, social reality requires established places of worship large enough for her regular plenary gatherings. Thus, as Karl Rahner writes, "Rather than entering a temple which walls off the Holy from the godless world outside, [humanity in Christ] sets up in the open expanse of God's world *a sign* proclaiming that not in Jerusalem alone but everywhere, in Spirit and in truth, God is adored, experienced, and accepted as gracious liberator."[30] Before the Edict of Milan (313) the church met in the homes of some of her more wealthy members or in modest, tenement-like buildings purchased for that purpose.[31] With religious freedom came many new converts so that house churches were no longer able to hold their now-larger assemblies. Nor were existing pagan temples well-suited for Christian worship, since they "had been designed to shelter an image, not to accommodate a congregation of both [laity] and clergy."[32] In his care for the church, the emperor Constantine (272–337) bestowed public dignity on bishops equal to that of Roman magistrates and turned some existing basilicas into Christian places of worship. He built others as well, such as the Lateran basilica (312/3–20) and St. Peter's (324–29) in Rome and the Holy Sepulcher in Jerusalem (325/6).[33]

The term "basilica" derives from the Greek word *basileus* (king) and in ancient times denoted a particular type of large meeting hall where a ruler gave audiences or magistrates heard law cases. Richard Krautheimer notes that "neither to Constantine nor to anyone, whether pagan or Christian, in the early fourth century a church was a religious building of the same character as a temple. Churches rather . . . were meeting halls for the congregations (*basilicae ecclesiae*) or meeting halls for burial and funeral rites (*basilicae quae coemeteria*). But they were also audience halls of the Lord."[34] Thomas Mathews adds that Christians adapted

> the Roman civic basilica by turning it ninety degrees on its axis. Thus, what had been a broad, colonnaded interior mall stretching right and left of the entering visitor became a long processional tunnel of space leading the visitor compellingly from the entrance to the holy of holies, the altar space at the opposite end of the nave. Because Christians generally faced east to pray, their basilicas conformed by pointing their nave to the east. The adoption of this building form—a roof of timber and tile covering three or five parallel corridors, the central one higher and wider than the side ones—determined the plan that cathedral architecture would follow throughout the Middle Ages. Already in 324–329 Constantine's "Old" St. Peter's in Rome contained the layout of Notre Dame in Paris nine hundred years later.[35]

Not everywhere in early Christianity were all stages of the eucharistic liturgy celebrated at one end of a basilica-style church. According to Klaus Gamber, "In the basilicas built under the Emperor Constantine and in North Africa the altar was situated approximately at the center of the central nave," and the laity stood in the side naves facing inward toward the liturgical action around the altar,[36] whereas in ancient east Syria it was the reading from Scripture that held this central location, on a "bema," or platform, on which were seated the presiding bishop/ presbyter and his accompanying ministers. In this configuration the presider, after the opening prayers and readings, moved for the eucharistic prayer to the apsidal altar at the east end of the building where along with the rest of the assembly he stood praying eastward, in the direction Christ was thought to have ascended into heaven and from which he would return again like the rising sun.[37] "At least since the turn of the [second] millennium it has been the universal, accepted rule in East and West that all altars are so constructed that the priest faces eastward with the people."[38] Up until the late twentieth century, therefore, even when Christianity lost a sense of an eastern orientation, the priest proclaimed the eucharistic prayer almost universally with his back to the people, facing outward with them toward God, who infinitely transcends his created world: "I lift up my eyes to the hills. / From where does my help come? / My help comes from the LORD, / who made heaven and earth" (Ps 121:1-2).

Thus, the shape of the subsequent major architectural styles up to our own day—Romanesque, Gothic, Renaissance, baroque, neoclassical, neo-Gothic, and more modern endeavors—has continued this predominantly processional floor plan.[39] And if it is true, as Louis-Marie Chauvet contends, that "liturgical space speaks . . . as Christian space, as do the objects and actors which in interaction make it up, manifesting metaphorically the mystery of Christ and metonymically the ecclesial communion in time and space,"[40] then one might conclude from this dominance of processional architecture that the church has seen herself throughout the centuries primarily as a pilgrim community, a church on the way:[41] "For here we have no lasting city, but we seek the city which is to come. Through [Jesus Christ] then let us continually offer up a sacrifice of praise to God, that is, the fruit of lips that acknowledge his name" (Heb 13:14-15).

Upon entering a typical Catholic church, therefore, one's eye is drawn immediately down the main aisle toward the opposite end of the building where stands the altar on a central axis in the raised area of the sanctuary. Above the altar, either in painted or mosaic images on the apsidal or flat sanctuary wall or in representational figures in stained-glass windows, is typically found iconography of Christ and the church triumphant, the heavenly Jerusalem toward which all Christian life in this world is directed: "So then you are no longer strangers and sojourners, but you are fellow citizens with the saints and members of the household of God, built upon the foundation of the apostles and prophets, Christ Jesus himself being the cornerstone, in whom the whole structure is joined together and grows into a holy temple in the Lord; in whom you also are built into it for a dwelling place of God in the Spirit" (Eph 2:19-22). The statue or image of the Blessed Virgin Mary typically found in Catholic churches at the left side of the altar (as seen from the nave) quietly testifies to the fundamental vocation that all the members of the church share with her of cooperating in Christ's work of salvation: "Let it be done to me according to your word" (Luke 1:38). As an image of his human mother, it also proclaims the full humanity of Christ himself. The image of St. Joseph to the right of the altar combines with it to symbolize the essential role Christian marriage and family life have in Christ's work of salvation. St. Joseph's flowering staff, signaling the purity of his virginity, is also a subtle theological reminder of Christ's full divinity. And, located along both side walls of the nave, the traditional fourteen Stations of the Cross give eucharistic worshipers the oftentimes needed assurance of God's awareness of and compassion for whatever they might be suffering in their lives, how in the saving events of Christ's passion all human suffering has been taken up and transformed into the fullness of life.

The visual progression from the entrance to the apse has often been accentuated in church architecture, beginning with the ancient Roman basilica, by a parallel series of columns or piers on both sides of the central nave. Given the church building as a symbol of the universal church both in this world and in the next, it is not surprising that the similarity of columns to upright human figures lined up in majestic instancy toward the sanctuary has given rise to identifying them with the apostles on whom, metaphorically, rests the structure of the universal church (Gal 2:9) and whose unswerving devotion invites contemporary believers to imitate their following the Lord into glory.[42] According to Louis-Marie Chauvet, "Metonymically [such objects] link the assembly to past generations which have handed down to it the living tradition of the church and the totality of Christian communities which, by communion, form the one church of Christ."[43]

Beginning with the fourth-century Lateran basilica and old St. Peter's in Rome, processional churches have more often than not included a transept or transept-like area in their construction. This nave-like extension at the eastern end of the building, perpendicular to the central nave, originally provided needed space to manage the flow of large liturgical processions. However, because the cruciform floor plan that resulted recalls Christ's saving death on the cross (apse area as head, transept as arms, and nave as combined trunk and legs), it became and remained dominant in church architecture in both East and West up to our own time. Indeed, this human body–like structure symbolizes not only the crucified body of Christ, but also how within the church building his sacrifice is realized once again in the liturgical self-offering of the members of his Body, the church. Pointing simultaneously toward all four directions of the compass, the cruciform structure connotes as well both the universality of God's salvation in Christ and the catholicity of the church as sacrament of that salvation.

It is true that although the vast majority of church buildings in the Western church through the centuries have been processional, in late antiquity Byzantine Christianity made the dome—a 360-degree spin of the Roman arch on its axis—its central architectural feature. Realized most dramatically in Justinian's Constantinopolitan Church of Hagia Sophia (532–37), the high circular dome by imitating the canopy of the heavens (cf. Amos 9:6) is an effective symbol of God's overarching providence and authority. Whereas Western processional architecture recalls Christ's horizontal human journey across time into eternity, the domal, vertical architecture of the East emphasizes more his unchanging divinity and the identity of the church's earthly liturgy with that of heaven. In traditional Eastern iconography the circular perfection of a church's dome is often echoed in an apsidal image of Christ *Pantocrator* ("all powerful") with a massive rounded head, signaling again his divine authority and immutability: "Jesus Christ is the same yesterday and today and forever" (Heb 13:8).

Given its compelling power to symbolize transcendence, it is not surprising that sooner or later the dome would make its appearance in Western processional church architecture as well. Erected in the 1420s, Brunelleschi's dome over the transept crossing of the cathedral of Florence began a practice that would be imitated across the Renaissance, baroque, and neoclassical periods and in larger church buildings such as cathedrals well into the nineteenth and twentieth centuries. The new St. Peter's Basilica in Rome (1506–1626), Sir Christopher Wren's Anglican Cathedral of St. Paul's in London (1677–1708), and the Cathedral of the Assumption in Baltimore (1806–21) are some of the more famous of many such domed processional churches throughout the world.

As Jungmann points out, the Western church in reaction to the fourth-century Arian heresy placed preponderant stress on Christ's divinity.[44] This led in turn to increased clericalism and an overemphasis on Christ's transcendence, resulting in a distancing of the altar from the nave of the church by an expanded chancel or sanctuary area, obscuring for the laity any sense of God's dwelling in the midst of his people. With the Second Vatican Council's (1962–65) emphasis on the church as both the Body of Christ (e.g., 1 Cor 12:27) and the people of God (1 Pet 2:9-10), presiders at the Eucharist in renovated churches throughout the Catholic world began facing the people from the other side of the altar, now brought forward toward and sometimes even into the nave, resulting in a sense of the whole community's being gathered together at a common family table.

Immediately after the council, however, these same theological emphases led in some places to the removal of almost all traditional signs of transcendence, such as statues of saints and noble furnishings, and sometimes even to locating the altar so into the midst of the assembly as to suggest that its sanctifying power originates solely from the community that completely surrounds it.[45] However, the vast majority of processional church renovations since the council have succeeded, through a judicious symbolic balance of immanence and transcendence, in communicating not only God's saving presence in the midst of the assembly but his absolute otherness as well, doing so by bringing the altar far enough forward to overcome its erstwhile excessive distance from the faithful and yet, by a relative separation, still calling the assembly beyond itself to complete union with God in the world to come. At the same time, many new churches are being built with appropriately shortened and widened naves and with transept seating directed toward the altar in order to create a greater sense of solidarity and participation of all in the eucharistic event.

In regard to the proper balance of transcendence with immanence, Chauvet asks,

> What is prayer if not a game? It is a game of negotiating the right distance between human beings and God, between presence and absence; it is a game which allows the believing subject to maintain relations with God by maintaining separation from God. This is truly a difficult task, since it calls for a fundamental detachment from the self and from the God to which the self attaches itself, and it inevitably results in wounds, as Jacob found in his struggle with God by the brook Yabbok (Gen 32:23-33). But this wound to narcissism is fruitful, since it is the result of a trial of strength with a God who "resists." Thus liturgical space, by virtue of its precarious character as transitional space, seems eminently suitable for the precarious character of prayer in which the trial of relations with God takes place, with a God who, inviting his children to bring the most human features of their lives to him, accepts the risk of seeing himself manipulated as an immediate presence, but accepts it only to the degree that he has an opportunity: that of teaching them at their expense to assume his absence and thus to convert their desires.[46]

Probably because the Letter to the Hebrews sees in Jesus the typological fulfillment of the Old Testament altar (13:10), patristic writers in the East and West came to regard the Christian altar as a symbol of Christ,[47] a tradition continued on into our own day as is evidenced by the current

Easter Preface V: "[Jesus] showed himself the Priest, *the Altar*, and the Lamb of sacrifice" (emphasis added). In most places after Vatican II the altar in Catholic churches has been moved forward toward the congregation, at the very heart of the building, in cruciform churches where the transept crosses the nave. Because the church is a ritually symbolic building, placing the altar toward the center invariably suggests symbolically how the Eucharist celebrated at the altar is actually a centering of one's whole life on Christ. The processions, too, that take place throughout the liturgy (entrance, offertory, and communion), leading to and from the altar, teach symbolically how true human identity can be found only in Christ, who in turn sends forth believers with the grace needed for an apostolically effective and joyful life in the world.

With Vatican II greater emphasis has been placed also on both the ambo, from which the Scriptures are proclaimed, and the presider's chair, from which the liturgy is introduced and completed and the opening and closing presidential prayers are proclaimed. Ambo, chair, and altar are constructed typically in the same style and of the same materials and set in visible relationship to each other to signify that the activities performed at each are integral to the single eucharistic event. Thus, the church's self-offering in Christ (altar) is in response to the scriptural account of salvation (ambo) and led by one ordained as sacramental representative of the whole church from her apostolic beginnings in Christ (chair).

Through the centuries the typical distances between altar, ambo, and chair in Catholic church sanctuaries have been sufficiently ample for noble movement among them by presider and liturgical ministers not only to mark the transition from one part of the liturgy to the next, but also to symbolize humankind's dignity and preciousness in the eyes of God. For, in the words of Romano Guardini, the "soul . . . must learn not to be continually yearning to *do* something, to attack something, to accomplish something useful, but to play the divinely ordained game of the liturgy in liberty and beauty and holy joy before God."[48] To create sanctuaries, then, so constricted in size that generous ritual movement is no longer possible serves only to foster a solely pragmatic, productionist mentality inimical to Christian life and liturgy. Where Christian worship appears restricted to the spoken word alone, soon only what is totally explainable is regarded as meaningful. The liturgy then becomes robbed of its power to ritualize bodies in the mysteries of salvation for fuller Christian living in the world, as well as to convey how in the eyes of God all authentically human comings and goings in this world are sacred.

Excessively high or remote sanctuaries are also deleterious to the church's faith by their wrongly implying that it is the presider alone, and not the whole assembly with presider at the head, who offers the Eucharist. At the same time, some sanctuary elevation is needed to allow those in the nave, even when standing, to enter actively by means of visual contact into the offering being made in the sanctuary area and to symbolize both the soul's movement of earth to heaven ("Lift up your hearts") and the supreme, exalted importance of the Eucharist itself in Christian life.[49] In contrast, theater-like churches where the floor of the nave is scaled downward toward a sanctuary below invariably act as countersymbols, suggesting that the gathered faithful are mere passive observers, that the liturgy is no more than a dramatic performance set before them for their entertainment or moral edification, and that in their superior position they as onlookers are the final arbiters of its value and meaning.

In addition to being processional, church buildings through the centuries have typically also been marked by high ceilings eliciting feelings of awe and unlimited freedom in God's presence: "For my thoughts are not your thoughts, / neither are your ways my ways, says the LORD. / For as the heavens are higher than the earth, / so are my ways higher than your ways / and my thoughts than your thoughts" (Isa 55:8-9). According to Hans Urs von Balthasar, "For good reasons the Middle Ages built their cathedrals so large that they could never be filled by liturgical acts."[50] "Roman churches," writes Jean-Yves Quellec, "embrace silence, give it birth and nurture it. The Gothic cathedral arches silence toward the heavens by its very shape."[51] Although intended primarily for corporate worship, through the ages the church building functioned also as the church's home, the place where in silence and prayer (Matt 21:13) she finds out once again—not only in liturgy but through architecture, furnishings, and sacred art as well—who and what she is: "the household of God" (Eph 2:19) that stretches across space, time, and eternity; and the Body of Christ in this world.

The practice in recent times of locating the baptismal font just inside the front entrance, opposite the altar on the main aisle's central axis, is another *lex orandi* expression of the church's faith, namely, that entrance into the eucharistic community of Christ takes place only through the sacrament of baptism, the commitment of one's whole life to the Lord in his church. Holy water fonts traditionally placed just inside the entrances of Catholic church buildings act as comparable reminders of Christian initiation, inviting those entering to renew their commitment by retracing the baptismal sign of the cross on their forehead, chest, and shoulders with water blessed for that purpose.

Although on coming to church for a Sunday morning Eucharist most Catholics may not be aware of even half of the liturgical symbols thus far set forth in this chapter, all are fully conscious that, besides being places of worship, typical church buildings are also designed to reflect the nature of the church that gathers in them. Thus St. Caesarius of Arles (470–543) states, "Every time we come to church, we ought to make our own souls be what we want the church itself to be. Do you want a clean church? Do not soil your soul with evildoing. Do you want a light-filled church? God grant your soul not to be a dark place but alight with good works. As you seek to enter a church building, so God seeks to enter your soul: 'I will dwell in them and walk about in them.'"[52]

Entering the church, blessing themselves with holy water, and possibly being greeted by the presider or a minister of hospitality, parishioners arriving for Sunday Eucharist next proceed down the aisle to find a place in one of the pews. As "chairs" too large to accommodate just a single individual, pews participate in the symbolic action of the Eucharist itself of gathering believers into the one mystery of Christ. The occasional need to "slide in" to make room for others only adds to this symbolism by recalling how every effort to "make space for" others in life makes one aware of and grateful for God's love. Because pews are designed to be shared, no one is discriminated against because of size, and little children, instead of being separated on single chairs, can slide between mother and father as their attention wanes, thus also allowing families to stay families, caring for one another, through the whole course of the liturgy. On the other hand, the individual chairs that have replaced pews in some churches, or in parts of some churches, provide a comparable sacramental witness—namely, how, along with the clergy on chairs in the sanctuary, all individuals in the church have a special place in God's kingdom, the equal dignity before God of being loved infinitely in the one mystery of Christ.

Having taken their seats, those arriving for Sunday Eucharist are not surprised by the folding kneeler attached to the pew or chair in front of them, a familiar feature in almost all Catholic churches. Although in ancient times people almost universally stood when they prayed, especially in public ("And when you shall stand to pray . . ." [Mark 11:25]),[53] for over a thousand years worshipers have also been called upon to kneel at certain points in the Roman Rite liturgy, so that kneelers are a great help. As part of the church building they witness to how prayer to God demands the total involvement not only of one's mind and heart but of one's whole body as well, and how, in order to live honest to themselves as creatures, human beings must regularly adore and glorify God as the source of all life and holiness: "At the name of Jesus *every knee should bow,* in heaven and on earth and under the earth, and every tongue confess that Jesus Christ is Lord, to the glory of God the Father" (Phil 2:9-11; emphasis added). Kneelers also remind liturgical participants that without personal prayer in their lives to foster faith, liturgical prayer itself soon becomes empty and meaningless, and liturgical action mere magic. Catholics arriving for Sunday Eucharist, therefore, typically spend a few moments on their knees preparing themselves for the awesome action that they together with the presider are about to perform.

Notes, Chapter Four

[1] Louis-Marie Chauvet, *Symbol and Sacrament: The Sacramental Reinterpretation of Christian Existence*, trans. Patrick Madigan, SJ, and Madeleine Beaumont (Collegeville, MN: Liturgical Press, 1995), 390 (italics in original). See also A. M. Roguet, OP, "The Whole Mass Proclaims the Word of God," in *The Liturgy and the Word of God* (Collegeville, MN: Liturgical Press, 1959), 67–83.

[2] E.g., Pius XII, "Allocution," in *The Assisi Papers* (Collegeville, MN: Liturgical Press, 1957), 229–30 (= *Acta Apostolicae Sedis* 48 [1956]: 711–25).

[3] Bishops' Committee on the Liturgy (BCL), Environment and Art in Catholic Worship (Washington, DC: National Conference of Catholic Bishops, 1978), no. 28.

[4] Thierry Maertens, *Assembly for Christ: From Biblical Theology to Pastoral Theology in the Twentieth Century* (London: Darton, Longman & Todd, 1970), 3–4; See also Joyce Ann Zimmerman, "Liturgical Assembly: Who Is the Subject of the Liturgy?" *Liturgical Ministry* 3 (Spring 1994): 41–51; and Catherine Vincie, *Celebrating Divine Mystery: A Primer in Liturgical Theology* (Collegeville, MN: Liturgical Press, 2009).

[5] Maertens, *Assembly*, 15.

[6] Ibid., 20–22.

[7] Ibid., 29. E.g., Isaiah 66:18-23. Note also Psalm 68:29, 35: "Because of your temple at Jerusalem / kings bear gifts to you. . . . Awesome is God in his sanctuary, / the God of Israel, / he gives power and strength to his people."

[8] Ibid., 23.

[9] Ibid., 31.

[10] Ibid., 52.

[11] Pierre Grelot, "Du sabbat juif au dimanche chrétien," *La Maison-Dieu* 124 (1975): 22.

[12] Ibid., 41–43 (emphases in original).

[13] Ibid., 41.

[14] David Coffey, "The Common and the Ordained Priesthood," *Theological Studies* 58 (1997): 233–34.

[15] Cf. Chauvet, "Description of the Structure of Christian Identity," in *Symbol and Sacrament*, 161–89.

[16] Maertens, *Assembly*, 72, 77.

[17] Cf. Grelot, "Du sabbat," 41. No solid evidence exists of a Eucharist more often than weekly, however, prior to the third century. Cf. Paul F. Bradshaw and Maxwell E. Johnson, *The Origins of Feasts, Fasts, and Seasons in Early Christianity* (Collegeville, MN: Liturgical Press, 2011), 11.

[18] E.g., Didache 14: "On the Lord's own day gather together and break bread and give thanks, having first confessed your sins so that your sacrifice may be pure" (Michael W. Holmes, ed., *The Apostolic Fathers* [Grand Rapids, MI: Baker Books, 1992], 267). "The Christian is constituted in the Sunday Eucharist and the Sunday Eucharist in the Christian; . . . neither can exist without the other" (Theodericus Ruinart, ed., *Acta martyrum Saturini, Dativi et aliorum plurimorum martyrum in Africa* [PL 8:696B]). Cf. chap. 2 for a fuller discussion of this question.

[19] Bradshaw and Johnson, *The Origins*, 13. Most scholars today believe that, because the Jewish day begins and ends with sundown, the early church held its weekly Lord's Supper on Saturday evenings; see, e.g., J. C. J. Metford, *The Christian Year* (New York: Crossroad, 1991), 10; Paul F. Bradshaw, *Eucharistic Origins* (New York: Oxford University Press, 2004), 69; and Martin Connell, *Eternity Today: On the Liturgical Year*, vol. 2 (New York: Continuum, 2006), 5–6. Matias Augé, however, in "The Liturgical Year in the First Four Centuries," in *Handbook for Liturgical Studies*, vol. 5, *Liturgical Time and Space*, ed. Anscar J. Chupungco, OSB (Collegeville, MN: Liturgical Press, 2000), 135–38, argues for Sunday evening, echoing Willy Rordorf in *Sunday: The History of the Day of Rest and Worship in the Earliest Centuries of the Christian Church* (London: SCM Press Ltd., 1968), 200–205.

[20] Noële M. Denis-Boulet, *The Christian Calendar*, trans. P. J. Hepburne-Scott (New York: Hawthorn Books, 1960), 32.

[21] Note that the "first quarter" moon in the Northern Hemisphere appears as a bright capital *D*, whereas in the Southern Hemisphere it appears as an enclosed capital *C*—and just the opposite in both cases for the "third quarter" moon.

[22] Denis-Boulet, *The Christian Calendar*, 10–18.

[23] Augé, "The Liturgical Year," 135–38. In regard to the meaning of 1 Cor 11:26, "For as often as you eat this bread and drink this cup, you proclaim the Lord's death until he comes," see Grelot, "Du sabbat," 23.

[24] J. M. R. Tillard, "Le dimanche, jour d'alliance," *Sciences ecclésiastiques* 16 (1964): 226.

[25] Karl Rahner, "Sunday, the Day of the Lord," in *Theological Investigations*, vol. 7, trans. David Bourke (New York: Herder and Herder, 1971), 205–10.

[26] Tillard, "Le dimanche," 230.

[27] Adolf Adam, *The Liturgical Year: Its History and Meaning after the Reform of the Liturgy* (New York: Pueblo, 1981), 40.

[28] PL 8:711A: "Sine dominico non possumus."

[29] Chauvet, *Symbol and Sacrament*, 276 (italics in original).

[30] Karl Rahner, "How to Receive a Sacrament and Mean It," *Theology Digest* 19:3 (Autumn 1971): 229 (emphasis added).

[31] Richard Krautheimer, *Early Christian and Byzantine Architecture*, 3rd ed. (Middlesex, England: Penguin Books Ltd, 1979), 25, 29–30; J. Stevenson, ed., "The 'Edict of Milan,' 313," in *A New Eusebius: Documents Illustrative of the History of the Church to A.D. 337* (London: SPCK, 1960), 301.

[32] Krautheimer, *Early Christian and Byzantine Architecture*, 41.

[33] Richard Krautheimer, "The Constantinian Basilica," *Dumbarton Oaks Papers* 21 (Washington, DC, 1967): 117–40.

[34] Ibid., 129.

[35] Thomas Mathews, *The Clash of Gods: A Reinterpretation of Early Christian Art* (Princeton, NJ: Princeton University Press, 1993), 94.

[36] Klaus Gamber, *The Reform of the Roman Liturgy: Its Problems and Background* (San Juan Capistrano, CA: Una Voce Press; and Harrison, NY: The Foundation for Catholic Reform, 1993), 158.

[37] Noële M. Denis-Boulet, "L'autel dans l'antiquité chrétienne," *La Maison-Dieu* 29 (1952): 46–47. John Damascene (ca. 676–ca.754) writes, "When ascending into heaven, He rose toward the East, and that is how the Apostles adored Him, and He will return just as they saw Him ascend into heaven. . . . Waiting for Him, we adore Him facing East. This is an unrecorded tradition passed down to us from the Apostles" (*De fide orthodoxa* IV, 12 (*PG* 94:1136), quoted in Gamber, *The Reform*, 162–63).

[38] Joseph A. Jungmann, SJ, "The New Altar," trans. John J. Galvani, SJ, *Liturgical Arts* 37 (1968): 37. In churches where the apse is located at the west end of the building, as in St. Peter's in Rome, the main celebrant in facing east also looks out upon the congregation, which itself was also turned eastward in prayer.

[39] At the same time, newer building materials and the twentieth-century liturgical movement leading to Vatican II reforms have resulted in a whole variety of attempts at more effective spatial arrangements in both newly constructed and renovated church buildings. Cf. R. Kevin Seasoltz, OSB, "In the Celtic Tradition: Irish Church Architecture," in *Ars Liturgiae: Worship, Aesthetics and Praxis, Essays in Honor of Nathan D. Mitchell*, ed. Clare V. Johnson (Chicago: Liturgy Training Publications, 2003), 231–52, and *A Sense of the Sacred: Theological Foundations of Christian Architecture and Art* (New York: Continuum, 2007), 221–88. Cf. also Mark A. Torgerson, *An Architecture of Immanence: Architecture for Worship and Ministry Today* (Grand Rapids, MI: William B. Eerdmans Publishing Co., 2007).

[40] Louis-Marie Chauvet, "The Liturgy in its Symbolic Space," in *Liturgy and the Body* ed. Louis-Marie Chauvet and François Kabasele Lumbala (Maryknoll, NY: Orbis Books, 1995), 36.

[41] Cf. Jungmann, "The New Altar," 39.

[42] François Louvel, "Le mystère de nos églises," *La Maison-Dieu* 63 (1960): 21. William Durandus (1230–96) interprets church columns rather to be symbols of the bishops supporting the structure of the universal church, with apostles as their bases (*Rationale divinorum officiorum* I, 1:27).

[43] Chauvet, "The Liturgy in its Symbolic Space," 30.

[44] Joseph A. Jungmann, SJ, "The Defeat of Teutonic Arianism and the Revolution in Religious Culture in the Early Middle Ages," in *Pastoral Liturgy* (New York: Herder and Herder, 1962), 1–101.

[45] "The sanctuary in the center of the building is not the answer." James F. White, "Liturgy and the Language of Space," in *Symbol: The Language of Liturgy* (New York: Federation of Diocesan Liturgical Commissions, 1982), 62.

[46] Chauvet, "The Liturgy in its Symbolic Space," 35–36.

[47] "The identification of Christ and the altar is a notion already current among the Greek fathers, the apostolic fathers, as well as the ante-Niceans and the authors of the fourth century. . . . The Latin fathers made the same identification beginning with St. Ambrose." O. Rousseau, OSB, "Le Christ et L'autel: Notes sur la tradition patristique," *La Maison-Dieu* 29 (1952): 34–35.

[48] Romano Guardini, "The Playfulness of the Liturgy," in *The Spirit of the Liturgy*, trans. Ada Lane (New York: Benziger Brothers, 1930), 106 (emphasis in original).

[49] Cf. Catherine Bell, "Ritual Oppositions and Hierarchies," in *Ritual Theory, Ritual Practice* (New York: Oxford University Press, 1992), 101–6.

[50] Han Urs von Balthasar, "Unmodern Prayer," in *Elucidations*, trans. John Riches (San Francisco: Ignatius Press, 1998), 177.

[51] Jean-Yves Quellec, "Silence in the Liturgy," in *Symbol: The Language of Liturgy* (Brooklyn, NY: Federation of Diocesan Liturgical Commissions, 1982), 66.

[52] Caesarius of Arles, *Sermon* 229, quoted in the Office of Readings of the Liturgy of the Hours for November 9: Dedication of the Lateran Basilica.

[53] For example, when in various places people began kneeling during the eucharistic liturgy, the Council of Nicea (325) explicitly forbade the practice on Sundays and during the season of Easter: "Because there are some who kneel on the Lord's Day and in the days of Pentecost (the fifty days of Easter), that all things may be uniformly performed in every parish or diocese, it seems good to the Holy Synod that the prayers by all to God be made standing" (c. 20).

Chapter Five

The Introductory Rites

T he General Instruction of The Roman Missal (GIRM) states that the purpose of the introductory rites "is to ensure that the faithful, who come together as one, establish communion and dispose themselves properly to listen to the Word of God and to celebrate the Eucharist worthily" (no. 46).[1]

The Entrance Procession

When the hour arrives for the celebration, a cantor typically announces the opening song. At the start of the music all stand to welcome the presider, deacon or reader, and acolytes who proceed forward toward the sanctuary as the community begins to sing.

Standing

Because of its many television replays, Phil Mickelson's joyful leap upward as he won his first Masters is familiar to golf fans around the world. The congregation's rising together at the beginning of Mass embodies a similar joy, that of Christ's resurrected life being relived once again in the eucharistic celebration. Antonio Donghi suggests that this "common posture of the body exhibits that the people are aware that their lives are an upward course toward the fullness of communion with

God in glory." Within the liturgy standing is "an act of praying faith that proclaims to the world that salvation comes from on high: 'I lift up my eyes to the hills. / From where does my help come? / My help comes from the Lord, / who made heaven and earth' (Ps 121:1-2)."[2]

"To stand up," says Romano Guardini, "means that we are in possession of ourselves. . . . We stand, as it were, at attention, geared and ready for action."[3] Like Sigmund Romberg's "Stout-Hearted Men" whose singing and marching "shoulder to shoulder"[4] emboldens them to fight for what they believe, the members of the assembly by rising up together experience a similar empowerment, a faith-animated joy in performing the liturgical action.

Procession

According to Joseph Gelineau, a liturgical procession is a kind of march: "The human person who marches—not simply wanders about, or is dragged along like a slave, or driven by the tyranny of passionate desire or the turbulence of human affairs—understands with their feet that they are engaged in a spiritual work and that their march, when done in faith, is supernatural."[5] In a march, mere walking is charged with life and rhythm that seem to cry out for melody. And because it is a communal and not a solitary activity, its rhythm and melody stir people to sing the purpose of their marching to each another: "I was glad when they said to me, / 'Let us go to the house of the Lord!'" (Ps 122:1).

Singing Together in Procession

That the same word listed in a dictionary takes on different shades of meaning within different situations opens up the possibility of its having meaning of some kind within almost any situation. We have already seen an example of this in our chapter 2 discussion on metonymy: General McAuliffe's using the word "nuts," denoting edible nuggets yielded by trees, to indicate the worthlessness of the Germans' ultimatum. The fact, however, that a ritual as a human activity is by definition to be repeated unchanged within any historical context signifies the intended universality within all situations of the meaning of that particular ritual, a universality present in and realized by that ritual itself. A major characteristic of music is precisely its patterns of repetition, so that music is a major bearer of meaning within any ritual. Music consists essentially in a deliberate isolation of the intonational dimension of human vocal communication in order to (a) communicate meaning by the universal significances of various tones, intensities, and paces of all human speech and to (b) instance the nobility of being human by dwelling in the auditory beauty of human speech as the essential mode of human expression.[6]

According to liturgical theologian Edward Foley, what differentiates music from mere noise is that in music we experience intention behind the arrangement of its sounds, so that it is fundamentally a communication event, exemplifying the social nature of being human and uniting its listeners as one.[7] Hans Bernard Meyer notes how for St. Paul the purpose of every kind of singing in the church is to build up the community, to foster unity in Christ (cf. 1 Cor 12-14).[8] By calling participants into relationship with God and with one another, liturgical music is a powerful symbol of how God calls all to God's Self in a network of relationships in Christ.

Because of music's ability to unify people, the entrance processional song serves to gather believers more fully in the Lord as a liturgical assembly. And the assembly's liturgical song both participates already in the heavenly song of praise that will last forever (cf. Rev 4:8) and provides voice for the rest of creation: "Let the sea roar, and all that fills it; / the world and those who dwell in it! / Let the floods clap their hands; / let *the hills sing for joy* together / before the LORD, for he comes / to judge the earth" (Ps 98:7-9; emphasis added).

Gelineau explains why singing *in procession* is particularly suited to the historical nature of Christian salvation:

> With a pilgrimage, space is transformed into duration and the route becomes history. The "way" of God is the history of salvation, and the church progresses and is on pilgrimage to meet her savior who comes. The chant . . . brings together in an instant the past, the present, and the future, and it does so not by denying time but by submitting to it, . . . imitating and signifying the *hodie* ("today") of the liturgy, the present of sacred time which at the same time is memorial, presence, and anticipation. . . . Just as melody does not exist except in the fleeting present and is always necessarily new although it repeats the airs of the past and only progresses into the future, God is among his people on march as One who has already come and is coming.[9]

Entrance Procession

The entrance procession of the Roman Rite originated out of fourth-century Roman stational liturgies. Popes as bishops of Rome journeyed

from their home basilica to celebrate the Eucharist in one of the presbyteral churches of the city. Just as emperors in late antiquity never went
out except accompanied by a retinue and greeted by crowds with signs
of honor along the way, so too with the peace of Constantine were popes
as state officials accorded the same distinction.[10] The entrance procession,
maintaining its identity through the ages, is therefore a "person-centered
procession,"[11] intended to welcome the ordained eucharistic presider.

At the same time, the entrance procession exists "strictly and completely for the people."[12] According to Louis-Marie Chauvet, "The first
liturgical function of the priest is to sacramentally manifest a double
connection: a metaphorical connection to Christ who presides, and a
metonymic connection to the whole Church, since 'liturgical actions are
not private actions, but celebrations of the Church' [*Sacrosanctum Concilium* 26]."[13] Indeed, the fact that the priest-presider is essential to the
existence of any particular eucharistic assembly by virtue of his having
been ordained at another time and in another place to represent *perma-
nently* the headship of Christ in the universal church demonstrates how
any assembly as liturgical symbol of Christ and his church is the embodiment of a mystery larger than just the physical sum of its own members.
By the arrival of an ordained presider sent from outside into the midst
of those already gathered for worship, the assembly in Christ is fully
established as a metonym of the larger church and humanity as a whole.
This liturgical symbolism of the assembly in turn is completed only with
the dismissal at the end of the liturgy where the congregation is itself
sent outside, dispersed into the world to continue the church's apostolic
mission of gathering all into the one Body of Christ: "Jesus suffered
outside the gate in order to sanctify the people through his own blood.
Therefore let us go forth to him outside the camp, bearing abuse for him.
For here we have no lasting city, but we seek the city which is to come"
(Heb 13:12-14).

The ultimate focus of the entrance procession as "person centered,"
therefore, is on Christ himself in whose name the priest as a metaphor
or "type of Christ" arrives to preside at the church's liturgy. As part of
the church's eucharistic celebration of the saving events of Christ's paschal
mystery, the entrance procession also recalls how the children of Jerusalem greeted the Lord with palms and singing on his way to the temple
just days before he died (see Mark 11:1-11 and parallels). Although this
episode in Christ's life is celebrated more explicitly each year in the
church's Passion Sunday procession, it forms part of church's liturgical
typology at Sunday Eucharists throughout the year as well. Thus, in their

rising and singing as the presider comes in, gathered believers are made to recognize that what happened two thousand years ago to bring definitive release and life to the whole world is starting to happen once again in the very persons, objects, and actions of the liturgy into which they themselves are being caught up as participants.

Psalmody and Hymnody

In regard to the opening song of the Eucharist, the GIRM states:

> In the Dioceses of the United States of America there are four options for the Entrance Chant: (1) the antiphon from the Missal or the antiphon with its Psalm from the *Graduale Romanum* as set to music there or in another setting; (2) the antiphon and Psalm of the *Graduale Simplex* for the liturgical time; (3) a chant from another collection of Psalms and antiphons, approved by the Conference of Bishops or the Diocesan Bishop, including Psalms arranged in responsorial or metrical forms; (4) another liturgical chant that is suited to the sacred action, the day, or the time of year, similarly approved by the Conference of Bishops or the Diocesan Bishop. (no. 48)

Since the reforms of the Second Vatican Council, the opening song in parishes throughout the United States has been almost universally a version of the fourth option: a selection from a hymnal or song book chosen to fit the action, feast, and/or season of the year. Robert Taft provides some historical background for why entrance antiphons and their accompanying psalms (option 1) first came to be substituted in this way by the singing of hymns or other nonbiblical songs.

According to Taft, the Christian practice of singing psalms at the liturgy has roots that go probably as far back as the New Testament itself (cf. 1 Cor 14:26; Eph 5:18-20; Col 3:16-17; Jas 5:13; and Rev 5:8-9).[14] Later church fathers, such as Gregory Nazianzen (d. ca. 390), Ambrose of Milan (d. 397), Augustine (d. 430), and Caesarius of Arles (d. 542), witness to the great success of congregational psalmody, praising their people for their beautiful and enthusiastic performance.[15] For the "soft points" of the eucharistic liturgy—the opening procession, the procession and preparation of gifts, and the communion procession (that is, those necessary actions which of themselves are performed without words)— particular biblical psalms were chosen for singing, verses from which fit either those actions or the feast or season being celebrated.[16] During the Middle Ages in the West, nonscriptural antiphons were created for responsorial psalmody sung during these "soft points." For various reasons they were then expanded so that only choirs were able to sing them, thereby for the most part ending the practice of congregational psalmody at the Eucharist even up until our own day (except for the post–Vatican II responsorial psalm after the first reading).[17]

The reasons given by the fathers of the church for congregational psalmody, says Taft, are that psalms (a) are divinely revealed; (b) were used by Christ and the apostles; (c) contain "everything found in all the other books of the Bible: history, law, prophecy, admonition, morality"; and (d) stir up love of God, calm passions, teach wisdom, stimulate tears of repentance, and so forth.[18]

In regard to the biblical value of the Psalms, Hans Renckens notes that canticles in the Bible are literary forms of liturgical practice. Just as individual canticles, such as Mary's *Magnificat* (Luke 1:46-55), indicate in what way the surrounding prose account is to be understood, the Psalms do the same for the Bible as a whole. They are not simply some texts among others, but the text par excellence, the life of all the others. Originating out of the temple liturgy of sacrifice as a sacrifice of praise, the Psalms are the inspired Word of God expressed in the faith appropriation of the ancient Israelite community (thus they are a type of "symbolic exchange" discussed above in chapter 1).[19] According to Joseph Gelineau, "In Christian worship, psalmody holds the first place, both in law and in fact. Psalms and biblical canticles rank before all lyrical composition of merely ecclesiastical origin, since they are the inspired word of God." He adds, "The hymn is to psalmody what decoration is to architecture or what preaching is to the reading of Holy Scripture."[20]

In his 1903 *moto proprio* on sacred music, *Tra le sollecitudini*, Pope Pius X enshrines Gregorian chant[21] as the norm for all liturgical music in the Roman Rite.[22] Pope Pius XII in 1955, however, approved the use of vernacular hymnody at "read Masses" (*missa lecta*),[23] thereby "giving official recognition to the entrance hymn, offertory hymn, communion hymn, exit hymn pattern familiar to many U.S. worshiping communities."[24] As Frank Quinn points out, Pius XII did so because it was the only way at the time for the congregation at "Low Masses" to participate through singing at the liturgy.[25]

The use of hymnody to cover the liturgical "soft points" of the three eucharistic processions, however, can be somewhat problematic. In order to sing hymns with their multiple verses, worshipers have to focus mainly on the printed lyrics found in their hymnals, whereas with responsorial psalmody, because they sing only an easily memorized antiphonal refrain, they are freed to participate in the entrance procession not only by song, but visually as well. One suggested way of overcoming this obstacle is to choose only those hymns which, as with responsorial psalmody, have the congregation sing a repeatable refrain in response to verses chanted either by a choir or preferably—to be more easily understood—by a single cantor.[26]

Another drawback to singing hymns during eucharistic processions stems from their self-contained nature as artistic compositions. In a 1982 document the Bishops' Committee on the Liturgy (BCL) of the then-denominated United States Catholic Conference states that because a hymn is a poetic unity, it "should not be ended indiscriminately at the end of the procession." Nor should the music "extend past the time necessary for the ritual." Consequently, "metrical hymns may not be the most suitable choices" in these situations.[27] Nevertheless, Quinn holds open the possibility that, "since metrical songs can be performed in a number of ways, if the musician is conscious of the purpose of that rite,[28] some of the problems of hymn singing at this moment might be overcome."[29]

If hymnody is chosen for the opening hymn, A. C. Vernoolij offers some time-tested advice. He suggests that although musical expressions of human emotion, such as lamentation, are at home in the church, as transitory and subjective in nature they should only be sung by a single individual (e.g., during the time of reflection after Communion). Religious chant by the whole assembly or by a person in whom the community raises its voice (such as the presider) is by tradition never too pronounced or wavering, nor does it vary too much in its dynamic, nor does it have a melody that is too expressive. Vernoolij quotes the sixteenth-century musician Valero Bona: "When you write pieces for the church, do not use the black notes, that is, rapid notes as in a madrigal. Neither use a lot of notes. For in the church everything ought to take place with gravity and devotion."[30]

Entrance Antiphon

It is possible that, with the new English translation of the Roman Missal, there may be a rebirth in our time of congregational psalmody at the Eucharist. And so we turn our attention to the entrance antiphon for the Ninth Sunday in Ordinary Time.

The word "antiphon," according to Ian Coleman, originated in the fourth century and transliterates not a Greek noun, a thing (*antiphōnē*), but the neuter form of a Greek participle, an activity (*antiphōnon*): that of "answering back." Witnessed to by the Liturgy of St. John Chrysostom,

Egeria's *Travels*, and the Rule of St. Benedict, the short reply sung on special feast days by a choir in response to psalm verses chanted by a cantor was taken from a text other than the psalm itself, chosen to fit the particular feast or season. This type of psalm response alone was known by the technical term "antiphon," an example of which occurs on "Gaudete Sunday," the Third Sunday of Advent: "Rejoice in the Lord always; again I say, rejoice. / Indeed, the Lord is near." Taken from Philippians 4:4-5, this antiphon "answers back" the verses of the accompanying psalm, interpreting them in light of the overall celebration of which it is a part. On less festive days the people's or choir's response was taken from the accompanying psalm itself, some particular verse highlighting the psalm's overall meaning.[31] Thus, the "entrance antiphon" for the Ninth Sunday of the Year has come to be classified under this later, more generic use of the word "antiphon."[32]

The entrance and communion antiphons assigned to any given Sunday of the year remain the same throughout its three-year cycle of scriptural readings (A, B, and C), so that apparently no thematic connection was intended between these Sunday antiphons and their respective sets of readings. The entrance antiphon for the ninth Sunday, therefore, along with the psalm from which it was taken (Ps 25:16, 18)—"Look on me and have mercy on me, O Lord, / for I am alone and poor. / See my lowliness and suffering / and take away all my sins, my God"—would simply serve the general purpose all entrance rites have of uniting the assembly and preparing hearts and minds for the sacred mysteries. Accordingly, the wording of the antiphon fosters an awareness of both the Lord's awesome majesty ("Look on me") and the participants' creaturely need for God's saving presence in their lives ("lowliness," "alone and poor"), while instilling a deep confidence in faith that this liturgical expression of yearning is itself an assurance of God's benevolence ("have mercy on me") and a joyful manifestation of the Spirit's life-giving power within them ("my God"): "No one can say Jesus is Lord except by the Holy Spirit" (1 Cor 12:3); "When we cry, 'Abba! Father!' it is the Spirit himself bearing witness with our spirit that we are children of God" (Rom 8:15b-16).

Members of the Procession

The entrance procession is typically led by an acolyte vested in a cinctured alb, bearing a processional cross with its fixed image of Christ facing the direction of the procession. This sacred image of the Crucified recalls

St. Paul's words to the Corinthians: "When I came to you, brethren, I did not come proclaiming to you the testimony of God in lofty words or wisdom. For I decided to know nothing among you except Jesus Christ and him crucified" (1 Cor 2:1-2). The cross at the forefront of the procession thus presages how what is about to take place deals wholly and exclusively with Christ's paschal mystery and its implications for Christian living.

The fact that most if not all in procession wear albs, white-sleeved tunics down to their feet,[33] symbolizes how all in the church—not only those processing in but also those in the pews participating visually and by singing—have by their baptism "put on the Lord Jesus Christ" (Rom 13:14) and so share already in his resurrected life (cf. Rev 7:9, 13-14).

Less typically, though often enough, two vested acolytes following the cross carry lighted candles on candlesticks to be placed near the altar, continuing a medieval Roman practice: "Two honorific (civic) candles which preceded the Pope on every occasion and which at Mass were placed behind the altar."[34] In pre-Christian times lit torches were looked upon as natural accompaniments of any joyful procession, such as the comings and goings of the emperor and, with the peace of Constantine, of the pope as well.[35] In the early church the religious use of lights was thought alien to the spiritual nature of Christian worship. By the fifth century, however, that judgment was reversed. In 406 St. Jerome observes that "throughout the churches of the East lights are kindled when the gospel is to be read, and that with the sun shining: not so as to scatter darkness, but to display signs of rejoicing."[36] St. Isidore of Seville in the seventh century writes, "The lights are lit by [acolytes] and carried . . . to give a sign of joy, in order that, under the type of light, that bodily light may be displayed of which we read in the gospel: he was 'the true light' (John 1:9)."[37] Ministers in albs carrying lit candles are then symbols also of Christian life itself, recalling how all in the church were clothed at their baptism in white garments and given a lighted candle:

> You have been enlightened by Christ.
> Walk always as children of the light
> and keep the flame of faith alive in your hearts.
> When the Lord comes, may you go out to meet him
> with all the saints in the heavenly kingdom.[38]

Often, too, following behind the acolytes, a reader typically dressed in ordinary clothes brings in the Lectionary, which she or he will set open on the ambo—or a deacon, vested in a dalmatic over an alb, carries in the Book of the Gospels to be laid on the altar.[39] That the scriptural Word of God—in particular the Book of the Gospels—is honored in procession is another typological reminder: that it is Christ himself, the Word of God, who speaks in the church when the Scriptures are proclaimed (cf. SC 7) and their meaning expounded by one of his ordained representatives.

At the end of the procession comes the presider wearing, over an alb and a stole, a festive green chasuble, the color prescribed for Sundays in Ordinary Time. Green vestments, reminders of the green earth, identify Ordinary Time as a time of steady growth in the life of Christ:

> For as the rain and the snow come down from heaven,
>   and do not return thither but water the earth,
> making it bring forth and sprout,
>   giving seed to the sower and bread to the eater,
> so shall my word be that goes forth from my mouth;
>   it shall not return to me empty,
> but it shall accomplish that which I purpose,
>   and prosper in the thing for which I sent it. (Isa 55:10-11)

The form of the chasuble, by encircling the presider's head and draping over his lower body's articulation into arms and legs, highlights the spiritual dimension of the human person[40] and therefore how the church's liturgy is primarily an offering of mind and heart to the Lord, a worship in spirit and in truth (cf. John 4:23). The chasuble's beauty, also symbolic, declares that all in the church, though sinners, are infinitely precious in God's sight—that God in his boundless love is like the father of the Prodigal Son who, even before any repentance is shown, runs out and greets his returning son with a kiss and has him clothed in the finest robe (cf. Luke 15:11-32).

In the ancient world, as we have seen, to occupy the last place in the procession was normally a symbol of honor. At the same time, because victorious Roman generals returning to the city trailed those they conquered in battle behind them like trophies, the last place could also be a sign of humiliation, leading St. Paul to say, "As servants of Christ and stewards of the mysteries of God . . . God has exhibited us apostles *as last of all*, like men sentenced to death; because we have become a spectacle to the world, to angels and to men. We are fools for Christ's sake" (1 Cor 4:1, 9-10; emphasis added). Hence, the presider's coming at the end of the entrance procession led by the crucifix teaches not only how all in the church are infinitely precious in God's sight, but also that only by following Christ in his sufferings do Christians actually experience his triumph as well.

Reverencing the Altar

When all in the procession reach the base of the steps before the sanctuary, they stop and make a deep bow of reverence toward the altar. Then as each goes to his or her place in the sanctuary, the presider and deacon proceed up the stairs to kiss the altar on its opposite side before going to their chairs.

The honoring of sacred images and objects with a kiss was common to ancient religions and was adopted early on by the church. Reverencing the altar in this way had various meanings attached to it.[41] As the place where the celebration of Christ's death and resurrection takes place, the altar is linked sacramentally to the cross, the Last Supper table, the heavenly altar of the Lamb (Rev 6:9), the church as "living stones" (1 Pet 2:5), and Christ himself (Heb 13:10).[42] It has other biblical overtones as well (e.g., Luke 7:45). That this kiss is the first action of the priest and deacon as they enter the sanctuary points powerfully to where the heart of the church lies, and to the willing submission owed to the Lord for his infinite goodness and love. It thus helps in preparing all in the church for the sacred actions about to take place.

Opening Words and Greeting

Sign of the Cross

As the singing is brought to an end, the presider leads the congregation in making the large sign of the cross, touching his forehead, chest, left shoulder, and then right shoulder, while pronouncing the words "In the name of the Father, and of the Son, and of the Holy Spirit," to which all respond, "Amen."

Jungmann tells us that this formula, together with its accompanying action, originated in the Middle Ages as a "petition for God's blessing," an acknowledgment that "we begin the holy action in the power that comes from the triune God through the Cross of Christ."[43] It is instruc-

tive that the presider's first liturgical words, "In the name of the Father
. . .," are a free-floating prepositional phrase, so that the subject and
verb are understood: "*We begin this holy action* in the name of the Father
. . ." In other words, instead of having participants *say* what they are
doing, the rite simply has them *do* it, suggesting how the Eucharist as a
ritual is primarily a human practice, an action, not an intellectual communication *about* an action. In making the sign of the cross "in the name
of the Father . . .," therefore, the presider in effect leads the assembly
into the whole drama of salvation history: the creative, saving, and sanctifying activities of the Blessed Trinity.

It should be noted furthermore that faith, one's relationship to the
living God, both demands prayer and *is* prayer in its deepest reality and
fullest expression.[44] Consequently, even those parts of the eucharistic
ritual which are not prayer in the strict sense of explicitly saying prayers
are nevertheless enacted within an overall address and context of prayer
("In the name of the Father . . ."), so that the Eucharist in all of its
parts—readings, homily, processions, greeting of peace, and so forth—is
actually one lovingly conscious, self-offering response in faith to God by
the church in order to grow into greater union with God. Hence, although it may be true to say that the liturgy as a whole is not "prayer" in
the narrow sense of the word, yet as rite it is a "dancing before the Lord"[45]
where all is deliberately performed in his sight and for his glory. And so
it *is* prayer, *ritual* prayer: a form of shared Christian life itself, but stylized
as an interpersonal encounter with God in and through an officially
established pattern of mutual self-giving among the gathered members
of the church community.[46]

On reaching the altar, the pope, up until the ninth century at least,
marked his forehead with the sign of the cross.[47] Early Christians in their
daily lives also marked themselves, others, and objects in this way, sometimes to ward off evil spirits and at other times to signify blessing and
sanctification. In the liturgy, however, the sign of the cross has always
been connected to baptism.[48] Just as Christians enter the community of
the church by their baptism into Christ's death and resurrection, so by
their regular celebrations of the Eucharist they are nourished to keep
living and growing as members of his Body.

The larger sign of the cross used in the entrance rites today was never
actually a part of the Mass until the Vatican II liturgy. Previously, it had
been associated with the eucharistic liturgy only as an introduction to
the prayers at the foot of the altar made quietly by the priest and acolytes
before Mass began. Transferred to its current location in the new liturgy,

it has become somewhat problematic. Because for Catholics all prayer normally begins with the sign of the cross, its presence here suggests that it begins the Eucharist as well, whereas, as we have seen, the Eucharist has already begun with the entrance procession and its opening song. Obviously, then, when some presiders introduce the sign of the cross with words like "Let us begin as we always do, in the name of the Father . . .," they only exacerbate the problem. On the other hand, as a concise formula of the totality of the church's faith, the sign of the cross for those who see, hear, and trace it on themselves catches them up in its significance and power and, prompting a ready response of "Amen!" brings about an even deeper entrance into the liturgical action, their participation in Christ's saving mystery.

"Amen"

The congregation's "Amen" to the sign of the cross marks the first occurrence of this word in the eucharistic ritual. A. Molieu notes that "Amen," borrowed from the Hebrew, has three interrelated liturgical meanings: (a) an assertion of commitment, as at the end of the Creed; (b) agreement or participation in a prayer enunciated by someone else, as at the end of the eucharistic prayer; and (c) a wish to see something accomplished, as at the end of the Our Father.[49] It is safe to say that this particular "Amen" is one mostly of commitment: a personal act of faith in the Blessed Trinity and in each Divine Person's respective activity in the work of creation and salvation. Molieu adds that the book of Revelation calls Christ himself "the Amen" (3:14), the authentic witness of God.[50] Every pronouncement of this word as a faith response to some prayer or belief of the church, then, is also a participation in the very mystery of Christ, "the originator and fulfiller of our faith" (Heb 12:2).[51]

Greeting

After the sign of the cross, the presider, opening his arms in a gesture of welcome, pronounces one of three possible ritual greetings, the most elaborate of which, taken from 2 Corinthians 13:13, is typically used on Sundays: "The grace of our Lord Jesus Christ, / and the love of God, / and the communion of the Holy Spirit / be with you all." The congregation responds heartily, "And with your spirit."

Together with its response, *Et cum spiritu tuo* (And with your spirit), the *Dominus vobiscum* (The Lord be with you) greeting taken from Ruth

2:4 occurs for the first time in the history of the church's liturgy as part of the introductory dialogue to the eucharistic prayer of the so-called *Apostolic Tradition*, various parts of which date from the third or early fourth century. It has become adopted into almost all liturgies, Eastern and Western, ever since.[52]

The GIRM states that "by means of the Greeting [the presider] signifies the presence of the Lord to the assembled community. By this greeting and the people's response, the mystery of the Church gathered together is made manifest" (no. 50). At the same time, as Bernard Botte among others has shown, *Dominus vobiscum* is not a declaration, "The Lord *is* with you,"[53] but a true greeting, "The Lord *be* with you," similar to the one the risen Jesus used with his disciples, "Peace be with you" (Luke 24:36; John 20:19), and those which begin St. Paul's epistles, such as "Grace to you and peace from God the Father and our Lord Jesus Christ" (Gal 1:3).[54]

Both Botte and Michael K. Magee demonstrate that the appearance of the word *spiritus* in the response, *Et cum spiritu tuo*, stems from its use in some New Testament greetings: 2 Timothy 4:22; Galatians 6:18; Philippians 4:23; and Philemon 25.[55] Much ink has been spilled about the recent change in translation of the congregation's response, *Et cum spiritu tuo*, from "And also with you" to "And with your spirit." Whereas Jungmann surmised that *spiritus* represents a Semitism signifying a person's self,[56] its meaning here is found rather in St. Paul's careful distinction between *psyche* (soul) and *pneuma* (spirit), as in "'The first man Adam became a living being [*psyche* (soul)]'; the last Adam [Christ] became a life-giving spirit [*pneuma*]" (1 Cor 15:45).[57] Citing the biblical exegete Ceslas Spicq, Magee concludes that "in St. Paul's anthropology, as in significant passages of the Old Testament, the term *spiritus* might be described as referring not simply to the person as such, but to that superior part or faculty in him which comes directly under the influence of God's action."[58]

Church fathers must have noted early on that the greeting of 2 Timothy 4:22, "The Lord be with your spirit," was addressed scripturally to an ordained[59] leader in the church. In any event, because the liturgical *Dominus vobiscum* calls for the *Et cum spiritu tuo* response, the Council of Hippo in 393 issued the first church legislation forbidding anyone but a bishop, priest, or deacon to deliver it. At the same time, as Magee observes, "if the Lord is to be with [the people] in a particular way that is effected by and embodied in the liturgical celebration, by virtue of which they are united to him and to each other, it is also because of the

Lord's presence to the spirit of the one who stands before them as the Lord's minister." And so the "And with your spirit" response "addressed to a cleric expresses a reality which is the very opposite of any inappropriate 'clericalism.' For it constitutes an acknowledgment that what the cleric is about to offer the people is . . . a pure gift of God that must be revitalized afresh in order to be of service to all."[60]

As part of an authentic human encounter, this greeting and its response at the same time both share in the liturgy's overall identity as prayer ("May the Lord be with you") and constitute a formal introduction to its dialogical nature as well ("And with your spirit").

Improvisational Introduction

In regard to this stage in the Mass, the GIRM makes the following allowance: "After the greeting of the people, the Priest, or the Deacon, or a lay minister may very briefly introduce the faithful to the Mass of the day" (no. 50).

According to Joseph Gelineau, "Purely repetitive ritualism takes no account of the people who are celebrating nor of the events which influence them. It forgets that the 'sacraments are for people' and that the liturgy is our history."[61] That is why, before proceeding any further, it is helpful that the presider, in addition to giving a foretaste of what is to come, say some improvisational words contextualizing the eucharistic celebration within the contemporary world of the congregation in front of him. When these remarks are very brief, well prepared, and reverent, they help to make everyone aware not only of the sacredness of the action they are about to perform, but also of how it is meant to speak to the whole meaning of their lives.

Penitential Act

The fact that all three Synoptic Gospels report John the Baptist "preaching a baptism of repentance for the forgiveness of sins" as a preparation for the coming of Christ (Mark 1:4 and parallels) is a strong witness to the essential role repentance has in the work of salvation. Listed in the Missal after the greeting are three possible options for the penitential act, with seven more available in appendix VI for use within the dioceses of the United States. On Sundays during Ordinary Time, the most typical choice might be the *Confiteor*, which before Vatican II was part of the preparatory prayers at the foot of the altar. The presider's introduction for each of the three options is the same: "Brethren (brothers and sisters), let us acknowledge our sins, / and so prepare ourselves to celebrate the sacred mysteries."

A brief moment of silence follows.

Then presider and congregation say together:

> I confess to almighty God
> and to you, my brothers and sisters,
> that I have greatly sinned,
> in my thoughts and in my words,
> in what I have done and in what I have failed to do,
>
> *And, striking their breast, they say:*
>
> through my fault, through my fault,
> through my most grievous fault;
>
> *Then they continue:*
>
> therefore I ask blessed Mary ever-Virgin,
> all the Angels and Saints,
> and you, my brothers and sisters,
> to pray for me to the Lord our God.

St. Paul's teaching in Romans that "if you confess with your lips that Jesus is Lord and believe in your heart that God raised him from the dead, you will be saved" (10:9) witnesses to how the words we speak are not only informative but performative as well. By imparting information about the world in which we live, spoken words also have causal, trans-formative effects upon us and others who live in that world. That is why Paul tells the Ephesians, "Let no evil talk come out of your mouths, but only such as is good for edifying, as fits the occasion, that it may impart grace to those who hear" (Eph 4:29). The penitential act of the liturgy, like Paul's faith confession, is also a confession with the lips. That it occurs as part of the church's liturgical expression of faith in Jesus' lordship and resurrection is confirmation that it shares in the same saving power. We have all in our lives had the experience of wanting to take back idle words that may still injure others long after they fell from our lips. That same yearning to undo or mitigate the effects of the past is expressed in the *Confiteor* prayer's repetitious phrase "through my fault, through my fault, / through my most grievous fault," accompanied by the striking of the breast (cf. Luke 18:13). In light of St. Paul's teaching, when the words of the *Confiteor* are prayed with faith and love, they not only help "take back" injurious thoughts, words, and actions of the past, but by having participants repent them to the Lord and to each another, they actually help change those hurtful deeds into vehicles now of their common sanctification.

With the closing words of the prayer ("therefore I ask blessed Mary ever-Virgin, / all the Angels and Saints, / and you, my brothers and sisters, / to pray for me to the Lord our God"), the members of the assembly become aware that they stand not only before the Lord and one another but before the whole court of heaven as well: the Blessed Virgin Mary and all the angels and saints, as if already at the Last Judgment, invited to participate in the wedding banquet of the Lamb. By asking all the blessed to intercede for them, participants are also made conscious of being one with the whole Body of Christ, which reaches from this world into the next and goes back in history to its earliest members. And also, the ritual uniqueness of simultaneously asking and being asked the same favor by the rest of the assembly both symbolizes the universal need for forgiveness and, as part of the Spirit-inspired liturgy of the church, intensifies faith confidence in God's willingness in Christ to forgive.

The presider next prays, "May almighty God have mercy on us, / forgive us our sins, / and bring us to everlasting life." The congregation replies, "Amen." One cannot help noticing that, following immediately upon the ending petition of the *Confiteor*, because this forgiveness prayer was just *requested of all* by each individual member of the assembly, it is *on behalf of all* that the presider now offers it.

The fact that the rubrics introduce this prayer with the words "The absolution by the Priest follows" has prompted church authorities to state, "A clear distinction must always be kept between the sacramental absolution received in the Rite of Penance and the ritual absolution performed during the Penitential Act at Mass."[62] Nevertheless, even if it be only a "ritual absolution," the very use of the word "absolution" indicates that the prayer has at least some salutary, absolving effect. As Enrico Mazza points out, "We must realize, however, that it is still a liturgical rite: If a person is truly contrite and converted in God's sight, and if the entire hierarchically organized assembly asks God to forgive, it is not possible to think and act as if nothing has happened."[63] As we have tried to illustrate here, the fact that both the *Confiteor* prayer and the ritual absolution are made as part of the church's liturgical expression of faith endows them with sanctifying power. At the same time, it is also true that any unconfessed *grave* sin on one's conscience thwarts the full needed effect of those prayers and so requires confession and the reception of sacramental absolution before participating in full communion with the other members of the church (cf. 1 Cor 11:27-32). As David Coffey indicates:

> Only [the sacrament of reconciliation] addresses the divine word of forgiveness to the individual contrite sinner. . . . Just as the Eucharist never replaces baptism though it fulfills it, so it never replaces reconciliation, though it fulfills it also. . . . The forgiveness of grave sin, the direct effect of reconciliation, cannot now be an effect of Holy Communion, which is a "sacrament of the living." . . . Holy Communion, like any of the sacraments, effects only what it signifies, and given the actual existence of the sacrament of reconciliation, it does not signify reconciliation, even indirectly. . . . A person conscious of grave sin should receive the sacrament of reconciliation before receiving Holy Communion.[64]

Kyrie

The *Kyrie* came into the Roman Missal "through the litany of the saints sung in processions to stational Masses, Rogations, ordinations, and processions to and from the font at Easter Vigil."[65] By the late fifth century the pope's eucharistic entrance procession was accompanied by the introit psalm until it reached the altar area; the Litany of the Saints, ending with multiple *Kyrie*s, was then sung. A century later Pope Gregory the Great (590–604) dropped the litany on nonfestal days, keeping the repetition of *Kyrie, Christe, Kyrie eleison*. Later still the litany was omitted on Sundays as well.[66]

And so, although the phrase "have mercy" in the second form of the penitential act may suggest only sorrow for sin, this was not always the case. According to Peter Jeffery,

> Historically, the word *eleison*—the second person singular, first aorist imperative active of *eleeō*—was used in emotional situations of entreaty or supplication. Persons making the entreaty would be in a state of great anxiety because they were utterly powerless to act on their own behalf. The person being asked was in complete control of the situation, and therefore utterly free to grant or withhold the favor. . . . Prior to its appearance in Christian liturgy . . . *Kyrie eleison* expressed the

anxious entreaty of a powerless individual addressing an all-powerful lord. . . . But this did not necessarily mean that the petitioner had done anything wrong, or needed to acknowledge guilt or sin. That meaning only occurs sometimes.[67]

On the other hand, given the decline in the practice of sacramental reconciliation ever since Vatican II, expressions of penitence in the context of the Eucharist might actually be helpful in creating consciousness of the Lord's goodness and the extreme cost on the cross of our salvation. In any event, without some awareness in Christian life of our wretchedness without God, we human beings end up not really knowing either ourselves or the God who loves us, a condition against which St. Augustine prayed so earnestly, *Domine Jesu, noverim me, noverim te*, "Lord Jesus, that I might know myself, that I might know you,"[68] evidently meaning that the one necessarily involves the other.

Two options for the *Kyrie* exist in the current edition of the Roman Missal:

℣. Lord, have mercy.	℟. Lord, have mercy.
℣. Christ, have mercy.	℟. Christ, have mercy.
℣. Lord, have mercy.	℟. Lord, have mercy.

Or:

℣. Kyrie, eleison.	℟. Kyrie, eleison.
℣. Christe, eleison.	℟. Christe, eleison.
℣. Kyrie, eleison.	℟. Kyrie, eleison.

Regarding the *Kyrie*, the GIRM states:

> After the Penitential Act, the *Kyrie, eleison* (*Lord, have mercy*), is always begun, unless it has already been included as part of the Penitential Act. Since it is a chant by which the faithful acclaim the Lord and implore his mercy, it is usually executed by everyone, that is to say, with the people and the choir or cantor having a part in it.
>
> Each acclamation is usually pronounced twice, though it is not to be excluded that it be repeated several times. (no. 52)

The fact that the *Kyrie* is among those parts of the Mass that the GIRM states "are in principle meant to be sung," especially "on Sundays and Holydays of Obligation" (no. 40), also indicates that its primary meaning is not one of repentance but one of joy: recognition of the lordship of God. Its position here, therefore, is meant not to echo the sentiments of the penitential act, but to recognize both the transcendence of God and our human dependence on God for all that we have and are in this world. Thus, whether by singing or saying the *Kyrie*, worshipers are deepened in their awareness of the holiness of the task they have begun and the awesomeness of the God they worship. The specified option in the 2002 edition of the Roman Missal of chanting the untranslated version of the *Kyrie* (*Kyrie eleison, Christe . . .*), in addition to having that recognition resonate by song through their whole being, also allows participants to experience their sacramental oneness with the whole church, the Body of Christ that stretches not only across the world but back through the centuries as well.

Gloria in Excelsis Deo

In regard to the Gloria, the GIRM states, "The *Gloria in excelsis* (*Glory to God in the highest*) is a most ancient and venerable hymn by which the Church, gathered in the Holy Spirit, glorifies and entreats God the Father and the Lamb. The text of this hymn may not be replaced by any other. It is intoned by the Priest or, if appropriate, by a cantor or by the choir; but it is sung either by everyone together, or by the people alternately with the choir, or by the choir alone. If not sung, it is to be recited either by everybody together or by two choirs responding one to the other" (no. 53).

The earliest version of the Gloria, a hymn of praise, originated in the ancient Eastern church as part of Morning Prayer. Adopted in the West, it underwent various modifications before reaching its present form. It was already long in use for the pope's nighttime Christmas Masses when Pope Symmachus (498–514) allowed it to be sung for all bishops' Sunday Masses and feast-day Masses for martyrs as well. The same permission began spreading in the eighth century also to presbyteral Sunday and feast-day Masses, so that by the end of the eleventh century it had become the universal practice in the West.[69]

The hymn opens with the song of the angels taken from Luke 2:14. Its 2010 English translation, "Glory to God in the highest / and on earth peace to people of good will," represents a change from the earlier "Glory to God in the highest / and peace to his people on earth." The newer version rests on what critical scholarship regards as better textual authority for the Lukan passage,[70] and it obviously reflects more closely the *bonae voluntatis* of the Roman Rite Latin. Jungmann argues that the "good will" (*eudoxia*) referred to here is God's good will, God's favor and grace. Thus "people of good will" are those to whom, by God's grace and selection, the Good News of God's kingdom has been proclaimed: "May God be given glory in the highest and may [people] in His grace find peace!"[71]

Beginning with the song of the angels, the Gloria unites earth to heaven in its praise of God. Then the following five-part asyndeton, "We praise you, / we bless you, / we adore you, / we glorify you, / we give you thanks for your great glory," like unending, incoming waves of the sea, inundates worshipers with the realization of how absolutely impossible it would be for the recipient of the praise, the "Lord God, heavenly King, / O God, almighty Father," ever to be sufficiently honored by all his creation.

The Gloria next applies the same rhetorical device to the praise of the Son, addressing him with a series of five separate vocatives: "Lord Jesus Christ, Only Begotten Son, / Lord God, Lamb of God, Son of the Father." Here an asyndeton again piles praise upon praise by standing all of Christ's glorious titles next to each other, as if to multiply each in its unimaginable sublimity by all the others.

Following this pleonastic address, the hymn continues to praise the Lord Jesus, but now in the form of a threefold petition: "[Y]ou take away the sins of the world, have mercy on us; / you take away the sins of the world, receive our prayer; / you are seated at the right hand of the Father, have mercy on us." The repetition of "you take away the sins of the world" highlights how the Son's eternal glory is fully realized also in time by his great work of salvation on behalf of all humankind. And that the first response of "have mercy on us" is changed first to "receive our prayer" and then back again to "have mercy on us" not only creates poetic beauty, but suggests also that both refrains share the same meaning and that the focus of the prayer is not on humanity, but exclusively on the immense glory of God.

Finally, the hymn ends in the form of a doxology within a doxology, glorifying the incarnate Son by means of another asyndeton, "For you alone are the Holy One, / you alone are the Lord, / you alone are the Most High, / Jesus Christ." The repeated use of the phrase "you alone" takes all focus off anyone else and yet at the same time extols the Son's glory as fully one with the Father's along with that of the Holy Spirit in the Blessed Trinity: "with the Holy Spirit, / in the glory of God the Father. / Amen." (Cf. John 17:5: "Father, glorify me in your own presence with the glory which I had with you before the world was made").

The Collect

According to the GIRM, "Next the Priest calls upon the people to pray and everybody, together with the Priest, observes a brief silence so that they may become aware of being in God's presence and may call to mind their intentions. Then the Priest pronounces the prayer usually called the 'Collect' and through which the character of the celebration finds expression" (no. 54).

Silence

At one point in the mystifying lyrics to Simon and Garfunkel's iconic 1966 song "Sounds of Silence," the artists seem to suggest that, like T. S. Eliot's "Hollow Men" (1925), modern society is devoid of depth because it is filled with people who talk without speaking and hear without listening. That is why those called-for short periods of silence within the liturgy have become especially important. Within the world of faith they act as a kind of antidote to the emptiness often found in secular culture. As we read in the Psalms, "Be still, and know that I am God" (Ps 46:10). Jean-Yves Quellec notes how "a moment of silence before the actual beginning of the service . . . makes a sort of sheltering screen for recollection. . . . People do not form a congregation on their own. They are called together: they must be able to hear the call which brings them together; they are not there only for the purpose of being an assembly, but rather to let themselves be seized by the One who gave himself up for them."[72] Quellec continues: "The interval of silence between the celebrant's 'Let us pray' and the collect ought not be neglected. . . . This pause points out that the Christian assembly is not a shapeless mass. The 'we' of prayer does not erase individuality: the collect must be what its name implies. Silence here gives each person a chance to exist before God, while joining a community of persons; it tightens the bonds between the individuals and gives them their true meaning."[73]

The Origin and Construction of the Collect

Gerard Moore, in his comprehensive study of post–Vatican II Mass collects, cites Bernard Capelle to show that various fourth- to ninth-century church writers identify the collect as a prayer made by the priest on behalf of the community at the end of a litany, psalm, or short period of silent prayer that sums up (*colligere*) the petitions the people have made. According to Capelle, its essential nature is that of petition.[74] The first evidence of collect-type prayers in the Roman liturgy occurs around the middle of the fifth century.[75] Up until that time the eucharistic liturgy began immediately with the readings. Jungmann theorizes that the entrance, offertory, and communion processions were brought to conclusion with a presidential prayer corresponding to today's collect, a prayer over the offerings, and a prayer after Communion, respectively.[76]

Collect-type prayers have their origin in Roman pagan prayer. Offered by the presider in the name of all, they consist most commonly in (a) an address to God, (b) a motivating cause referring to some attribute of God or some aspect of human existence, (c) a petition, and (d) a purpose clause.[77] The Latin originals are composed according to the Roman rhetorical device known as *cursus*. "By arranging the accents in the last syllables of a literary unit or clause according to a fixed set of rules (the *cursus*), the prayer took on a certain rhythm and harmony."[78]

The very existence of the so-called Verona Sacramentary, a seventh-century compilation of new collect-style prayers and prefaces for each liturgy, "indicates a movement away from the creation of fresh prayers for each liturgy, a preference for well-styled prayer formulae, and a willingness to use well-written prayers in diverse liturgical contexts."[79] According to Christine Mohrmann, fifth-century Christians thought the dignity of divine worship required highly stylized language, even if it could not be easily understood. "While modern post-Reformation sensibilities place much more emphasis on hearing and understanding each word, this was not necessarily a major concern for earlier Christians."[80]

The Collect for the Ninth Sunday in Ordinary Time

After the brief silence, the presider opens his arms in the ancient *orans* position of prayer,[81] with hands turned toward the heavens in a gesture at once of both offering and receiving. Wearing a traditional, more expansive chasuble, the presider by stretching out his arms creates with the folds of the garment the visual effect of a half oval whose lines sweep upward from ankles to both hands, further emphasizing with their beauty the upward direction of the prayer that he offers.[82]

The original Latin of the collect for the Ninth Sunday in Ordinary Time is taken from the eighth-century Old Gelasian Sacramentary (*Reginensis* 316), and it reads: "Deus, cuius providentia in sui dispositione non fallitur, te supplices exoramus, ut noxia cuncta submoveras, et omnia nobis profura concedas. Per Dominum." The new English version of the Roman Missal translates it as follows:

> O God, whose providence never fails in its design,
> keep from us, we humbly beseech you,
> all that might harm us
> and grant all that works for our good.
> Through our Lord Jesus Christ, your Son,
> who lives and reigns with you in the unity of the Holy Spirit,
> one God, for ever and ever.

As Moore demonstrates, the phrase "all that would harm us" is balanced in the prayer by the parallel phrase "all that works for our good." On the one hand, then, the prayer makes participants aware that, because of the fallen state of creation, they have need for God's help in their weakness. On the other hand, God's caring "providence" and power (which "never fails in its design") give them confidence that God will both listen to and fulfill their prayer. That the prayer occurs as part of the preparatory rites suggests that worshipers are both asking and expecting that God will grant them the help that they need, doing so first of all in the liturgy itself through the upcoming Liturgy of the Word and Liturgy of the Eucharist.

To be noted also is how the last sentence of the prayer in the new translation is actually a prepositional phrase and not a sentence at all: "Through our Lord Jesus Christ . . ." As such, it witnesses at once to both the divinity and the humanity of Christ, to how all divine benefits —including those recognized in the present prayer—come to humanity only in and through the Second Person of the Blessed Trinity made flesh, and to how only through the humanity of the same Lord Jesus is it possible for the church now to offer her own petitions and sacrifice of praise. Thus, by not identifying one to the exclusion of the other, the prepositional phrase allows for petitioning the full agency of Christ's humanity *and* divinity in bestowing the object of the prayer.

Once again the congregation responds with "Amen." This time its primary meaning is agreement with and participation in the prayer just proclaimed. Because the whole assembly is the subject of the liturgical action, the "Amen" is needed for the full legitimacy, so to speak, of the prayer. It is a "signing on the dotted line," if you will, the full personal appropriation by all in the assembly of the vision and commitment publically offered in the prayer for their approval. And so, with its official "Amen," the congregation sits down in readiness to hear the Word of God in the readings.

Notes, Chapter Five

[1] The General Instruction of The Roman Missal, 3rd ed. with adaptations for use in the Dioceses of the United States of America, was confirmed by decree of the Congregation for Divine Worship and the Discipline of the Sacraments on March 26, 2010 (Prot. n. 1464/06/L). Proper adaptations for the United States were confirmed on July 24, 2010 (Prot. n. 577/10/L).

[2] Antonio Donghi, *Words and Gestures in the Liturgy*, trans. William McDonough, Dominic Serra, and Ted Bertagni (Collegeville, MN: Liturgical Press, 2009), 12.

[3] Romano Guardini, *Sacred Signs*, trans. Grace Branham (St. Louis, MO: Pio Decimo Press, 1955), 22–23.

[4] From the operetta *New Moon* (1927), music by Sigmund Romberg and lyrics by Frank Mandel, Laurence Schwab, and Oscar Hammerstein II.

[5] Joseph Gelineau, SJ, "Les chants de procession," *La Maison-Dieu* 43 (1955): 74–75.

[6] I am indebted for most of this analysis on the nature of music to a source that I have unfortunately not been able to rediscover.

[7] Edward Foley, OFM Cap., "Toward a Sound Theology," in *Ritual Music: Studies in Liturgical Musicology* (Beltville, MD: Pastoral Press, 1995), 107–26.

[8] Hans Bernhard Meyer, SJ, "Singen und Musiziern: C. Im Neuen Testament," in *Gestalt des Gottesdienstes*, ed. H. B. Meyer et al. Gottesdienst der Kirche: Handbuch der Liturgiewissenschaft series, (Regensburg: Verlag Friedrich Pustet, 1987), 145.

[9] Ibid., 75–76.

[10] Bernard Botte, OSB, "Processionis Aditus," in *Miscellanea Liturgica in Honorem L. Cuniberti Mohlberg*, vol. 1 (Roma: Edizioni liturgiche, 1948–49), 19–127.

[11] H. A. J. Wegman, "'Procedere' und Prozession: Eine Typologie," *Liturgisches Jahrbuch* 27 (1977): 32–34.

[12] Ibid., 34.

[13] Louis-Marie Chauvet, "La présidence liturgique dans la modernité: le chances possible d'une crise," *Questions liturgiques* 83 (2002): 149.

[14] Robert F. Taft, SJ, "Christian Liturgical Psalmody: Origins, Development, Decomposition, Collapse," in *Psalms in Community: Jewish and Christian Textual,*

Liturgical, and Artistic Traditions, ed. Harold W. Attridge and Magot E. Fassler (Leiden-Boston: Brill, 2004), 8n4.

[15] Ibid., 23.

[16] E.g., for communion, Ps 34:9: "Taste and see that the LORD is good!"; Taft, "Christian Liturgical Psalmody," 24–28, 30–31.

[17] Ibid., 31–32.

[18] Ibid., 24.

[19] Hans Renckens, "Le chant de la disapora," in *Fides Sacramenti, Sacramentum Fidei*, eds. Hans Jörg Auf der Maur, Leo Bakker, Annewies Van de Bunt, Joop Waldram (Assen, The Netherlands: Van Gorcum, 1981), 5, 7.

[20] Joseph Gelineau, SJ, *Voices and Instruments in Christian Worship: Principles, Laws, Applications*, trans. Clifford Howell, SJ (Collegeville, MN: Liturgical Press, 1964), 67, 183.

[21] Ibid., 193: "It was not until the ninth century that the name 'Gregorian' was given to the chant of the Roman liturgy. The [people] of those days wanted to endow the chants with the prestige and authority attached to the name of Pope Gregory the Great (590–604). Later on this kind of music was often called 'ecclesiastical chant,' and later still it was called 'plain chant.'

"Gregorian chant is the chant of the Roman church. It consists of those melodies which the Roman church [= the Roman Rite liturgy] has retained in the books approved by the Holy See and which are proposed, sometimes as of obligation, sometimes as recommended and sufficient, for the execution of the ritual texts." The corresponding note, n. 419, reads, "The only authentic Gregorian chant is that which is contained in the 'typical' Vatican editions or has the approval of the Sacred Congregation of Rites for use in a particular church or religious community."

[22] Pope Pius X, *Tra le sollecitudini*, Instruction on Sacred Music, November 22, 1903, no. 3: "Gregorian Chant has always been regarded as the supreme model for sacred music, so that it is fully legitimate to lay down the following rule: the more closely a composition for church approaches in its movement, inspiration and savor the Gregorian form, the more sacred and liturgical it becomes; and the more out of harmony it is with that supreme model, the less worthy it is of the temple" (http://www.adoremus.org/MotuProprio.html).

[23] Pope Pius XII, *Musicae Sacrae Disciplina*, December 15, 1955.

[24] Jan Michael Joncas, *From Sacred Song to Ritual Music: Twentieth-Century Understanding of Roman Catholic Music* (Collegeville, MN: Liturgical Press, 1997), 16.

[25] Frank C. Quinn, OP, "Hymns in Catholic Worship," *Liturgical Ministry* 4 (Fall 1995): 147.

[26] Gelineau, *Voices*, 188–89.

[27] Liturgical Music Today: A Statement of the Bishops' Committee on the Liturgy on the Tenth Anniversary of Music in Catholic Worship (Washington, DC: United States Catholic Conference, 1982), no. 19, quoted in Frank C. Quinn, OP, "Liturgical Music as Corporate Song 2: Problems of Hymnody in Catholic Worship," in *Liturgy and Music: Lifetime Learning*, ed. Robin A. Leaver and Joyce Ann Zimmerman, CPPS (Collegeville, MN: Liturgical Press, 1998), 308. For a summary of reasons against the use of hymnody in the eucharistic liturgy, see Kevin W. Irwin,

"Musical Contretemps," *America* 156 (June 13, 1987): 492. "The Snowbird Statement on Catholic Liturgical Music" by a group of prominent Catholic liturgical theologians and musicians, on the other hand, lists reasons why hymnody at the Eucharist "deserves today stronger encouragement" (Salt Lake City, UT: Madeleine Institute, 1995), no. 19.

[28] For a discussion regarding the purpose of the entrance rite, see Michael James Molloy, "Liturgical Music as Corporate Song 3: Opportunities for Hymnody in Catholic Worship," in *Liturgy and Music*, ed. Leaver and Zimmerman, 334.

[29] Quinn, "Problems of Hymnody," 320.

[30] A. C. Vernoolij, "La musique comme liturgie," *Questions liturgiques* 83 (2002): 194.

[31] Ian Coleman, "Antiphonality: Notes Towards a Theology of Liturgical Form," *Communio* 29 (Spring 2002): 134, 136–37.

[32] For a full explanation of how antiphonal psalmody differs from both responsorial psalmody and alternating psalmody, see Taft, "Christian Liturgical Psalmody," 17–23.

[33] For the symbolism of white as a liturgical color and the theological significance of liturgical vestments, see John D. Laurance, SJ, "Liturgical Vestments," in *The New Dictionary of Sacramental Worship*, ed. Peter E. Fink, SJ (Collegeville, MN: Liturgical Press, 1990), 1306, 1312–14.

[34] A. J. MacGregor, *Fire and Light in the Western Triduum: Their Use at Tenebrae and at the Paschal Vigil*, Alcuin Club series (Collegeville, MN: Liturgical Press, 1992), 49.

[35] E. G. Cuthbert F. Atchley, *A History of the Use of Incense in Divine Worship* (London: Longmans, Green and Co., 1909), 155.

[36] Jerome, *Adversus vigilantium* (PL 23:346), as quoted in translation in Atchley, *A History*, 183.

[37] Isidore of Seville, *Etym.*, VIII, 12 (PL 82:293), as quoted in translation in D. R. Dendy, *Use of Lights in Christian Worship* (London: SPCK, 1959), 80.

[38] Rite of Christian Initiation of Adults, in *The Rites of the Catholic Church*, vol. 1, study ed. (Collegeville, MN: Liturgical Press, 1990), no. 230.

[39] The GIRM: "[O]n or next to the altar are to be placed candlesticks with lighted candles: at least two in any celebration, or even four or six, especially for a Sunday Mass or a Holyday of Obligation. . . . Likewise, on the altar or close to it, there is to be a cross adorned with a figure of Christ crucified. The candles and the cross with the figure of Christ crucified may also be carried in the procession at the Entrance. On the altar itself may be placed a *Book of the Gospels* distinct from the book of other readings, unless it is carried in the Entrance Procession" (no. 117).

[40] Laurance, "Liturgical Vestments," 1306.

[41] For the history and multiple meanings over the centuries ascribed to kissing the altar, see Joseph A. Jungmann, SJ, *The Mass of the Roman Rite*, vol. 1 (New York: Benziger Bros., 1951), 311–17.

[42] Rite of Dedication of An Altar, in *The Rites of the Catholic Church*, vol. 2, study ed. (Collegeville, MN: Liturgical Press, 1991), nos. 1–5.

[43] Jungmann, *Mass of the Roman Rite*, vol. 1, 296–97.

[44] Edward J. Kilmartin, SJ, *Christian Liturgy I: Theology and Practice* (Kansas City, MO: Sheed and Ward, 1988), 46: "The liturgy is primarily a prayer." Note also the title of Aimé-Georges Martimort's classic handbook on the liturgy: *L'Eglise en Prière* (*The Church at Prayer*).

[45] 2 Sam 6:21: "And David said to Michal, '. . . I will make merry before the LORD.'" Cf. also Romano Guardini, "The Playfulness of the Liturgy," in *The Spirit of the Liturgy*, trans. Ada Lane (New York: Benziger Brothers, 1931), 85–106 (German original: *Vom Geist der Liturgie* [Freiburg: Herder, 1919]).

[46] Cf. Kilmartin, *Christian Liturgy I*, 77.

[47] Cyrille Vogel, "Le signation dans l'église des premiers siècles," *La Maison-Dieu* 75 (1963): 37. Cf. Tertullian, *De corona* (ca. 211) III, 4 (PL 1:80).

[48] Originating from Christ's instruction in Matt 28:18 (cf. Jungmann, *Mass of the Roman Rite*, vol. 1, 296). Cf. also Vogel, "Le signation," 40, 49; *Hippolytus: A Text for Students*, trans. Geoffrey J. Cumming, Grove Liturgical Study series 8 (Bramcote, Notts.: Grove Books, 1976), no. 41: "By signing yourself with moist breath and catching your spittle in your hand, your body is sanctified down to your feet. For when (prayer) is offered with a believing heart as though from the font, the gift of the Spirit and the sprinkling of baptism sanctify him who believes"; and Leo the Great, *Sermo* 4:1–2 (PL 54:148–49).

[49] A. Molieu, "Amen," in *Catholicisme: Hier—Aujourd'hui—Demain*, I, ed. G. Jacquemet (Paris: Letouzey et Ané, 1948), 441.

[50] Ibid.

[51] Cf. chap. 1 above.

[52] Ibid., 232; Michael K. Magee, "The Liturgical Translation of the Response, '*Et Cum Spiritu Tuo*," *Communio* 29 (Spring 2002): 155–58.

[53] *Pace* W. C. Van Unnik, "*Dominus Vobiscum*: The Background of a Liturgical Formula," in *New Testament Essays: Studies in Memory of Thomas Walter Manson, 1983–1958*, ed. A. J. B. Higgins (Manchester: Manchester University Press, 1959).

[54] Bernard Botte, OSB, "*Dominus Vobiscum*," trans. Peter M. J. Stravinskas, *Antiphon* 14, no. 2 (2010): 231 (French original: *Bible et vie chrétienne* 62 [March/April 1965]: 33–38).

[55] Botte, "*Dominus Vobiscum*," 231–32; Magee, "Liturgical Translation," 161–62.

[56] Jungmann, *Mass of the Roman Rite*, vol. 1, 363.

[57] Magee, "Liturgical Translation," 162.

[58] Ibid., 163, citing P. C. Spicq, OP, *Les épitres pastorales* (Paris, 1947), 397.

[59] Cf. 1 Tim 4:14; 2 Tim 1:6.

[60] Magee, "Liturgical Translation," 167.

[61] Joseph Gelineau, SJ, "Conclusions," in *Growing in Church Music: Proceedings of a Meeting on "Why Church Music?" Strawberry Hill, London, England* (Washington, DC: Universa Laus, 1979), 56.

[62] United States Conference of Catholic Bishops, Committee on Divine Worship, *Newsletter* XLVII (July 2011): 26; The GIRM states: "The rite concludes with the Priest's absolution, which, however, lacks the efficacy of the Sacrament of Penance" (no. 51).

⁶³ Enrico Mazza, *The Celebration of the Eucharist: The Origin of the Rite and Development of Its Interpretation*, trans. Matthew J. O'Connell (Collegeville, MN: Liturgical Press, 1998), 264n7.

⁶⁴ David Coffey, *The Sacrament of Reconciliation* (Collegeville, MN: Liturgical Press, 2001), 63–64.

⁶⁵ Peter Jeffery, "The Meanings and Functions of *Kyrie Eleison*," in *The Place of Christ in Liturgical Prayer: Trinity, Christology, and Liturgical Theology*, ed. Bryan D. Spinks (Collegeville, MN: Liturgical Press, 2008), 192.

⁶⁶ John Baldovin, SJ, "*Kyrie Eleison* and the Entrance Rite of the Roman Eucharist," *Worship* 60, no. 4 (July 1986): 344.

⁶⁷ Jeffery, "The Meanings," 144, 150.

⁶⁸ Augustine, *Soliloquies* II, 1, 1 (CSEL 89:45).

⁶⁹ Jungmann, *Mass of the Roman Rite*, vol. 1, 346–59.

⁷⁰ Cf. *Novum Testamentum Graece et Latine*, eds. Nestle-Aland (Stuttgart: Deutsche Bibelgesellschaft, 1984), 157.

⁷¹ Jungmann, *Mass of the Roman Rite*, vol. 1, 351.

⁷² Jean-Yves Quellec, "Silence in the Liturgy," in *Symbol: The Language of the Liturgy*, ed. Anthony Sherman et al. (n.p.: Federation of Diocesan Liturgical Commissions, 1982), 66.

⁷³ Ibid., 66–67.

⁷⁴ Gerard Moore, SM, *Vatican II and the Collects for Ordinary Time: A Study in the Roman Missal (1975)* (San Francisco: Catholic Scholars Press, 1998), 10–11, citing Bernard Capelle, OSB, "*Collecta*," in *Travaux liturgiques de doctrine et d'histoire*, vol. 2 (Louvain: Abbaye du Mont César, 1962), 195.

⁷⁵ Moore, *Vatican II*, 19.

⁷⁶ Joseph Jungmann, SJ, *Public Worship: A Survey* (Collegeville, MN: Liturgical Press, 1957), 94–95, quoted in Moore, *Vatican II*, 31.

⁷⁷ Moore, *Vatican II*, 13.

⁷⁸ Ibid., 16.

⁷⁹ Ibid., 20.

⁸⁰ Ibid., 19–20, 22n34.

⁸¹ As depicted repeatedly in early Christian catacomb art.

⁸² Cf., e.g., the apse mosaic of the sixth-century church of Sant' Apollinare in Classe in Ravenna, Italy, with its image of Saint Apollinaris in a chasuble and with arms outstretched in the *orans* position. Unfortunately, today's squarish, "continental-style" chasuble, draping heavily directly downward from both arms, no longer provides the same upward sweeping visual effect.

Chapter Six

The Liturgy of the Word

The General Instruction of the Roman Missal (GIRM) describes the purpose and content of the Liturgy of the Word:

> The main part of the Liturgy of the Word is made up of the readings from Sacred Scripture together with the chants occurring between them. As for the Homily, the Profession of Faith, and the Universal Prayer, they develop and conclude it. For in the readings, as explained by the Homily, God speaks to his people, opening up to them the mystery of redemption and salvation, and offering spiritual nourishment; and Christ himself is present through his word in the midst of the faithful. By silence and by singing, the people make this divine word their own, and affirm their adherence to it by means of the Profession of Faith; finally, having been nourished by the divine word, they pour out their petitions by means of the Universal Prayer of the Faithful for the needs of the whole Church and for the salvation of the whole world. (no. 55)

Origins of the Liturgy of the Word

As we have seen, Thierry Maertens in his biblical study lists proclamation of the scriptural Word, including a homiletic "breaking open" of the Word, among the four essential characteristics of any true liturgical assembly.[1] "The proclamation of the Word and its explanation in the homily resulted in the solidarity of the assembled people."[2] Until recently most scholars held that the Liturgy of the Word originates out of the fixed pattern of the Jewish Saturday morning synagogue service and that the Liturgy of the Eucharist, in imitation of the Last Supper, derives from the ritual meal celebrated in Jewish homes on Friday evenings to inaugurate the Sabbath. Yet, as Paul Bradshaw points out, we have no evidence of what shape the Sabbath morning service might have taken in the first century. Furthermore, "the Jewish meal tradition itself seems to have included what might be called 'an informal ministry of the word,' the custom of surrounding the repast with religious discourse and the singing of hymns."[3] According to Ambroos Verhuel, "Although the ritualized Liturgy of the Word in preparation for the Eucharist is not verified before the middle of the second century, the union of the Word and the Eucharist is not for that fact any less a very ancient biblical datum. Are the farewell words of Christ at the Last Supper anything other than a proclaiming word preceding the institution of the Eucharist? And when, on the road to Emmaus, the Lord opens the Scriptures to the discouraged disciples, is it not in view of making their hearts ardent so that they might recognize him in the breaking of the bread?" (Luke 24).[4]

According to Philippe Béguerie, the "Bible was born of the liturgy, from its very beginnings, from the most ancient texts of the holy book."[5] It originated as Scripture out of its liturgical role as an expression of faith: "I have told the glad news of deliverance / in the great congregation" (Ps 40:9). Angelus Häussling lays the theological foundation for this assertion:

> The goal of the economy of salvation is community in the Mystery revealing itself and the believers accepting that revelation—a *sacrum commercium* (a holy exchange). This community exists only when the Other is grasped in his essential reality. He, however, who traditionally has been called "God," has shown himself essentially as One calling for a response, as a personal partner, as someone always greater but yet listening to us. Therefore prayer, that is, speech in response to God, belongs to the very nature of faith. The life of Jesus, then, would not be adequately accounted for if his prayer were not mentioned. In the same way, the believing Church, seriously accepting God as the God he is, can exist only if she prays.[6]

Just as the canon of Old Testament Scripture, then, is itself the result of a selection among multiple oral and, later, written traditions by their use in the communal worship of the ancient Israelite community[7]—the prayer exercise of her faith—so was the first-hand liturgical witness by the apostles to God's saving deeds in Christ (e.g., Acts 20:7-11) written down in New Testament texts to be announced anew in other liturgical celebrations.[8] "By its very constitution, the Bible is made for public reading: this is the reason . . . why 'ecclesiality' belongs to it not accidentally but essentially."[9] Through liturgical usage the church came to recognize the essential content of her apostolic faith in Christ crystalized in the totality of those particular writings, and so early on the church regarded them as canonical.[10] The whole Bible, then, originates as Scripture out of the church's *lex orandi*, that is, from its role in the church's liturgical worship.

Because for Christians the principle of intelligibility for any passage of Scripture, as for all human life in general, is Jesus Christ in his saving events, his paschal mystery,[11] the full Bible as the book of the church is made up of both Old and New Testaments taken together: the Old to be read in light of the New and the New as fulfilling the Old. Consequently, "a Liturgy of the Word during Mass that consists only in a reading from the Gospel would be insufficient. For the Gospel and the history of Christ that it recounts are completely incomprehensible without the Scripture that precedes it (the Old Testament)."[12]

The Liturgy of the Word as "Cultural Memory"

If, as we know, individuals attain to a sense of their personal identity through memory, associating particular moments from their past into a kind of internal biography, societies do the same. However, a society's memory can never remain purely interior or psychological. In order to be shared, it has to be objectified outwardly in symbolic and ritual forms of communication, especially since the defining origins of any society typically antedates the life spans of its current members and their own individual memories. Hence the need for public anamnesis (memorial) of the origins of any given religious society to insure its continuance into the future, an anamnesis enacted both at holy sites and at sacred times to help symbolize that society's divinely established, perduring validity.[13] By such ritual memorial, participants experience themselves as contemporary with the group's origins and so are plunged together more deeply into its core identity. Deuteronomy 26 provides a particularly clear example of this phenomenon.

By their memorial of the exodus as the defining event in Israelite history, those making the sacrificial offering in Deuteronomy 26 experience their solidarity ("us," "we") with their ancestors who emerged from Egypt ages earlier as a "nation, great, mighty, and populous":

> When you come into the land which the LORD your God gives you for an inheritance and have taken possession of it, and live in it, you shall take some of the first of all the fruit of the ground, which you harvest from the land that the LORD your God gives you, and you shall put it in a basket, and you shall go to the place which the LORD your God will choose, to make his name to dwell there. . . .
>
> And you shall make response before the LORD your God: "A wandering Aramean was my father; and he went down into Egypt and sojourned there, few in number; and there he became a nation, great, mighty, and populous. And the Egyptians treated us harshly, and afflicted us, and laid upon us hard bondage. Then we cried to the LORD the God of our fathers, and the LORD heard our voice, and saw our affliction, our toil, and our oppression; and the LORD brought us out of Egypt with a mighty hand and an outstretched arm, with great terror, with signs and wonders; and he brought us into this place and gave us this land, a land flowing with milk and honey. And behold, now I bring the first of the fruit of the ground, which you, O LORD, have given me." And you shall set it down before the LORD your God, and worship before the LORD your God; and you shall rejoice in all the good which the LORD your God has given to you and to your house, you, and the Levite, and the sojourner who is among you. (Deut 26:1-2; 5-11)

By ritually remembering how God through the exodus transformed nomadic Hebrews into God's people—providing them with their own land—worshipers directly experience in the tangible fruit that they offer not only the land from which it came but also the land as a gift from God through those events long ago, and therefore they experience those saving events themselves.

Because of such experiences of God's saving activity in her liturgical assemblies, Israel came to see that such assemblies themselves were the result of God's calling his people together ("When you come into the land . . .") and that God is the source also of the very words in which the memorial is enacted, so that, as Reinhard Messner points out, "the anamnesis of God here is fundamental: it is God who recalls his redemptive action."[14] That the sacred text is to be performed only at "the place which the LORD your God will choose" witnesses also to how everything about the commemorative ritual is part of God's initiative and so shares likewise in God's saving power.

On the other hand, the saving anamnesis of God is realized only through Israel's own anamnetic performance of the rite. In other words, by their memorial, worshipers are taken up into the work of their own salvation—a further instance of "symbolic exchange" as treated above in chapter 2. For if God speaks himself out to Israel through historical "signs and wonders," Israel truly "hears" and therefore receives God's saving word in those deeds only by offering herself back to God in "cultural remembrance" of them. The Bible, then, is the Word of God in the words of human beings. Israel herself, as depicted in Deuteronomy 26, by offering and consuming the memorialized first fruits of the land, becomes in turn God's word to the world, called on to manifest God's own unconditional and undeserved generosity to herself by sharing those gifts along with her whole life, in celebration in God's love ("you shall rejoice")—not only among her own members but with all others who come her way as well ("sojourners").

If the exodus in all of its parts—liberation from Egypt, Sinai covenant and law, gift of the Promised Land—constitutes Israel's founding origins, then the church's originating events are those of Christ's paschal mystery: his life, death, resurrection, and future coming in glory as witnessed to in the New Testament. In the words of St. Paul, "We preach Christ crucified, . . . the power of God and the wisdom of God" (1 Cor 1:23-24). However, "the Liturgy of the Word of the anamnetic kind is not a simple act of reading or of a presentation of texts. It is a ritual enactment; it is a symbolic action and not a mere word-act."[15] By liturgically recalling Christ's saving events, including how on the night before he died he handed himself over to his disciples in the form of bread and wine for their salvation, the church, too, becomes one with the events that she memorializes, or rather that God through the church's liturgical celebration memorializes in her midst: "The word of the Lord."

Nor is the church's memorial one of bringing only past events to life in the present. Even within Old Testament history itself Israel began to look for a future, definitive enactment of God's salvation: "Remember not the former things, / nor consider the things of old. / Behold, I am doing a new thing; / now it springs forth, do you not perceive it? / I will make a way in the wilderness / and rivers in the desert" (Isa 43:18-19).[16] According to New Testament faith, that predicted future has already been fully realized in Christ's paschal mystery. There is, then, "no purely future eschatology in the New Testament. The end of history has intervened into history itself. In the death of Jesus and in the resurrection of the Crucified One, it is already realized. . . . The anamnesis of Christ is a memory of the future, an anticipation of the fulfillment of the world in the kingdom of God. It is able to be this inasmuch as it consists essentially in a here-and-now encounter with the risen and therefore present Christ."[17] Consequently, St. Paul exhorts the Colossians: "If you have been raised with Christ, seek the things that are above, where Christ is, seated at the right hand of God. . . . For you have died, and your life is hid with Christ in God. When Christ who is our life appears, then you also will appear with him in glory" (Col 3:1, 3-4).

The Liturgy of the Word as Consecratory

In his reflections on the relationship of the Liturgy of the Word to the Liturgy of the Eucharist, Chauvet appeals to St. Augustine's famous adage regarding the nature of a sacrament: "The word enters upon a material element and it becomes a sacrament, itself also a kind of a visible word" (Accedit verbum ad elementum, et fit sacramentum, etiam ipsum tanquam visibile verbum).[18] In the past one might have understood Augustine's *verbum* (word) here to mean only what is known in traditional Catholic sacramental theology as the essential "form" of a sacrament: those verbal formulae such as "I baptize you in the name of . . ." or "I absolve you . . ." without which sacraments do not take place. However, by applying Augustine's adage to the relationship of the Liturgy of the Word to the Liturgy of the Eucharist, Chauvet in effect suggests that when Christ alive in the church speaks to a historically unique liturgical assembly through the reading and homiletic application of Scripture, the Liturgy of the Word itself becomes in a way a sacramental Word. The defining context of meaning within which the upcoming eucharistic prayer takes place, and is therefore to be understood, is that which is revealed especially in the reading of the gospel and its explication by sacramentally ordained leadership, the church's apostolic authority.[19] Within this context, then, believers come to recognize Christ in a new way in the breaking of the bread (cf. Luke 24). Thus, if sacraments truly cause by signifying as we saw in chapter 1, the whole Liturgy of the Word actually contributes to the prayer's consecratory effect on the assembly's offerings of bread and wine.

It is only because the memorialized original saving events of Christ's life, death, and resurrection themselves took place within human history that they are able to save human beings, who themselves, as temporal beings, necessarily live each within their own historical time and place. For Chauvet, then, without a preliminary Liturgy of the Word, the Liturgy of the Eucharist would celebrate "a timeless Christ" and endorse "the semi-gnostic Christianity that Paul (and others) struggled against."[20] In the words of Aimon-Marie Roguet, "Without the liturgy of the Word, the Eucharistic celebration is incomplete, it runs the risk of turning into a kind of magic or routine devotion."[21] As is well known, it was the theoretical disengagement of the words of consecration, *Hoc est enim corpus meum* (For this is my body), from their moorings within the whole anamnetic eucharistic celebration that led outsiders to regard them as a kind of magical incantation: "hocus-pocus."

Therefore, although the Christ received in Communion "is the same yesterday and today and forever" (Heb 13:8), each successive Liturgy of the Word reveals him fully present there in ever-new ways in the breaking of the bread, that is, in the lives that participants share together in Christ. For it is only through the Liturgy of the Word, revealing Christ alive in their contemporary world both within them and around them, that members of each new liturgical assembly are able to see not a Gnostic Christ existing independent of history, but rather a Christ whose presence in the Eucharist is one with all the moments of their own lives, both "today" (*hodie*) and into the future: "O that today you would listen to his voice!" (Ps 95:7; cf. Heb 3:7).

The Lectionary

"After some hesitations in the first centuries, where the acts of the martyrs or certain apocryphal gospels were read, it was considered as a fixed rule, beginning with Pope Damasus (+ 386), to read only the inspired texts of Sacred Scripture."[22] During her earliest years the church at each eucharistic liturgy seems to have read, as long as time would allow, complete books of the Bible straight through from beginning to end (*lectio continua*). On feast days, however, particular pericopes were chosen (*lectio selecta*) as were deemed appropriate to the life of the martyr or the saving event being celebrated. Furthermore, the fact that liturgical presiders at the time were able to improvise the eucharistic prayer suggests that they had similar freedom to choose scriptural readings for a given liturgy.[23]

The oldest witness to the existence of a book of scriptural readings is found in Gennadius (fl. 470). However, there is no doubt that, given the influence of Jewish synagogue practices on Christian liturgy, lists of readings were in use much earlier.[24] For "from the synagogue come such patterns as the semicontinuous reading of a biblical book over a sequence of Sundays (Jewish synagogue traditions read the Torah—the first five books of the Hebrew Scriptures—in a continuous one-year or three-year sequence of Sabbaths), and the pairing of passages from different parts of the Bible at each celebration (Jewish tradition selected an excerpt from the Prophets, called a *haftorah*, to explicate the Torah pericope of the day)."[25] The usage common to Gallican, Milanese, Mozarabic, and other rites was to have three readings at the Eucharist: Old Testament, epistle, and gospel. The Roman Rite alone, up until the post–Vatican II reforms, knew only an epistle and a gospel, and those only in a one-year cycle.[26]

According to Normand Bonneau, whereas the practice of *lectio continua* affirms that all Scripture "is inspired by God and profitable for teaching" (2 Tim 3:16), "*lectio selecta*, which evolved along with the festal season, underscores the significance of the present event being celebrated and its importance in the ongoing history of salvation."[27] "*Lectio continua* in the current Lectionary takes the adapted form of semicontinuous reading and provides the distinctive trait of the Sundays in Ordinary Time."[28] On these Sundays the Synoptic Gospels are read in semicontinuous fashion across a three-year cycle (Matthew, Year A; Mark supplemented by John, Year B; and Luke, Year C).[29] On the other hand, because the current Roman Rite Lectionary for Sundays of the Year is also "totally oriented to the Paschal Mystery of Christ,"[30] the Old Testament readings have been *selectively* chosen to provide a typological connection to the particular gospel passage of the day, to illustrate how Jesus Christ, who in his life, death, and resurrection acted proleptically in a saving way through Old Testament realities, is alive and active in a similar way in the church's liturgy and throughout the lives of believers today.

Because the second of the three biblical readings is taken semicontinuously from New Testament nongospel writings, it has no predetermined thematic connection to either the Old Testament reading or the gospel passage for the day. However, if the "first reading from the Old Testament evokes the story of salvation of which Jesus in the gospel reading is the climax, . . . [the] second reading from the apostolic writings models how the early Christians interpreted the Paschal Mystery of Jesus' death and resurrection and provides examples of how believers can appropriate it in their lives."[31]

Ordinary Time, then, "paces the faithful through the difficult fidelity of discipleship."[32] Furthermore, "by hearing the words of Scripture made alive in their midst and by opening themselves to their transforming power, the believing community both writes itself into the story and is in turn shaped by the story. The result is a new text or narrative, a combination of old and new. [At any particular liturgical celebration, never] before has the specific interplay between these texts and these people occurred, never will it occur again in this particular way, for liturgy celebrates God's salvation made present and effective for the community here and now assembled."[33]

The Readings for the Ninth Sunday in Ordinary Time, Year A

As noted at the end of the previous chapter, after the introductory rites all in the assembly sit down in preparation for hearing the Word of God proclaimed in their midst. In this context, then, being seated is itself an act of faith, embodying the attitude of complete openness to God into one's life: "Speak, LORD, for your servant hears" (1 Sam 3:9).

First Reading: Deuteronomy 11:18, 26-28, 32

The lector ascends to the ambo[34] and announces the first reading for the Ninth Sunday in Ordinary Time with the words "A reading from the Book of Deuteronomy" and then proceeds to read:

> Moses told the people,
>   "Take these words of mine into your heart and soul.
> Bind them at your wrist as a sign,
>   and let them be a pendant on your forehead.
>
> "I set before you here, this day, a blessing and a curse:
>   a blessing for obeying the commandments of the LORD, your God,
>   which I enjoin on you today;

a curse if you do not obey the commandments of the L ORD,
    your God,
but turn aside from the way I ordain for you today,
to follow other gods, whom you have not known.
Be careful to observe all the statutes and decrees
that I set before you today."

At the end of the reading the lector proclaims, "The word of the Lord," to which all in the assembly respond, "Thanks be to God." As Messner observes, "This is not a more or less optional 'thank you' as much as it is an acclamation—a public, ritualized, and communal announcing of commitment to the proclaimed Word of God. Acclamations are legal actions, binding those who make them."[35] In other words, "Thanks be to God" is like the acclamation the ancient Israelites made in answer to Moses' proclaiming the book of the covenant: "All that the LORD has spoken we will do, and we will be obedient" (Exod 24:7). In the same way, then, eucharistic participants, understanding the first reading as addressed to themselves ("The word of the Lord"), commit themselves by this response to "take" God's "words into" their "heart and soul," not "to follow other gods" but to "obey the commandments of the Lord," and so to deserve his promised "blessing."

If the reading is done well—that is, if the English words are pronounced accurately and distinctly, phrases and sentences flowingly, in a public voice, not by attempting to play the role of God through sanctimonious cadences or long emotional pauses, but by speaking out in a normal human way the faith of the church—it will have the best chance of being heard and appropriated by the whole congregation. The brief period of silence that follows then allows the Word to resonate through the minds and hearts of all in the assembly, eliciting reflections, for example, on what "other gods" might exist in their lives, what "commandments of the Lord" seem most difficult to keep, or what yearnings they might have to be "heart and soul" one with the Lord.

Next, the cantor ascends the ambo to lead the responsorial psalm. He or she does so from the ambo because the psalms are themselves part of Sacred Scripture.

Responsorial Psalm: Psalm 31:2-3, 3-4, 17, 25

After intoning and then leading the assembly in repeating the refrain, "Lord, be my rock of safety," words taken from the psalm itself (v. 3b), the cantor proceeds to the strophes, after each of which the assembly again responds with the same refrain.

> In you, O LORD, I take refuge;
>> let me never be put to shame.
> In your justice rescue me,
>> incline your ear to me,
>> make haste to deliver me!
>
> R̶y̶. Lord, be my rock of safety.
>
> Be my rock of refuge,
>> a stronghold to give me safety.
> You are my rock and my fortress;
>> for your name's sake you will lead and guide me.
>
> R̶y̶. Lord, be my rock of safety.
>
> Let your face shine upon your servant;
>> save me in your kindness.
> Take courage and be stouthearted,
>> all you who hope in the LORD.
>
> R̶y̶. Lord, be my rock of safety.

Whereas psalm chants are used elsewhere in the Roman Rite liturgy to accompany processions,[36] the responsorial psalm has no other purpose than to be sung and listened to as part of God's scriptural Word. And because it is intended primarily to be a proclamation of the Word of God rather than just a musical event, if for some reason it cannot be chanted, it should still be recited and not simply replaced by some other musical composition.[37]

Peter Jeffery has demonstrated that the responsorial psalm entered the Roman Rite Mass during the pontificate of Pope Celestine I (422–32).[38] Although by tradition it immediately follows the first reading, its original purpose was not as a response to that reading, but so that the faithful could enter more fully into God's Word by their share in the chanting of the psalm. "Nevertheless, this [supposed] correspondence [between reading and psalm] played a strong part in the revision of the Lectionary by the postconciliar commission."[39] As a result, the current responsorial psalms are chosen to echo the content of the Old Testament readings that precede them.[40]

As we have seen, the opening reading for the Ninth Sunday taken from Deuteronomy 11 entreats all in the assembly to rely on God alone as their Lord. The psalm refrain then supplies a response to that call: "Lord, be my rock of safety." And the verses that follow deepen this commitment by a variety of phrases on the same theme: "You are my rock and my fortress"; "In you, O LORD, I take refuge"; "[M]ake haste to deliver me!"; "[S]ave me in your kindness"; and so forth.

It has already been noted in the previous chapter how, according to Ian Coleman, "antiphon" originates not from *antiphōnē* (a response) but from *antiphōnon* (answering back): it is "not a noun, but the neuter form of a participle. The word also derives, not from *phōnē* (voice) but from *phōnein* (to give voice, speak, or sing), that is, a verb having the meaning of 'to reply, gainsay.' Thus the use of the participle identifies an action rather than a thing—an 'answering back' rather than an 'opposing voice.'"[41] On the basis of this understanding Coleman discovers within this dialogical interplay between the responsorial psalm and the first reading a whole theology of liturgy that he calls "antiphonality." In regard to the responsorial psalm, then, what the congregation does is appropriate the essential content of the psalm's verses, sung by the cantor, by voicing it back, *antiphōnon*, in the words of the refrain. By doing so the congregation also shares in the responsorial psalm's larger, overall function of voicing back the content of the first reading.

Coleman points to the Reproaches (*Improperia*) of the Good Friday liturgy as the prime example of what he means by "antiphonality." Sung by a cantor *in persona Christi* in response to the *Trisagion* ("Holy is God, / Holy and Mighty, / Holy and Immortal One, / have mercy on us"), the Reproaches ("My people, what have I done to you? / Or how have I grieved you? Answer me!") reveal by placing these words in Jesus' mouth how the hidden reality of his divinity and the horrible injustice of human rejection are both at work in the saving events of his passion and death, during which he made no reproach ("He was oppressed, and he was afflicted, / yet he opened not his mouth" [Isa 53:7]). In other words, *res ipsa clamat* (the reality itself cries out), so that the antiphonal response gives voice to the unspoken depth of what was proclaimed in the scriptural reading. Thus, "to the brute facts of the Passion, related in the preceding liturgy of the word (in particular [the reading of the Passion narrative]), this rite is antiphonal [as] an 'opposing voicing.'"[42] By a divided chorus the same "I" is made to "answer back" to itself, to oppose its own voice, "creating dialogue out of apparent monologue, with the aim of a unity of heart and mind in those who embrace it."[43]

Here Coleman observes how "consistently throughout the history of the liturgy, the antiphon and all that is antiphonal has not been the preserve of the clergy. The opposing voice is a lay voice . . . not the voice of the Sanctuary, [but] a mediate voice."[44] It is, in fact, through the fundamentally dialogical, antiphonal nature of the eucharistic liturgy as a whole ("The Lord be with you," etc.) that the church experiences God and that God sacramentally manifests God's Self. For Christian liturgy is nothing else than authentic human living stylized to highlight its fundamental reality as participation in the saving events of Christ. Just as all true human living consists in a dialogical self-giving of human beings to each other in everyday word and action—loving God in others and others in God—so is the liturgy itself dialogical, however in a more intense, symbolic way designed to send the Christians back into the world consciously empowered in a new way to live more fully their common life in Christ. As Edward Kilmartin defines it, "Liturgy is primarily the exercise of the life of faith under the aspect of being together 'in the name of Jesus' for the realization of communion, the sharing and receiving, between God, community, and individual, in a coordinated system of ministerial services."[45] It is no surprise, then, that antiphonality is the very essence of Christian liturgy.

As we have seen, human beings dwell in language, and so it is in the *physical* sounding of the word that its meaning is both realized and communicated within this temporal and spatial world. The fact that the root of "antiphon" is *phōnē*, "voice," points to how human speech communicates through various tones and stresses, suggesting that antiphons be sung and not simply said, in precisely the same spirit of an opposing voicing.[46] For the sacramentality of God's Word emerges most clearly when this antiphonal voicing is couched in the *physicality* of melodious sounds, allowing participants as embodied creatures to express more fully and thus enter more completely into their sacramental nature as Christ's Body in this world. "Our mistake lies in seeking for the sort of 'objectivity' of message in the liturgy that both a 'Form-critic' and a 'Redaction-critic' seek for in Scripture; to get behind the text. Whilst this may be entirely appropriate for the scientific study of ancient texts, the tradition of antiphonality should alert us to its absurdity in the celebration of the liturgy. For 'getting behind the text' implies that there is an immediacy to be sought out and found, where antiphonality points us towards mediacy."[47] In other words, if human beings dwell in language, they do so precisely in the sounds of language: its physicality, which in the context of the liturgy is the mode also of its sacramentality.

Just as by the responsorial psalm the assembly "voices back" to God and thus appropriates the basic content of the previous Old Testament reading, so through the Liturgy of the Eucharist with its more concentrated celebration of the paschal mystery of Christ's life, death, and resurrection does it "voice back," and so more fully appropriate, the proclamation of God's Word in the Liturgy of the Word. In fact, the eucharistic liturgy as a whole consists in an antiphonal response of thanksgiving to God for the fullness of God's Word in Christ throughout history.

In each instance, then, what would otherwise have been a monologue becomes, through antiphonality, dialogue, in which the fuller Word of God is not only heard but also existentially appropriated by all in the assembly through ritual actions and voicings. Through antiphonality God's Word is revealed to be not some unchanging, purely objective set of ideas lying behind the words of Scripture to be uncovered through linguistic and exegetical analysis, but dialogically alive and ever new in each new assembly's encounter with the living God who speaks to his people in and through their lived faith response to God in return. For just as in the Holy Spirit the Father spoke himself out completely into the incarnated humanity of his Son Jesus precisely through Jesus' own "antiphonal" response of faith in return, so too, according to Coleman,[48] does the church participate as the Body of Christ in this same trinitarian dialogue-in-unity by means of the fundamentally antiphonal reality of the Eucharist.

Second Reading: Romans 3:21-25, 28

After a brief pause of silence, the second reader ascends the ambo and announces the second reading: "A reading from the Letter of Saint Paul to the Romans."

> Brothers and sisters,
> Now the righteousness of God has been manifested apart from the law,
>   though testified to by the law and the prophets,
>   the righteousness of God through faith in Jesus Christ
>   for all who believe.
> For there is no distinction;
>   all have sinned and are deprived of the glory of God.
> They are justified freely by his grace
>   through the redemption in Christ Jesus,
>   whom God set forth as an expiation,
>   through faith, by his blood.
> For we consider that a person is justified by faith
>   apart from works of the law.

Again the lector ends the reading with "The word of the Lord," and the assembly makes the same acclamation of commitment to the Lord in his Word, "Thanks be to God."

As we have seen, the pericopes of the second reading on Sundays are selected semicontinuously from nongospel books of the New Testament. The A Cycle of readings begins the letter to the Romans on this, the ninth Sunday, and continues it on through the twenty-fourth Sunday. As semicontinuous, then, these readings would have had no intended thematic connection to either the first reading (Old Testament) or the gospel passage of the day. However, as part of the Christian Bible, all three readings share in the common purpose of proclaiming God's salvation in Christ.

Read in the wake of Deuteronomy 11, the passage taken from Romans acts for Christians as both a corrective and a revealer of that first reading's deeper significance. As a corrective: whereas in regard to the dictates of the Mosaic law Deuteronomy prescribes that believers should "[b]ind them at your wrist as a sign, and let them be a pendant on your forehead," the Romans reading insists that, with the coming of Christ, "[n]ow the righteousness of God has been manifested apart from the law," so that, although "all have sinned and are deprived of the glory of God," nevertheless all "are justified freely by his grace through the redemption in Christ Jesus" so that such technical observances of the law are no longer required ("For we consider that a person is justified by faith apart from works of the law"). In other words, if anything in the Old Testament when read literally seems to deny the fullness of God's Word in Jesus Christ, it may when read figuratively actually help to reveal the deeper meaning of those saving events. Thus, the action of binding God's commandments on one's wrist and forehead becomes, when read in light of the New Testament, metaphorical for the need to keep God's laws always in mind and to have them securely fixed in one's heart. Such, after all, would have been the original metaphorical purpose of the Old Testament practice in the first place. The same could be said for all other such problematic Old Testament expressions—for example, that all of Israel's enemies be put to the sword (1 Sam 15:3) or that the heads of Babylonian babies be crushed on the rocks (Ps 137:9). Although if taken literally they would be reprehensible from a New Testament perspective, when read in a typological fashion, they become hyperbolic figures of speech for the unchanging truth throughout the whole Bible that absolute adherence is owed by all to God in Christ, who is the fullness of God's self-revelation and sole savior of all humankind.

On the other hand, by claiming that God's salvation in Christ is "testi-fied to by the law and the prophets," Romans acts, in light of Christ's paschal mystery, also as a revealer of Deuteronomy 11's deeper meaning, in particular its call for "obeying the commandments of the Lord, your God." Consequently, the observance of God's biblical Word called for by Deuteronomy, far from being precluded by faith in Christ, is fully realized only through it.

In addition, the words of St. Paul—"the redemption in Christ Jesus, whom God set forth as an expiation, through faith, by his blood"—when proclaimed as part of the Eucharist, confirm the church's faith that the eucharistic offering is itself a participation in Christ's saving, outpouring death on the cross.

Some moments of silence after the reading allow the Word of God to echo in the hearts and minds of the faithful and so to prepare them to hear Christ speak once again through the upcoming gospel and homily.

Alleluia: John 15:5

The cantor then intones the Alleluia refrain, and all in the church stand and repeat it:

> Alleluia, alleluia.

After he or she sings the verse, the congregation repeats the refrain:

> I am the vine, you are the branches, says the Lord;
> whoever remains in me and I in him will bear much fruit.
>
> ℟. Alleluia, alleluia.

If a deacon is present, he turns to the presider to receive a blessing before announcing the gospel; if there is no deacon, then the presider himself proceeds to the altar, bows, and prays silently, "Cleanse my heart and my lips, almighty God, / that I may worthily proclaim your holy Gospel." He then takes up the Book of the Gospels and, holding it high, carries it in procession to the ambo.

The presider's private prayer at the altar quoted above is the first of such prayers throughout the Eucharist known as "apologies:" declarations of the priest's unworthiness before an all-holy God.[49] Although it may seem illogical that such personal prayers are included within the ritual text of communal worship, precisely in their being personal they serve a very important liturgical function. For they help to create an overall atmosphere of prayer, of communication with God, witnessing publicly as they do to how all in the assembly need also to celebrate the liturgy in a spirit of personal prayer if the community's words and actions are to be more than a noisy gong or a clanging cymbal: "This people honors me with their lips, but their heart is far from me" (Matt 15:8).[50]

Reinhard Messner observes that the "gospel procession is an enactment of the coming of Christ, the *adventus Christi*, a representational symbol that announces his final coming 'in glory' and represents this ritually in the coming of his Word—the gospel."[51] That is why

> during this procession the Christ who comes is acclaimed by the Alleluia. It is precisely by the Alleluia chant that the gospel becomes an anamnesis of the future. This acclamation is found only one unique time in the New Testament, that is, in the extremely eschatological context of Revelation 19:6 where the definitive entrance into the kingdom of God and the eschatological celestial wedding feast are proclaimed. . . . It is with the acclamation of the Alleluia—an acclamation to the Resurrected One made visible in the gospel—that the Eucharist is enacted as a symbolic anticipation of the heavenly wedding feast and becomes an in-breaking of the future, of the kingdom of God. . . . [The] Alleluia has its significance . . . as the chant accompanying the procession of coming (*adventus*) to the ambo in which Christ, honored by light and incense, is received by his community.[52]

Immediately after the singing of the Alleluia, the presider once again greets the congregation, "The Lord be with you," and all respond, "And with your spirit." And then tracing a cross with his thumb over the symbol of the cross in the book at the top of the gospel pericope, the presider proceeds to sign his forehead, lips, and heart in the same way. As a kind of prayer in motion, this action says in effect, "May the gospel words read from these pages conform me in my thinking, in my speaking, and in my loving to the mystery of Christ's cross." All in the congregation sign themselves in the same way, thereby joining him in the same silent prayer.

Next, the presider announces, "A reading from the holy Gospel according to Matthew." The congregation responds, "Glory to you, O Lord." As Messner observes, "The gospel is a real encounter with the risen Christ; his presence is recognized by the acclamation. He comes among his own as the One whom God has raised; he comes from where his own themselves will certainly also be: the future promised to believers."[53] The presider then proclaims the gospel in a loud and clear voice.

Gospel: Matthew 7:21-27

Jesus said to his disciples:
    "Not everyone who says to me, 'Lord, Lord,'
    will enter the kingdom of heaven,
    but only the one who does the will of my Father in heaven.
Many will say to me on that day,
    'Lord, Lord, did we not prophesy in your name?
Did we not drive out demons in your name?
Did we not do mighty deeds in your name?'
Then I will declare to them solemnly,
    'I never knew you. Depart from me, you evildoers.'

"Everyone who listens to these words of mine and acts on them
    will be like a wise man who built his house on rock.
The rain fell, the floods came,
    and the winds blew and buffeted the house.
But it did not collapse; it had been set solidly on rock.
And everyone who listens to these words of mine
    but does not act on them
    will be like a fool who built his house on sand.
The rain fell, the floods came,
    and the winds blew and buffeted the house.
And it collapsed and was completely ruined."

Holding up the Book of the Gospels, the presider declares, "The Gospel of the Lord." The congregation responds with another acclamation, "Praise to you, Lord Jesus Christ."

The presider next kisses the open page of the gospel just read, saying quietly as he sets it down in front of him, "Through the words of the Gospel / may our sins be wiped away," while all in the congregation become seated to listen to the homily. As noted in chapter 5, to kiss a sacred object is an ancient sign of reverence. To touch one's mouth to something suggests the desire to take it in completely, to unite oneself fully to the object of one's reverence. And so, combined with this silent prayer, the action here of kissing the book witnesses to the sanctity of the words just read and to their power by Christ's death and resurrection to cleanse and renew the hearts and lives of all who absorb them into themselves in a spirit of faith.

The Homily

Chapter 3 above concluded that the church's unchanging faith is expressed and realized in the liturgy by means of (1) traditional rites (2) celebrating in an anamnetic, epicletic, and doxological way (3) the universality of God's salvation in Christ (4) as manifested typologically throughout creation and across salvation history but most especially in the rites themselves. It was noted also that the liturgical manifestation "of the church's faith likewise depends on the relative ability that any given individual or community has both spiritually and culturally to enter into . . . the objective faith content of her official rites." The homily at the Sunday Eucharist exists for no other purpose than to make this happen: to help all in the congregation see how Christ's paschal mystery as proclaimed in the readings is typologically realized in their lives as well within the contemporary world in which they live, including the liturgical celebration in which they are participating. In other words, it is not necessary that each local assembly develop new rites for each new liturgical celebration in order for it to express how the mystery of Christ is present within its own particular time and place in history. Because the traditional rites of the church are symbolic events, concrete universals of her age-old faith, when celebrated in light of the day's readings and the contemporary situation in which the assembly takes place, they have the potential to reveal how any given eucharistic celebration is a unique sacramental encounter with Christ.

The Homilist

The homily is a dialogical event. If the homilist preaches the apostolic faith of the church, his preaching has its intended effect only in its being also the faith of those to whom he preaches, the faith into which they were baptized and that called them into assembly in the first place. In the words of Anton H. M. Sheer, "The preacher speaks in the name of many and to many. . . . *Praedicatio Verbi divini verbum populi*" (The preaching of the divine Word is the word of the people).[54]

Furthermore, the sacramentally ordained homilist expresses the faith of the church not by the mere enunciation of words but rather by preaching out of his own *personal appropriation* of that faith. That is to say, the dialogue that takes place in the homily originates in and emerges out of the homilist himself. Notice, for example, the instruction given to new deacons during their ordination, "Receive the Gospel of Christ, / whose herald you now are. / Believe what you read, teach what you believe, / and practice [i.e., live] what you teach,"[55] and the following statement found in the prayer for the ordination of presbyters (priests) who themselves were previously ordained as deacons: "May he be faithful in working with the order of bishops, / so that the words of the Gospel may reach the ends of the earth, / and the family of nations, / made one in Christ, / may become God's one, holy people."[56] Thus, homilists are chosen and ordained by the church to be personal embodiments of the church's faith that they are called on to preach. In order to be effective in their preaching, therefore, they must keep alive by (a) prayer, (b) reading of Scripture, and (c) theological study the gift of the Spirit conferred on them for that purpose (cf. 1 Tim 4:14-16; 2 Tim 1:6-7).

By being persons of prayer they help assure that what they preach is not themselves but Christ alone. By their familiarity with the whole of Scripture, they are better able to read any passage within its larger scriptural context, especially that of Christ's paschal mystery, and so avoid any danger of fundamentalism. And by theological study they ensure that the faith they preach is that of the whole church and not simply some narrow personal vision. Only in being themselves sacramental types of Christ[57] in this way will they be able to recognize and witness credibly to the action of God in Christ in the lives of their hearers as well.

Just as the rest of the liturgy "speaks" the faith in symbolic language and ritual, so too is the homily itself most effective when it uses imagery that acts as a concrete universal in which each person in the assembly can find his or her own particular situation before the Lord. When this happens the whole assembly becomes united in a common experience of faith. Like Jesus himself who taught in parables taken from everyday life situations, a good homilist often begins with a story or some concrete image, phrase, or word as a metaphor of whatever faith insight he might have received out of his prayer on the scriptural readings. The legitimacy of this method is found not simply in the extrinsic similarities of our everyday world to the world of faith, but in the fact that all things in heaven and on earth have been created in Christ (Col 1:16) and therefore can be made to witness to his saving presence in our midst. At the same time, the homilist cannot simply stay with an illustrative story or image throughout the duration of the homily, or else he may very well end up preaching mere human wisdom and not the wisdom of God. At some point he must relate it to at least one of the scriptural readings in order to allow the other members of the assembly to experience what he discovered to be the deeper, Christ-centered significance of the image or story he uses.

The church actually encourages this process of relating Scripture to contemporary life by setting up a typological relationship between each Sunday's Old Testament reading and the gospel, providing the possibility for what might be called a "triangulation" among the historical situations of these two readings and that of the present assembly itself.

To begin with, it is obvious that the opening reading of the Ninth Sunday in Ordinary Time, taken from Deuteronomy 11, with its command that the ancient Israelites embody God's Word in their lives ("Take these words of mine into your heart and soul"), by paralleling the gospel passage taken from Matthew 7 ("Everyone who listens to these words of mine and acts on them . . ."), witnesses to the church's faith that the God of the Old Testament has become fully incarnate in Jesus Christ. And yet, when these two readings are proclaimed in relationship to the particular contemporary context in which a Sunday Eucharist is celebrated, this parallel discloses an even fuller faith understanding of God's activity in human history. For not only do the two passages taken side by side teach that just as the Israelites of old experienced salvation by their obedience to God's commands, so will Christians today also be saved by obedience to the Lord's Word in their lives. As part of a triangulation, they witness even more pointedly that just as Christ as the fullness of God's Word was at work within those Old Testament commands themselves to unite the ancient Israelites to God, so he is alive today as well—in the saving events of his life, death, and resurrection—to bring salvation to those who put their trust in him: "Although he was a Son, he learned obedience through what he suffered; and being made perfect he became the source of eternal salvation to all who obey him" (Heb 5:8-9). Thus, the well-chosen story, image, or phase taken from ordinary life provides the third leg in a triangulation that illustrates how this deeper mystery of Christ's salvation, revealed in Scripture as present already in Old Testament times, is at work now also in the lives of all in the assembly, most especially in their participation in the upcoming Liturgy of the Eucharist wherein they act in obedience to the Lord's command, "Do this in memory of me."

The typological relationship of a Sunday's Old Testament reading to the gospel is but one approach among many for relating the day's liturgy to the lives of participants. Indeed, the interrelationships among all three readings open up a myriad of other possibilities for this to take place, depending on the spiritual insight of the homilist in light of the needs of his hearers. The fact also that individual words act as metonyms of the whole context in which they occur makes almost any word or phrase in these readings a jumping-off point for articulating a whole Christian vision. In any event, whatever the means chosen, the ultimate purpose of any homily is to forge a deeper unity among all in the assembly in the one Christ and his mission to gather all the scattered children of God ever more fully into the one Body of Christ.

The Profession of Faith

The Niceno-Constantinopolitan Creed is a relatively late addition to the Roman Rite Mass. Its use at the Eucharist had already been a long-standing custom in the Gallican liturgy when, during a visit to Rome in 1014, Emperor Henry II pressured Pope Benedict VIII to include it in the Roman Mass as well. The pope complied, but restricted it to Sundays and those feast-day celebrations whose mysteries are named in its text.[58]

The practice of reciting the Creed in the eucharistic liturgy reportedly began in Antioch in 471 and was adopted in Constantinople in 511. With Byzantine expansion to the West, it migrated first to Spain in 589 to combat the Arianism of the Visigoths, and then into Gaul.[59] The Niceno-Constantinopolitan Creed is based on a baptismal confession that belonged most probably to a family of creeds used around either Antioch or Jerusalem[60] to which the ecumenical councils of Nicea (325) and Constantinople I (381) added doctrinal words and phrases formulated to counteract the Arian and Pneumatomachian heresies. In doing so, the council fathers changed the introductory words "I believe" to "We believe" in order to identify the resulting statement as the official faith of the church against those heretical attacks. The content of the Creed is expressed in "three sections, comprising our belief in God the Creator, in Christ our Lord, and in the goods of salvation. And what is more to the point in a baptismal profession, these three sections are linked with the naming of the three divine Persons."[61] It is noteworthy, therefore, that in adopting this conciliar Creed for use in the Eucharist, both the Byzantine[62] and the Latin Roman traditions reverted to using the first-person-singular "I believe" (*Credo*) form of a baptismal creed.

The current GIRM states, "The purpose of the Creed or Profession of Faith is that the whole gathered people may respond to the Word of God proclaimed in the readings taken from Sacred Scripture and explained in the Homily and that they may also honor and confess the great mysteries of the faith by pronouncing the rule of faith in a formula approved for liturgical use and before the celebration of these mysteries in the Eucharist begins" (no. 67). According to the GIRM, therefore, one purpose for reciting the Creed at this point in the liturgy is to provide an antiphonal response, an alternate voicing, to the faith proclaimed in the previous scriptural readings and their homiletic explanation, a response belonging once again primarily to the lay congregation.[63]

The use of the "I believe" form here is related to the GIRM's second stated purpose for its recitation, for it directs participants to celebrate the Eucharist precisely as a deepening of the faith they committed themselves to at their baptism. Furthermore, by making this personal declaration simultaneously with everyone else in the assembly, the "I" of the Creed is suddenly experienced also as the "I" of the assembly itself, thereby instilling a sense of *sacramental* solidarity with the universal church everywhere as one "complex person" in Christ.[64]

Space here does not allow a detailed liturgical commentary on every word and phrase of the Creed. However, a couple of reflections may be in order regarding the recent change in the English translation of *consubstantialem Patri* from "one in Being with the Father" to "consubstantial with the Father." Although various arguments might be given for either rendition, it seems important to note that the *idiosyncratic* nature of the word "consubstantial" highlights the uniqueness inherent in the doctrine itself to which it points: namely, that of all human beings Jesus of Nazareth alone, as the incarnate, only-begotten Son, is one in divinity with God the Father (*homoousios* = *consubstantialis*). Moreover, the fact that "consubstantial" exists precisely as a *nonscriptural* formulation within the church's official profession of faith makes it an effective liturgical symbol of another fundamental Catholic belief: namely, that Christ, who dwells within the church by the Holy Spirit, guides her "into all the truth" (John 16:14) "always, to the close of the age" (Matt 28:20), in great part through the church's magisterium, the official teaching office of the pope and the bishops.

The Universal Prayer

Still standing at his chair, the presider next introduces the prayer of the faithful, possibly alluding to some theme from the day's readings or homily in doing so. The deacon or some other minister then goes to the ambo and announces a series of six to eight specially prepared intentions, in response to each of which the assembly then voices an intercessory refrain such as "Lord, hear our prayer," directed immediately to God. The GIRM provides this instruction:

> It is for the Priest Celebrant to regulate this prayer from the chair. He himself begins it with a brief introduction, by which he calls upon the faithful to pray, and likewise he concludes it with an oration. The intentions announced should be sober, be composed with a wise liberty and in few words, and they should be expressive of the prayer of the entire community.
>
> They are announced from the ambo or from another suitable place, by the Deacon or by a cantor, a reader, or one of the lay faithful.
>
> The people, for their part, stand and give expression to their prayer either by an invocation said in common after each intention or by praying in silence. (no. 71)

The universal prayer came into existence undoubtedly because of the 1 Timothy 2:1-2 recommendation "that supplications, prayers, intercessions, and thanksgiving be made for all men, for kings and all who are in high positions, that we may lead a quiet and peaceable life, godly and respectful in every way." St. Justin Martyr witnesses that by the mid-second century in Rome, "common prayers" (*koinai euchai*) of this type were offered at Sunday Eucharists after the homily and before the eucharistic prayer.[65] The *Apostolic Tradition* and the writings of Clement of Alexandria, Tertullian, Origen, Cyprian, Athanasius, Ambrose, Chrysostom, Augustine, Ambrosiaster, and Prosper of Aquitaine all provide evidence that such common prayers were offered in their own respective communities as well.[66]

Paul De Clerck opines from what little documentation remains that between 250 and 320 the prayer of the faithful in Rome took the form still in use today in the solemn intercessions in the Good Friday celebration of the Roman Rite. Originally, after each intention was announced by the deacon and followed by the silent prayer of the faithful, the prayer ended with a simple "Amen." Only toward the end of the fourth century were the presider's summarizing collects added before each "Amen." This whole prayer structure was later replaced, probably by Pope Gelasius (492–96), with an Eastern litany-type prayer most likely borrowed from the churches of northern Italy. In this later form, similar to the one in use today, congregations responded to each intention with the refrain "Lord, hear and have mercy" (*Domine, exaudi et miserere*). For various reasons, the universal prayer disappeared from Roman usage altogether sometime in the following century, probably during the reign of Pope Vigilius (537–55).[67]

The current GIRM also states, "In the Universal Prayer or Prayer of the Faithful, the people respond in some sense to the Word of God which they have received in faith and, exercising the office of their baptismal Priesthood, offer prayers to God for the salvation of all" (no. 69). In response to the scriptural account of God's self-gift in Christ, by praying the universal prayer the assembly also takes responsibility for its baptismal commitment to share in Christ's priestly mission to the world. The prayer is called "universal," then, because by praying unrestrictedly for whole groups of people throughout the world, both Christian and non-Christian alike, participants are taken up *sacramentally* into Christ's work of universal salvation. In its universality and concrete embodiment in a local, historical assembly, the universal prayer is but one more enactment within the Eucharist of Christ's paschal self-offering.

Joan Llopis writes, "The four traditional forms of prayer—petition, adoration, thanksgiving and expiation—can be reduced to two: petition, which includes asking for forgiveness, and praise, which includes thanksgiving. . . . Thanksgiving and petition are not in conflict, . . . since to believe, in the last resort, means accepting life as grace and as a task, as reality and promise, as honor and responsibility." And so, "when we ask [God] for something, we are not trying to make him act in our place and violate the autonomous system of secondary causes, but we are making ourselves more aware of our responsibilities for the transformation of the world, not as independent beings, but as totally upheld by the power of God. . . . Indeed, if we are not prepared to do on our own account what we ask God in his mercy to do, we would be better not to write prayers."[68] Thus, the "universal prayer . . . is a prayer made directly by the faithful, exercising their priesthood, and it is an intercession open to all the needs of the church and the world."[69]

The GIRM adds,

> The series of intentions is usually to be:
> a) for the needs of the Church;
> b) for public authorities and the salvation of the whole world;
> c) for those burdened by any kind of difficulty;
> d) for the local community. (no. 70)

Here Llopis observes, "Christians cannot limit their concern to the narrow sphere of their individual needs—nor even those of their immediate community—but must be open to genuinely universal and ecumenical horizons. . . . Nonetheless it would be very unhelpful to those praying if there was [*sic*] no room in the prayer for the needs, desires, ideas, circumstances, events and varying conditions of local churches, communities and individuals."[70] Accordingly, Michael Kwatera recommends that although there "is no official directive regarding the number of intentions to be included, . . . there should be at least one intention from each of the [four] categories"[71] listed by the GIRM.

It may be helpful even today to note that in a 1992 report on the reception by Catholics throughout the world of the restored universal prayer, Jean-Louis Angué lists among the complaints made most frequently by respondents (1) timeless, prefabricated prayers taken from a book; (2) individualistic prayers not open to the universal; (3) moralizing prayers, aimed at conveying a message; (4) prayers at too fast a pace, with no time to interiorize them; (5) long and complex intentions; and (6) intentions announced directly to God and not to the people.[72]

After all the intentions have been announced and responses made, the presider in the name of all closes the rite with a final prayer made to God the Father, asking "through Christ our Lord" that the community's prayers be heard. All respond, "Amen," and sit while the presider and acolytes move down the sanctuary steps to await the procession of the gifts from the rear of the church.

Notes, Chapter Six

[1] Thierry Maertens, *Assembly for Christ: From Biblical Theology to Pastoral Theology in the Twentieth Century* (London: Darton, Longman & Todd, 1970), 19–21.

[2] Ibid., 20.

[3] Paul F. Bradshaw, *The Search for the Origins of Christian Worship*, 2nd ed. (New York: Oxford University Press, 2002), 121, 139.

[4] Ambroos Verheul, "Le pourquoi et le comment du Service de la Parole," *Questions liturgiques* 66 (1985): 210–11.

[5] Louis-Marie Chauvet, *Symbol and Sacrament: A Sacramental Reinterpretation of Christian Existence*, trans. Philip Madigan, SJ, and Madeleine Beaumont (Collegeville, MN: Liturgical Press, 1995), 191, quoting Philippe Béguerie, "La Bible née de la liturgie," *La Maison-Dieu* 126 (1976): 109.

[6] Angelus A. Häussling, OSB, quoted in Dwight W. Vogel, ed., *Primary Sources of Liturgical Theology: A Reader* (Collegeville, MN: Liturgical Press, 2000), 67–68, trans. John D. Laurance, SJ, from "Die Kritische Funktion der Liturgiewissenschaft," in *Liturgie und Gesellschaft*, ed. Hans-Bernard Meyer (Innsbruck, Wien, München: Tyrolia Verlag, 1970), 117–30.

7 Chauvet, *Symbol and Sacrament*, 190–95.

8 Ibid., 197.

9 Ibid., 192.

10 "Only with the lists of the late 4th cent., viz., those of Athanasius, Augustine, and the councils of Hippo (393) and Carthage III (397) do we come to evidence of common agreement in much of the church," though "the subapostolic writings, like *1-2 Clem.*, *Did.*, *Herm.*, and *Barn.* continued to be considered Scripture even into the 4th and 5th cents." Raymond E. Brown, SS, and Raymond F. Collins, "Canonicity," in *The New Jerome Biblical Commentary*, ed. Raymond E. Brown, SS, Joseph A. Fitzmyer, SJ, and Roland E. Murphy, OCarm. (Englewood Cliffs, NY: Prentice Hall, 1990), 1050–51.

11 Cf. Chauvet, *Symbol and Sacrament*, 476–89.

12 Reinhard Messner, "La liturgie de la parole pendent la messe: L'anamnèse du Christ mise en scène," *La Maison-Dieu* 243 (2005): 55.

13 Ibid., 44–46.

14 Ibid., 48. Here as an illustration Messner quotes Ps 74:2: "Remember your congregation, which you have gotten of old, / which you have redeemed to be the tribe of your heritage! / Remember Mount Zion, where you have dwelt."

15 Ibid., 56.

16 Ibid., 47–49.

17 Ibid., 51–53.

18 Chauvet, *Symbol and Sacrament*, 222; Augustine, *In Joannis Evangelium tractatus* 80, 3 (PL 35:1840). The fuller context helps explain Augustine's meaning: "*Jam vos mundi estis propter verbum quod locutus sum vobis.* Quare non ait, mundi estis propter Baptismum, quo loti estis; sed ait, *propter verbum quod locutus sum vobis*; nisi quia et in aqua verbum mundat? Detrahe verbum, et quid est aqua, nisi aqua? Accedit verbum ad elementum, et fit sacramentum, etiam ipsum tanquam visibile verbum. . . . Unde ista tanta virtus aquae, ut corpus tangat, et cor abluat, nisi faciente verbo: non quia dicitur, sed quia creditur? ([Jesus said,] "You are already made clean by the word that I have spoken to you" (John 15:3) Why did he not say, "You are clean because of baptism by which you were washed," but said rather, "because of the word that I spoke to you," except that even in the water it is the word that cleans? Take away the word, and what is water but [merely] water? The word enters upon a material element and it becomes a sacrament, itself also a kind of a visible word. . . . Whence then comes such great power to water that when it touches the body it also cleans the heart, if not from the activity of the word—not because it is spoken, but because it is believed?)

19 Hence the requirement that only those in holy orders proclaim the gospel and deliver the homily.

20 Chauvet, *Symbol and Sacrament*, 222.

21 Aimon-Marie Roguet, OP, "The Whole Mass Proclaims the Word of God," in *The Liturgy and the Word of God* (Collegeville, MN: Liturgical Press, 1959), 72.

22 Verheul, "Le pourquoi," 215.

23 Cf., e.g., Justin Martyr: "And on the day called Sunday, all who live in cities or in the country gather together to one place, and the memoirs of the apostles or the

writings of the prophets are read, as long as time permits." *First Apology* 67, in *Ante-Nicene Fathers*, vol. 1, ed. Alexander Roberts and James Donaldson (Buffalo: The Christian Literature Publishing Co., 1885–96), 186.

[24] Eric Palazzo, *A History of Liturgical Books: From the Beginning to the Thirteenth Century* (Collegeville, MN: Liturgical Press, 1998), 83–84. Regarding early liturgical improvisation, see Allan Bouley, *From Freedom to Formula: The Evolution of the Eucharistic Prayer from Oral Improvisation to Written Texts* (Washington, DC: Catholic University of America Press, 1981).

[25] Normand Bonneau, "The Sunday Lectionary: Underlying Principles and Patterns," *Liturgical Ministry* 5 (Spring 1996): 49–50.

[26] Palazzo, *A History*, 85; John Reumann, "A History of Lectionaries: From the Synagogue at Nazareth to Post–Vatican II," *Interpretation* 31, no. 2 (April 1977): 125: "The view that the Roman mass originally had three lessons, Old Testament, Epistle, and Gospel, for Sundays and festivals is not substantiated. Two pericopes were the norm, for example in the sixth century. The eventual series of Gospel lections has been traced back to the time of Gregory the Great in Rome, and the Epistles to Gaul, the two being combined around 800. Alcuin is credited with revising the lectionary."

[27] Bonneau, "Sunday Lectionary," 55.

[28] Ibid.

[29] Cf. Normand Bonneau, *The Sunday Lectionary: Ritual Word, Paschal Shape* (Collegeville, MN: Liturgical Press, 1998), 141–62.

[30] Ibid., 51.

[31] Ibid., 56.

[32] Ibid., 52; Bonneau also writes, "During Ordinary Time . . . Sunday after Sunday, the assembly gathers to receive the Lord's words and be inspired by his deeds. Week after week they walk in his footsteps, following him on the path which leads through death to new life" (ibid., 151).

[33] Ibid., 56.

[34] "In the ancient Roman basilicas [the gradation between nongospel readings and the gospel] was expressed [by their being] two ambos: one for the readings of less importance, less elevated and less ornate, the other more elevated and more richly elaborated, reserved to the reading of the gospel" (Verheul, "Le pourquoi," 216).

[35] Messner, "La liturgie de la parole," 57.

[36] Although the *Missale Romanum* of Paul VI no longer includes offertory antiphons, they are still provided in the post–Vatican II *Graduale Romanum*.

[37] GIRM 61: "If the Psalm cannot be sung, then it should be recited in such a way that it is particularly suited to fostering meditation on the Word of God." Cf. Dom Ambroos Verheul, "Le psaume responsorial dans la liturgie eucharistique," *Questions liturgiques* 73 (1992): 249.

[38] Peter Jeffery, "The Introduction of Psalmody into the Roman Mass by Pope Celestine I (422–32): Reinterpreting a Passage in the Liber Pontificalis," *Archiv für Liturgiewissenschaft* 26 (1984): 146–65.

[39] Verheul, "Le psaume responsorial," 237.

[40] GIRM 61: "The Responsorial Psalm should correspond to each reading and should usually be taken from the Lectionary."

[41] Ian Coleman, "Antiphonality: Notes towards a Theology of Liturgical Form," *Communio* 29 (Spring 2002): 134.

[42] Ibid., 143.

[43] Ibid., 144.

[44] Ibid., 146.

[45] Edward J. Kilmartin, SJ, *Christian Liturgy I: Theology and Practice* (Kansas City, MO: Sheed and Ward, 1988), 77.

[46] Coleman, "Antiphonality," 145.

[47] Ibid., 148.

[48] Ibid., 143–44.

[49] Cf. Cabrol, Fernand (1855–1937), "Apologies," in *Dictionnaire d'archéologie chrétienne et de liturgie*, ed. Fernand Cabrol and Henri Leclercq (Paris: Letouzey et Ané, 1920–53), 2591–601.

[50] Quoting Isa 29:13. Note also: "I hate, I despise your feasts, / and take no delight in your solemn assemblies. / . . . Take away from me the noise of your songs; / to the melody of your harps I will not listen" (Amos 5:21, 23).

[51] Messner, "La liturgie de la parole," 57.

[52] Ibid., 57–58.

[53] Ibid., 58.

[54] Anton H. M. Scheer, "Praedicatio Verbi Divini Verbum Populi?" in *Omnes Circumadstantes*, ed. Charles Caspers and Marc Schneiders (Kampen: J. H. Kok, 1990), 301.

[55] Ordination of a Deacon, no. 24, in *The Rites of the Catholic Church*, vol. 2, study ed. (Collegeville, MN: Liturgical Press, 1991), 35–36.

[56] Ordination of a Priest, no. 22, in *The Rites of the Catholic Church*, vol. 2, 35–36.

[57] For a fuller discussion of how the ordained presider acts as type of Christ in the church, see John D. Laurance, SJ, *"Priest" as Type of Christ: The Leader of the Eucharist in Salvation History According to Cyprian of Carthage* (New York-Bern-Frankfurt: Peter Lang, 1984).

[58] Joseph A. Jungmann, SJ, *The Mass of the Roman Rite*, vol. 1 (New York: Benziger Bros., 1951), 468–70.

[59] Ibid., 468.

[60] Berard L. Malthaler, OFM Conv., "Creeds," in *The New Dictionary of Theology*, ed. Joseph A. Komonchak, Mary Collins, and Dermot A. Lane (Wilmington, DE: Michael Glazier, 1987), 262.

[61] Jungmann, *Mass of the Roman Rite*, vol. 1, 463.

[62] Malthaler, "Creeds," 262.

[63] Thus, in the ancient Eastern liturgies, according to Jungmann, "the symbol is, as a rule, spoken by the people—thus in the Egyptian liturgies and mostly also in the Byzantine. Or it is spoken by a representative of the people. But it is never said by the priest" (*Mass of the Roman Rite*, vol.1, 468).

[64] Cf. chap. 2 above.

[65] Justin Martyr, *First Apology* 65; Geoffrey G. Willis, "The Prayer of the Faithful," in *Essays in Early Roman Liturgy*, Alcuin Club Collections series (London: SPCK, 1964), 3.

[66] Ibid., 77; Paul De Clerck, *La "prière universelle" dans les liturgies latines anciennes*, Liturgiewissenschafliche Quellen und Forschungen series (Munster: Aschendorff, 1977), 109.

[67] Ibid., 296–98, 313–14.

[68] Joan Llopis, "Is There Prayer in the Eucharist?" trans. Francis McDonagh, in *Asking and Thanking*, ed. Christian Duquoc and Casiano Florestan, Concilium series (London: SCM Press, 1990), 79, 81.

[69] Ibid., 82.

[70] Ibid., 83–85.

[71] Michael Kwatera, OSB, *Preparing the General Intercessions* (Collegeville, MN: Liturgical Press, 1996), 14.

[72] Jean-Louis Angué, "Le devenir de la prière universelle," *La Maison-Dieu* 192 (1992): 58.

Chapter Seven

The Liturgy of the Eucharist

aving progressed thus far into the book, the reader is presum-
ably well versed by now in the theology used here for reading
the *lex orandi* of the church's liturgy. It is obvious, however,
that no single theological vision—past, present, or future—could ever
do full justice to the Eucharist as the sacrament of Christ's paschal mystery. And so—in addition to the fact that limits of space prevent our
continuing to apply the same close reading to *all* aspects of the remaining
rites of the Mass—to make it clear that the attempts made here are not
seen as definitive, it will be left to the reader himself or herself to analyze
whatever prayers or rites are not thoroughly dealt with in the pages that
follow, doing so according to either this same theology or some other
approach that might more satisfactorily correspond to his or her own
ecclesial experience of the sacred mysteries.

The Preparation of the Gifts

After the Liturgy of the Word when everyone is seated, the ushers
take up the Sunday collection.[1] During this time, in preparation for the
upcoming rites, the congregation typically sings a hymn and the acolytes
prepare the altar by setting up the Missal, laying out the corporal and
purificators, and bringing over chalices and whatever bread containers
are needed for the distribution of Communion.

The Offertory Procession

The GIRM states, "The procession bringing the gifts is accompanied by the Offertory Chant, which continues at least until the gifts have been placed on the altar. The norms on the manner of singing are the same as for the Entrance Chant. Singing may always accompany the rite at the Offertory, even when there is no procession with the gifts" (no. 74). And so, after the collection has been taken up, the priest and acolytes rise and move down to the base of the sanctuary steps to receive the bread and wine brought forward by two or three members of the congregation enlisted beforehand for this purpose. Receiving them there, the ministers take the gifts to the altar, while the ushers bring forward the collection and typically place it at the base of the altar as symbolic of the self-offering of the congregation. At this point the GIRM observes: "It is a praiseworthy practice for the bread and wine to be presented by the faithful. . . . Even money or other gifts for the poor or for the Church, brought by the faithful or collected in the church, are acceptable; given their purpose, they are to be put in a suitable place away from the Eucharistic table" (no. 73).

Although the *Missale Romanum* of the Mass of Paul VI does not include offertory antiphons within its pages, the post–Vatican II *Graduale Romanum* does do so, but then only in Latin. The antiphon and opening verse of the offertory psalm for the Ninth Sunday in Ordinary Time are taken from Psalm 71: "Esto mihi in Deum protectorem et in locum refugii ut salvum me facias. *V.* Deus in te speravi: Domine, non confundar in aeternum,"[2] which the RSV translates: "Be to me a rock of refuge, / a strong fortress to save me. . . . In you, O Lord, / I take refuge; let me never be put to shame!" (Ps 71:3, 1). The words and sentiments of the antiphon, followed by the first verse of the psalm, afford a fitting accompaniment to the procession of gifts to the altar, given that it is through this liturgical symbol that the assembly, in response to the Liturgy of the Word, begins the action of *entrusting itself fully* into the hands of the Lord.

St. Justin Martyr in mid-second-century Rome notes simply that at this point in the liturgy "bread and wine and water are brought."[3] The first documentary indications of a *procession* of gifts are those made by the synods of Elvira and Nicea in the early fourth century,[4] whereas St. Isidore of Seville (560–636) is the first to name this part of the rite the "offertory" (*offertorium*),[5] a title it retains to this day, as we have seen, in some references made to it in the current Roman Missal. Some early church writers regard this action as already sacrificial. Tertullian (fl. ca. 200), for example, refers to the gifts of the faithful as an "offering" (*offerre*) directed to God,[6] and the third/fourth-century *Apostolic Tradition* calls them an "oblation" (*oblatio*).[7] St. Cyprian of Carthage (ca. 210–58) even chastises a rich woman for "coming to celebrate the Sunday Eucharist . . . without a sacrifice" (*dominicum celebrare . . . sine sacrificio venis*) since at Communion she would then have consumed that part of the sacrifice made by some poor person (*partem de sacrificio quod pauper obtulit sumis*).[8] "In the ancient Milanese and Roman liturgies, and probably also in the North African, the offering of the faithful was very closely bound up with the eucharistic sacrifice. . . . In Africa it was possible to bring one's offering to the altar day after day as Monica [the mother of Augustine] was wont to do. The priest himself received what was offered by the people, and in turn he offered these things to God."[9]

Niels Krogh Rasmussen observes how in the ninth century the substitution of unleavened for ordinary bread brought about a momentous change in the church's understanding of the Eucharist. For it then became possible to use small hosts, which in effect both eliminated the apostolic rite of breaking bread for sharing among participants and also disconnected the eucharistic offering from the assembly's diaconal service to the poor. "Even the role of the president of the assembly changes: he becomes *the celebrant* for the community which *assists* at his celebration. . . . The priest then offers *for* the people, who are able to associate themselves spiritually to his sacrifice but who are no longer conscious of being themselves the community which celebrates. The gifts (in money) offered at the offertory lose, by this fact, the profound meaning they originally had."[10] Accordingly, the earlier formula of the prayer that began the offertory rites was reworked in medieval times into "the first person singular ('this offering which *I*, your unworthy servant, offer to you' [*offero*])," thus evidencing that the community was understood no longer as celebrating, but as only assisting at the celebration of the priest.[11] Thus, in his official capacity the priest became regarded as acting only *in persona Christi* (in the person of Christ) and not also *in persona ecclesiae* (in the person of the church), thereby making present through memorial Christ's once-for-all self-offering on the cross, but doing so as something completely separate from a devotional self-offering made by the liturgical assembly.

Another result of this separation is evident in how these preparatory rites are commonly understood today. When the post–Vatican II Consilium entrusted with the reform of the Eucharist retitled the offertory "the preparation of the gifts" (*praeparatio donorum*), thereby reviving another ancient designation, its stated purpose for doing so was to avoid any anticipation of the "true offering of the sacrifice which will take place at the canon [eucharistic prayer]."[12] This concern resulted most likely from an ancient awareness, revived in the twentieth century, that not only do Christ's Body and Blood become present in every Eucharist, but so too do the saving events of his life, death, and resurrection.[13] And so, just as theologians throughout the second millennium tried to determine at what point in the Mass the bread and wine are converted into the Body and Blood of Christ—whether during the Last Supper narrative ("This is my body . . .") or the epiclesis (calling down of the Holy Spirit) of the eucharistic prayer—so too did many twentieth-century scholars theorize that the historical self-offering of Christ on the cross is realized once again *totally* within only a single, narrow portion of the Mass: the eucharistic prayer. Any mention of "offering" beforehand, therefore, was thought to be a misguided reduplication and so had to be avoided altogether.

And yet, as Alex Stock points out, "the theologian seems to want to ward off what appears to the historian of religions as most obvious: the identity of gifts and offering."[14] That is to say, the ritual act in which members of the congregation bring forward (*ob-ferre*) bread and wine evidences more than just a practical gathering and arranging of food-stuffs—a mere preparation of material gifts. The act itself is clearly the beginning already of the assembly's eucharistic self-offering in Christ. Stock regards it as a kind of "overture" to the whole Liturgy of the Eucharist.[15] Jozef Lamberts concurs: "Just as we have to underscore the importance of the communion rite together with the eucharistic prayer as a whole, so at the same time we have to discern the proper meaning of the rite of preparation of the gifts in the entire liturgy of the eucharist."[16] To use an analogy taken from the world of sports: just as a "balk" would be called on a pitcher in baseball were he to stop in the middle of his windup since by doing so, even though he had not completely delivered the ball to the catcher, he would be thought to have already "begun his delivery," so too does this set of rites already begin an action that, although realized *substantially* only in the eucharistic prayer, neverthe-less actually comes to full completion only in the reception of Holy Communion![17]

According to Joseph Gelineau, then, after the procession forward of the bread and wine "the Victim . . . is already represented by the sacred gifts placed upon the altar."[18] That is to say, since everything in the liturgy comprises one single act of the church's prayer, and since Christ dwelling within the members of his Body, the church, is both the source and the content of the faith by which she makes her prayer, the preparation of the gifts—beginning with the offertory procession—is also a manifestation and participation in Christ's own once-for-all self-offering in faith. Were this not the case, these rites would be spiritually meaningless or, even worse, a mere human effort to please God by presenting offerings in addition to and totally other than the saving sacrifice of Christ. But on the contrary, as we shall see more fully below, Christ in the Eucharist offers himself to the Father precisely in and through the self-offerings of the liturgical participants. In the words of Adolf Adam, "The sacrifice of Christ becomes sacramentally present insofar and only insofar as it is also the sacrifice of the church."[19]

The Blessing Prayers

The two opening prayers, which the Vatican II reforms created anew and added to the ancient Roman Rite, reflect this same understanding. According to the rubrics, "The Priest, standing at the altar, takes the paten with the bread and holds it slightly raised above the altar with both hands, saying in a low voice: 'Blessed are you, Lord God of all creation, / for through your goodness we have received / the bread we offer you: / fruit of the earth and work of human hands, / it will become for us the bread of life'" (23).

The rubrics give the following direction: "Then he places the paten with the bread on the corporal. If, however, the Offertory Chant is not sung, the Priest may speak these words aloud; at the end, the people may acclaim: 'Blessed be God for ever.'"

Here, as Stock points out, this *berakah*, a Jewish blessing-type prayer, prayed over the bread, imitates the blessing at the Seder meal pronounced over the matzah bread: "Blessed art thou, O Lord our God, King of the universe, who bringest forth bread from the earth"[20]—more or less the same blessing that Jesus would have prayed to begin the Last Supper meal. The opening *berakah* of the Liturgy of the Eucharist, therefore, is clearly intended as the beginning of the eucharistic meal, which will be completed only with the final prayer after Communion.[21]

Just as the single piece of matzah bread of the Seder blessing acts as a metonym for all the ways that God provides nourishment to his people throughout history, the ritually stylized bread of the Eucharist does the same. If according to Deuteronomy 26, as we saw in chapter 6, the ancient

Israelites recognized in the first fruits the Promised Land itself as God's self-gift from which they came, the church sees in the bread of her offering not only bread itself but also the earth from which it comes ("fruit of the earth"), and from which all else that is earthly comes as well, including the human lives of the offerers themselves and the energy given them to please God in all they say and do ("work of human hands").[22] But in pronouncing these blessings over the bread and wine, the church is conscious, first and foremost, that all life comes to humanity only in and through Jesus Christ in whom "all things were created, in heaven and on earth, visible and invisible" (Col 1:16), and who is therefore the fullness of God's "bread which came down from heaven . . . for the life of the world" (John 6:35, 51). According to St. Augustine, Jesus "took earth from the earth; because flesh is of the earth, he took flesh from the flesh of Mary. And because he walked here in this flesh, he also gave us this flesh to eat for our salvation" (cf. John 6:51).[23] In the offertory procession, therefore, and in this simple rite of recognizing themselves in the bread and wine as gifts from God in Christ, the eucharistic participants are already taking the first steps toward making the full offering of themselves in Christ in the eucharistic prayer, along with the priest, back to the Father. For, as metonyms of their lives on earth, the bread and wine already participate in the once-for-all self-offering of Christ himself, that is, in the same self-offering in which the universe as a whole, including the earth, was created in the first place (cf. Col 1:15-20).[24]

Between the two *berakoth*, one over the bread and the other over the wine, "The Deacon, or the Priest, pours wine and a little water into the chalice, saying quietly: 'By the mystery of this water and wine / may we come to share in the divinity of Christ / who humbled himself to share in our humanity'" (no. 24).

Taken from an ancient Christmas collect, this prayer regards the mixture of water and wine in the chalice as a "mystery," that is, a sacramental symbol. And its mystagogy, hinted at here, can be traced back to St. Cyprian of Carthage, who explains that because wine stands for Christ and the water signifies the people—that is, the rest of humanity taken up by Christ in his passion, death, and resurrection—it is the inseparable combination of both water and wine that constitutes the true *sacramentum* of those saving events.[25] The phrase "who humbled himself" in this brief, silent prayer recalls the Philippians hymn, which states, "And being found in human form he humbled himself and became obedient unto death, even death on a cross" (2:8).

Since the remaining prayers of the preparation of the gifts are "apologies," that is, more or less private prayers of the priest as we saw earlier, they are also prayed quietly.[26] This prayer, however, accompanying the mixture of water and wine—along with the two *berakoth* over the bread and wine—is spoken in the name of all the faithful ("we"), and so logically should be proclaimed aloud, were the rubrics changed to allow it.

The two blessing prayers—one over the bread and the other over the chalice—are among the most successful additions to the new liturgy. The faithful have embraced them so enthusiastically most probably because of how, within the liturgy, their concrete images celebrate the nobility and the preciousness in God's eyes of all that concerns the human family: "the earth," "the work of human hands," and "the fruit of the vine." This last phrase is taken from the Kiddush blessing that opens every Jewish feast day and Sabbath evening meal (cf. Luke 21:17-18). And the congregation's response whenever these prayers are spoken aloud is invariably enthusiastic: "Blessed be God for ever!"

The unfortunate though frequent choice of instrumental music to "cover over" what is commonly regarded as the purely utilitarian nature of the preparation of the gifts is all too reminiscent of elevator or airport music, that is, sounds intended solely to lessen boredom where nothing else seems to be happening. No matter how enjoyable, such wordless music at this point in the liturgy makes impossible any liturgical participation through hearing and responding to the prayers. And even when the prayers are said quietly, such melodic intrusions still remove the silence needed for "hearing" the "still small voice" (1 Kgs 19:12) of God, who might be "speaking" to one's heart through the sacred actions themselves. For, after all, such is the purpose of liturgical symbols.

Lavabo Rite and Closing Prayers

After the two blessing prayers and a short prayer made silently at the center of the altar, the priest turns to have his hands washed in the "lavabo" rite. Although once again the prayer is prayed quietly, the action speaks volumes about the need all in the assembly have for purification in mind and heart in order to enter worthily into the presence of the all-holy God.

The priest then returns to the center of the altar and says,

> Pray, brethren (brothers and sisters),
> that my sacrifice and yours
> may be acceptable to God,
> the almighty Father.

And the people rise and reply:

> May the Lord accept the sacrifice at your hands
> for the praise and glory of his name,
> for our good
> and the good of all his holy Church.

The invitation, in effect, exhorts each member of the assembly to ask that his or her individual offering ("my sacrifice and yours") be joined to that of all the others within the one, same self-offering of Christ. And so in the response, the congregation, in contrast to the invitation, regards the offerings already as a single "sacrifice." Furthermore, the congregation's prayer teaches a threefold purpose in making the sacrifice: (a) to give glory to God, (b) to benefit those who make the offering, and (c) to benefit the whole church as well, since, within the life of faith, each of these three necessarily includes the other two. Because it is only through the church that one is joined to Christ in the first place, the prayer ends by acknowledging the church's constitutional holiness, a holiness deriving from Christ's having surrendered himself up for her salvation (Eph 5:25-27).

The priest then prays aloud the "prayer over the offerings" for the Ninth Sunday in Ordinary Time:

> Trusting in your compassion, O Lord,
> we come eagerly with our offerings to your sacred altar,
> so that, through the purifying action of your grace,
> we may be cleansed by the very mysteries we serve.
> Through Christ our Lord.

The people again respond, "Amen," making their own the words and intentions of the prayer pronounced in their name.

The prayer over the offerings (*super oblata*) acts once again as kind of a collect prayer, reprising sentiments contained in the previous processional antiphon and the intervening prayers accompanying the rites. In the offertory antiphon for the Ninth Sunday in Ordinary Time taken from Psalm 71, as we have seen already, the church prays: "Be to me a rock of refuge, / a strong fortress to save me. . . . In you, O Lord, I take refuge; let me never be put to shame!" This concluding prayer therefore expresses this same spirit of total reliance on God: "Trusting in your compassion, O Lord . . ." It then identifies the "offerings," presented by the participants and purified by the "action of your [God's] grace," as saving "mysteries" through which they render service to God. That is to say, in the prayer over the offerings proclaimed by the priest, worshipers ask that, by God's "grace," their self-offerings as sacramental "offerings" ("mysteries") might be truly cleansing and effective in their lives.

The Eucharistic Prayer

The third characteristic of all liturgical assemblies, as we saw in chapter 4, is a faith commitment made in response to some proclamation of God's marvelous deeds in the past. For the ancient Israelites this response came most typically in the form of a ritual sacrifice (e.g., Exod 24). The primary mode through which the church gives her commitment is also sacrificial, and one in line with Hosea's exhortation to "take with you words and return to the Lord" (14:2): the eucharistic prayer as a sacrifice of praise.[27] Because spoken and enacted words create the worlds of meaning and value in which human beings live, by speaking and enacting in Christ his Word back to Father, the church actually becomes what she speaks: God's own Word to the world.

Relying on the common witness of St. Paul and the Synoptic Gospels,[28] theologians through the centuries have taken for granted that the Liturgy of the Eucharist in all of its historical manifestations derives ultimately from the Last Supper. Paul Bradshaw, however, has recently argued for the greater likelihood that the first Christian Eucharists originated out of apostolic imitation, after Jesus' death and resurrection, of his ministry of eating and drinking with all kinds of people.[29] For by means of this practice he manifested in his own person the arrival already of the eschatological kingdom of God (cf. Isa 25:6-8; 55:1-3), an arrival brought about fully by his death on the cross.[30]

In the late twentieth century various theories also emerged regarding the historical roots of the eucharistic prayer.[31] Cesare Giraudo, for example, postulates that it is a descendant of the *bipartite* Jewish prayer that accompanied the *Todah* sacrifice. That prayer combined (a) a grateful remembrance of God's wondrous deeds on Israel's behalf in the past with (b) a petition that those same blessings be continued on into the future.[32] Enrico Mazza, on the other hand, sees the eucharistic prayer developing out of the *Birkat ha-Mazon* that was prayed at the end of a Jewish meal,[33] with its *tripartite* structure of (a) a blessing of God for nourishing humankind, (b) thanking God for the Promised Land, and (c) petitions made for Israel, Jerusalem, and the Temple.[34] Although Bradshaw agrees that Christian eucharistic prayers stem from Jewish meal prayers,[35] he finds the available evidence insufficient to support the specificity of either theory: "[Mazza's] contention, however, is as difficult to sustain as is Giraudo's theory of an original bipartite structure, and Mazza has to exercise considerable ingenuity to force all ancient extant forms to fit within this particular framework."[36] At the same time, because of the historicity of salvation in Christ, Christian prayer in general does tend toward being bipartite in structure: "The movement of praise and gratitude is motivated by the recalling of the *mirabilia Dei*, the works of the past accomplished by God in favor of the one praying who, relying on the salvation already manifested in his or her favor, implores that this same salvific power be present to him or her right now. The anamnesis of the past becomes the guarantee of the future. This anamnetico-eplicletic dynamic is without doubt a fundamental motif in Jewish prayer and is the soil in which Christian prayer is rooted."[37] The current eucharistic prayers of the Roman Rite are no exception.

Eucharistic Prayer II

Although Eucharistic Prayer III is used most often on Sundays in Catholic parishes, Eucharistic Prayer II, because of its brevity, is also employed quite frequently, especially if some other part of the Mass is prolonged beyond its normal duration. To keep our study from expanding excessively, we therefore have chosen it here as well to be our "typical" eucharistic prayer.

Created as part of the post–Vatican II liturgical reform, Eucharistic Prayer II is based on the anaphora found in an ancient church order known as *The Apostolic Tradition* (AT), a compilation of second-to-mid-fourth-century prayer and disciplinary instructions on how to regulate church life and worship.[38] Because the AT prayer contains Jesus' Last Supper words ("This is my body," etc.), a feature not found in anaphoras before the fourth century, scholars conclude that in its present state it could not date prior to the late third century at the very earliest. On the other hand, being devoid of a *Sanctus* ("Holy, holy, holy . . ."), a feature common to most if not all eucharistic prayers by the mid-fourth century, neither could it have been composed in its present form much later than that mid-century mark, although some of its elements may have originated considerably earlier, from as far back as the mid-second century. Nor is it certain that in its present form it was ever even used in a liturgical setting and not simply created as an example of what an orthodox prayer should contain.[39] In any event, with a variety of additions and modifications, in 1969 the AT eucharistic prayer made its way, by the approval of the papal magisterium, into the post–Vatican II Roman Missal as Eucharistic Prayer II, and it has been celebrated throughout the Western church ever since. It exists today, therefore, in its modified condition, as an authentic witness to the faith of the universal church.[40]

Among the rubrics given for Eucharistic Prayer II in the text of the Roman Missal, we read, "Although it is provided with its own Preface, this Eucharistic Prayer may also be used with other Prefaces, especially those that present an overall view of the mystery of salvation, such as the Common Prefaces" (no. 99). The preface chosen for our study, Preface II of the Sundays in Ordinary Time, is based on the preface for the second Sunday after the Easter octave found in the *Gelasian Sacramentary*, a volume composed between 628 and 714.[41] As we shall see, this preface provides just such an overview of Christian salvation.

Beginning with the AT prayer itself, succeeding eucharistic prayers through the centuries have been introduced by a series of exchanges between priest and congregation. If at all possible, it is very important on Sundays especially that, along with this opening dialogue, the preface be sung. No other musical element in the course of the Eucharist has near the same power for communicating the momentous nature and beauty of the mysteries being celebrated. By means of the presider's a capella voice intoning the ancient melody, the whole assembly is more fully caught up into and ennobled by their grateful recollection of God's saving deeds.

The prayer begins with the ancient dialogue: "The Lord be with you," and so forth. Just as the Lord Jesus on the cross entrusted himself completely into the Father's care ("Father, into your hands I commit my spirit" [Luke 23:46]), the priest calls upon the gathered faithful in Christ to do the same: "Lift up your hearts." All respond, "We lift them up to the Lord." Invited next to give thanks to God, the congregation replies, "It is right and just." This simple, almost legal-sounding phrase helps to emphasize how absolute and sacred is the obligation human beings have to gratefully recognize God's infinite goodness as manifested and realized in the life, death, and resurrection of his only-begotten Son, Jesus Christ.[42]

Beginning the preface with arms extended so as to symbolically embrace the prayer of all, the priest then echoes the very same words, "It is truly right and just," and with additional phrases stresses further the same conviction: "It is . . . our duty and salvation, / always and everywhere to give you thanks." He proceeds next to add to this sense of indebtedness and solemnity by addressing the Father with a series of exalted appellations, "Lord, holy Father, almighty and eternal God," doing so "through Christ our Lord."

The priest then supplies the motive for the church's gathering each Sunday to do the Eucharist:

> For out of compassion for the waywardness that is ours,
> *he humbled himself* [Phil 2:8] and was born of the Virgin;
> by the passion of the Cross he freed us from unending death,
> and by rising from the dead he gave us life eternal." (emphasis added)

That is to say, as we saw in chapter 1, Christ accomplished our salvation within his own humanity: suffering death and rising to eternal life to unite the members of his Body to himself in his once-for-all self-offering to God the Father. The church here below therefore joins with the heavenly hosts in praising the Father's glory made fully manifest in Christ's paschal mystery, through which, according to Colossians 1:15-20, all things "visible and invisible" have been both created and redeemed:

> And so, with Angels and Archangels,
> with *Thrones and Dominions*,
> and with all the hosts *and Powers* [Col 1:16] of heaven,
> we sing the hymn of your glory,
> as without end we acclaim:
>
> *Holy, Holy, Holy Lord God of hosts.*
> Heaven and *earth* are *full of your glory* [Isa 6:3].
> *Hosanna* in the highest.
> *Blessed is he who comes in the name of the Lord.*
> *Hosanna in the highest* [Matt 21:9]. (emphases added)

The opening lines of this acclamation, taken from the prophet Isaiah's vision of the Lord (Isa 6:3), entered into the Jewish synagogue liturgy in connection with the *Shema* maybe as early as the second century.[43] They first made their way into the Christian Eucharist most likely in Egypt, "possibly as early as the second half of the third century under Dionysius the Great, bishop of Alexandria from 247–264."[44] Matthew 21:9, with a slight modification,[45] was then added by the church in Syria sometime around the mid-fourth century, and the whole acclamation as we have it today came into common eucharistic use in both East and West probably in the latter half of the fourth century.[46] The *Sanctus* acclamation continues the dialogical nature of the eucharistic prayer as the people's antiphonal response of praise to the presider's preface account of God's saving deeds in Christ.

Following the *Sanctus*, the priest stretches out his hands in prayer once again and continues: "You are indeed Holy, O Lord, / *the fount of* all holiness [Jer 17:13]" (emphasis added). He then joins his hands over the offerings, saying,

> Make holy, therefore, these gifts, we pray,
> by sending down your Spirit upon them like *the dewfall* [Num 11:9],
> so that they may become for us
> the Body and ✠ Blood of our Lord Jesus Christ.[47]

This section of the prayer is commonly known as the "consecratory epiclesis," a calling upon (*epi-kaleo*) the Holy Spirit to sanctify the gifts. The fact that the original AT eucharistic prayer includes no similar appeal to the Holy Spirit prior to the Last Supper narrative calls for a brief explanation for its appearance in the present form of the prayer.

As we shall see, in addition to the "consecratory epiclesis," a "communion epiclesis" follows the Last Supper narrative and asks that the Spirit sanctify participants through their sharing in the consecrated bread and chalice. Although scholars in the past have generally held that the double epiclesis derives from early Alexandrian liturgies,[48] this is no longer certain.[49] In any event, without mentioning the Holy Spirit the ancient Roman Canon also contains two parallel petitions that serve the same respective functions,[50] thereby supplying a precedent for including a "consecratory epiclesis" in the eucharistic prayers newly created after Vatican II. As Paul De Clerck points out, this addition has altered the theology of these prayers: "In contrast to a certain medieval tendency, transforming the Eucharist through the memory of the passion of the Lord, the epiclesis underlines that the Eucharist is only possible thanks to the gift of the Spirit, in other words, thanks to the resurrection of the Lord. For ecclesiastically the Eucharist is celebrated mainly on Sunday, the day of the resurrection, not on Thursday, seen as the day of its institution."[51]

> Joining his hands, the priest continues,
>
> At the time he was betrayed
> and entered willingly [Isa 53:10; John 10:18] into his Passion,
>
> > *He takes the bread and, holding it slightly raised above the altar, continues:*

he took bread and, giving thanks, broke it,
and gave it to his disciples, saying:

> *He bows slightly.*

TAKE THIS, ALL OF YOU, AND EAT OF IT, / FOR THIS IS MY BODY, WHICH
WILL BE GIVEN UP FOR YOU.

The priest shows the host to the people, places it on the paten, genuflects,
and continues,

> In a similar way, when supper was ended,

>> *He takes the chalice and, holding it slightly raised above the altar,
>> continues:*

> he took the chalice
> and, once more giving thanks,
> he gave it to his disciples, saying:

>> *He bows slightly.*

TAKE THIS, ALL OF YOU, AND DRINK FROM IT,
FOR THIS IS THE CHALICE OF MY BLOOD,
THE BLOOD OF *THE NEW* AND ETERNAL *COVENANT* [Jer 31:31],
WHICH WILL BE *POURED OUT* [Isa 53:12] FOR YOU AND FOR *MANY* [Isa 53:11]
FOR THE FORGIVENESS OF *SINS* [cf. Isa 53:5, 11].
DO THIS IN MEMORY OF ME. (emphases added)

The priest shows the chalice to the people, places it on the corporal,
genuflects in adoration, and announces, "The mystery of faith." The
congregation responds, "We *proclaim* your *Death*, O Lord, / and profess
your Resurrection / *until you come* again [1 Cor 11:26; emphases added]."

The first section of the eucharistic prayer unites the preface, *Sanctus*,
consecratory epiclesis, words of institution, and memorial acclamation
into a single, integrated whole: "Liturgical studies have demonstrated
that the Eucharistic Prayer is, as a whole, a memorial; as a whole, consecratory; as a whole, a sacrificial event; as a whole, epicletic (a prayer
namely for the coming of the Spirit and a prayer in the Spirit). In this
prayer as a whole a number of moments occur that explicitly articulate
one of those general characteristics, for example the special anamnesis
or the explicit offering. Yet, we must not let them function on their own
in isolation from the prayer as a whole."[52] The fact that the words of the
Last Supper narrative are capitalized in the printed text and their recital
is followed by elevations and genuflections may seem to suggest that

their performance is still regarded by official church theology as the sole cause of the transformation of bread and wine into Christ's Body and Blood. At the same time, it should also be noted that whereas in the pre–Vatican II *Missale Romanum* only the words spoken directly over the bread and chalice ("Hoc est enim Corpus meum . . ." and "Hic est enim Calix Sanguinis mei . . .") are emphasized in this way, the printed Missal of Paul VI gives equal typographical stress to the Lord's introductory instruction as well: "TAKE THIS, ALL OF YOU, AND EAT OF IT . . .," resulting in a significant shift in theological meaning. In other words, it is Christ in his saving events who is made present and effective in and through the consecrated bread and wine. These sacraments, therefore, are truly his Body and Blood—however, not in a purely static, objective way,[53] but as handed over and poured out for the salvation of the world, in order through Holy Communion to transform Eucharistic participants themselves into active embodiments of those same saving events. Thus, St. Leo the Great says, "What . . . was visible [in the life] of the Redeemer has passed over into the sacraments."[54]

In regard to the original meaning of the Last Supper narrative, Edward Kilmartin observes

> In the context of a Jewish meal the pregnant formula 'This is my body which is given for you' (Luke 22:19; 1 Cor 11:24) should mean: *This* (sharing of bread) *is* (has the meaning of sharing in) *my body* (my person as transitory earthly being and nevertheless principle of life in relation to others) *which is given for you* (become so by total dedication to the will of God). Since this sharing of bread establishes a relationship of identity of life between Jesus and the disciples and so a new principle of unity between the disciples, we can also paraphrase the bread words thus: You are my body, you who share this bread and eat it together.[55]

Thus, instead of the static, objectivist view of Christ's presence in the form of bread and wine that more or less dominated Western theology since the Berengar controversy in the eleventh century,[56] this printing change opens up the possibility of a more *relational* understanding of that same mystery, such as that which, according to Kilmartin, the apostles in the first century would have had: that Christ is fully present through the eucharistic bread and chalice, but in a totally *active* way, in the complete *self-offering* of his paschal mystery at once both to his Father and to the Father's children. Thus, as evidenced in this typographical change, Christ's presence in the consecrated elements is seen no longer as dependent on an isolated pronouncement of biblical words by an ordained presider, but as realized through the whole eucharistic liturgy as the assembly's appropriation of the faith of the universal church: its self-offering to the Father in the power of the Spirit through the once-for-all self-offering of Jesus Christ.

Furthermore, if, as we have seen, true Christian life is fundamentally an imitation of Christ, then the liturgy as a symbolic stylization of that life will necessarily also be typological, and especially so. It is only fitting then that, when recalling God's great deeds of salvation, the rite has the priest enter fully, even bodily, into the ritual recollection of Christ's saving events at this point in the prayer.[57] In fact, this same dramatization is apparently what occasions the memorial acclamation, for although the priest speaks the eucharistic prayer to the Father, the congregation addresses its acclamation to Christ, as if in response to the priest's performance of Jesus' words and actions at the Last Supper.[58]

A significant change that took place in the new translation is the use of the word "many," a Hebraism meaning "all," in the phrase "WHICH WILL BE POURED OUT FOR YOU [Luke 22:20] AND *FOR MANY* [Isa 53:12; Mark 14:24; Matt 26:28] / FOR THE FORGIVENESS OF SINS" (emphasis added). Taken from Last Supper accounts of Mark and Matthew, "many" functions here as it does in those scriptural passages as a metonymy for Isaiah's description of the "Suffering Servant," by whose suffering and death God brings about *universal* forgiveness of sins: "The Lord has laid on him / the iniquity *of us all.* . . . He *poured out* his soul to death, . . . yet he bore the sin of *many,* / and made intercession for the transgressors" (Isa 53:6, 12; emphases added; cf. also Rom 5:15). In other words, in light of Old Testament Scripture, it acts as an interpretative key for the salvation history meaning of Christ's own suffering and death. And the poetical use of "many" here also suggests the overwhelming numerical size of the human race saved by the death of Christ, providing an experience similar to that described in the Gospel of John: "There is a lad here who has five barley loaves and two fish; but *what are they among so many?*" (John 6:9; emphasis added).

The priest then extends his hands and begins the second part of the eucharistic prayer:

> Therefore, as we celebrate
> the memorial of his Death and Resurrection,
> we offer you, Lord,
> the *Bread of life* [John 6:35, 48]
> and the *Chalice of salvation* [Ps 116:13],
> giving thanks that you have held us worthy
> to be in your presence and minister to you. (emphases added)

According to Cesare Giraudo,[59] the theology of a eucharistic prayer can be discerned in great part from its literary, syntactical structure. Analyzing the first part of Eucharistic Prayer II, we find that the assembly, through the person and voice of the ordained presider, gives thanks to God the Father for sending the Son to bring about human salvation by his self-offering on the cross and by his ritualizing that self-offering at the Last Supper through the forms of bread and wine. Furthermore, according to the prayer, also integral to the Son's saving activity and obedience to the Father's will was the Son's Last Supper command to his disciples, "Do this in memory of me."[60] In other words, by her compliance with the will of the Son, it is the Father himself who is acting through the actions of the church to bring about her salvation. That the second part of the prayer begins then with the word "therefore" clearly signals that everything that follows is to be understood as the church's obedience to this command of the Lord.

Analyzing the grammar of this initial sentence, we find that the church's obedience consists in an offering ("offer" = main verb) that is both a memorial and an act of thanksgiving ("as we celebrate the memorial" and "giving thanks" = adverbial clauses). And yet, if, as the Letter to the Hebrews tells us, "we have been sanctified through the offering of the body of Jesus Christ once for all" (10:10), and if the church's Eucharist is not simply a mechanical repetition of what happened at the Last Supper and on Calvary, what does the Lord intend by the church's offering of bread and wine at the Eucharist? What precisely is meant here by Jesus' words "Do this in memory of me"? What, in the context of the Eucharist, are these elements intended to signify?

The story about the feeding of the five thousand in the Gospel of Mark may provide some direction in answering these questions:

> And when it grew late, his disciples came to him and said, "This is a lonely place, and the hour is now late; send them away, to go into the country and villages round about and buy themselves something to eat." But he answered them, "You give them something to eat." And they said to him, "Shall we go and buy two hundred denarii worth of bread, and give it to them to eat?" And he said to them, "How many loaves have you? Go and see." And when they had found out, they said, "Five, and two fish." . . . And taking the five loaves and two fish he looked up to heaven, and blessed, and broke the loaves, and gave them to the disciples to set before the people. . . . And they all ate and were satisfied. And they took up twelve baskets full of broken pieces and of the fish." (Mark 6:35-43)

Here, as we see, Jesus first asks his disciples to feed a huge hungry crowd of people. When the disciples recognize that they cannot do so out of their own limited resources, he takes up those same resources into his own self-offering to the Father, his prayer of blessing, only then to return them once again to the disciples with the instruction that they distribute them to the crowds. Miraculously, what before was totally insufficient to feed an immense multitude suddenly becomes a superabundance. That is to say, what the disciples were unable to accomplish by themselves they are empowered to do when what they have to give becomes part of Christ's own self-offering. In the same way does Christ now as "the bread of life" (John 6:48) continue to feed the whole world at the church's Eucharist, and again through the self-offering of believers themselves, symbolized by the intentionally small supply of bread and wine as a stylized expression of their own finitude. In the words of St. Paul, "For the sake of Christ, then, I am content with weaknesses, . . . for when I am weak, then I am strong" (2 Cor 12:9-10); "I can do all things in him who strengthens me" (Phil 4:13).

Consequently, according to the language of Eucharistic Prayer II, what the Lord is asking from the members of his Body, the church, in giving the command "Do this in memory of me" is that they offer themselves in and through Christ's own self-offering to the Father by means of the same bread and wine *as the symbols of themselves* that were brought forward earlier at the preparation of the gifts—products of the earth and work of human hands. What, then, Christians give thanks for in the church's eucharistic prayer is Jesus Christ in his life, death, and resurrection as the fullness of the Father's self-gift, a gift realized throughout all creation but made present to believers especially through their own self-offering. In the words of Louis-Marie Chauvet, "The Christian mode of appropriation is through disappropriation: the mode of 'taking' is by 'giving'— 'giving thanks.'"[61] Just as the Father gave himself fully to the incarnate Son, and to all humanity in him, through the Son's self-giving on the cross to the Father, so does the Son ask us to let him continue, now through our self-offering in him, to give himself both to the Father and to us: "Do *this* in memory of me." Accordingly, St. Augustine teaches, "If, then, you are the Body of Christ and his members (1 Cor 12:27), it is your sacrament that reposes on the Lord's table; it is your sacrament that you receive. To *that which you are* you respond, 'Amen,' and by responding you agree. For you hear, 'The Body of Christ,' and you respond, 'Amen.' Be a member of the Body of Christ that your 'Amen' may be true."[62]

As we remarked in an earlier chapter, the vocalists Barbra Streisand and Neil Diamond knew that they could use flowers to give themselves to each other in love. Jesus, too, was able to give himself to his disciples through the bread and wine of the paschal meal, and he asks us now, in him, to do the same for one another in his memory. However, whereas Streisand and Diamond could give themselves to each other in only a limited fashion through the products of the earth, the man Jesus, by actualizing the fullness of his divinity in his theandric self-giving on the cross, is able now to give his full resurrected self to us in the bread and wine of the Eucharist. He does so, however, by using the bread and wine of the meal by way of metonymy. That is to say, just as bread and wine act as metonyms for all the ways we human beings are nourished both physically and spiritually by God in his gifts throughout our lives, so too does Jesus offer himself in his physical ("body and blood") life, death, and resurrection through these same metonyms, but now as the "super-substantial" food of our lives, the absolute fullness of God's self-gift, which makes us in our reception of them his "bread" for one another and the world. Thus, as metonyms they become full typological realizations of Christ's self-offering presence.

In Western history this figurative dimension of the Lord's words and actions at the Last Supper became obscure, as we know, when theologians, especially by the ninth century, in trying to understand these dominical words,[63] wondered how bread and wine could become his objective, physical human body and blood, not understanding that although because of his resurrection shared bread and wine in this context are physical realizations of his full self-giving presence, so much so that he can truly be adored there,[64] they are such in a symbolic (sacramental), relational way. The fact is that already early on in church history, theologians had to guard against this same literalist tendency. For example, immediately upon quoting Christ's Last Supper words, "This is my body," the North African Tertullian felt compelled to add, "that is, '*a figure* of my body' [*figura corporis mei*]."[65] Likewise St. Cyril of Jerusalem in the fourth century.[66] In fact, the early form of the Roman Canon quoted by St. Ambrose includes the same explanatory phrase.[67]

In chapter 13 of his *Epistle* 63, St. Cyprian of Carthage (ca. 210–58) provides a further and even more explicit example of this patristic, figurative understanding of the church's liturgy. Laying the groundwork for this chapter earlier in the epistle by pointing out that in Scripture water symbolizes the people whereas wine always stands for Christ, Cyprian proceeds to argue:

For because Christ who bore us all *bore* even *our sins* (Isa 53:4, 11), we see that in the water is understood the people, but in the wine is shown the blood of Christ. But when the water is mingled in the cup with wine, the people are made one with Christ, and the assembly of believers is associated and conjoined with Him in whom it believes, and the association and conjunction of water and wine is so mingled in the Lord's cup that that mixture can no longer be separated. Consequently, nothing *can separate* the church—that is, the people established in the church, faithfully and firmly persevering in that which they have believed—*from Christ* (Rom 8:35) in such a way as to prevent their undivided love from always abiding and adhering. Therefore, in consecrating the cup of the Lord, water alone cannot be offered, even as wine alone cannot be offered. For if any one offers wine only, the Blood of Christ begins to be without us; but if the water be alone, the people begins to be without Christ; but when both are mingled and are joined to each other by a close union, there is completed a spiritual and heavenly *sacrament*.[68]

Given that for Cyprian water throughout Scripture symbolizes the people whereas wine symbolizes the blood of Christ, because in his "passion" (*passio* = Last Supper, suffering, and death) Jesus carried within himself the whole human race by his victorious love, for the chalice to be a true "sacrament" (that is, a truly representative sacred symbol of what actually happened on the cross—the unity of all humankind in Christ), it must contain both water *and* wine and in an inseparable (cf. Rom 8:35) mixture. According to Cyprian, then, by offering themselves in the spoken and enacted figurative "language" of the church's memorial of Christ's saving events, the members of the church, through the power of Christ dwelling within them, make it possible for God to give God's Self completely to them in Christ by their thus opening themselves to receive that infinite gift.

Thus, even if the Liturgy of the Eucharist may have originated in imitation of Jesus' meal ministry rather than the Last Supper meal, the ritual as ritual is not unimportant. From the very beginning it was also recognized that it is the risen Christ who calls his followers together, presides, and shares himself with them through the blessed chalice and blessed and broken bread (cf. Luke 14:30). The blessing of eucharistic bread and chalice did not originate out of any decision by the church to use them as expressions of her unity. As ritual manifestations and enactments of his theandric love on the cross, it is Christ who through them offers himself fully to the participants for their acceptance of that love and their unity in him: "The bread which we break, is it not a participation [*koinonia*] in the body of Christ? Because there is one bread, we who are many are one body, for we all partake in the one bread" (1 Cor 10:16-17). That is apparently why the church so emphasizes the dominical words in the printing of eucharistic prayers and has the presider genuflect after pronouncing them: "In this is love, not that we loved God but that he loved us and sent his Son to be the expiation for our sins" (1 John 4:10).

At the same time, the ritual is important ultimately because of its power to transform Christian lives through its transformation of bread and wine—that through them Christ comes to dwell within *us*, in our ways of thinking and acting in this world: "It is no longer I who live, but Christ who lives in me" (Gal 2:20). The Lord's injunction, then, "Do this in memory of me," refers as much to how, through his power working within us, we should pattern our lives on his own life of self-giving to God and neighbor as it does to our replicating the Last Supper *ritual* of that self-giving (cf. 1 Cor 11:17-33).

By entering as part of a liturgical assembly into the official prayer forms of the universal church, the individual worshiper appropriates as his or her own *the full scope of the church's faith* embodied both in those forms and in their communal celebration. Because Christ in his self-offering on the cross is the source and content of the church's faith, what the individual worshiper receives in return, then, is Christ symbolically realized in the bread and chalice first brought forward as his or her own liturgical self-offering, then consecrated, and then distributed in Holy Communion. Thus, even though all the baptized are but single members within the whole corporate Body of Christ, because their individual expression of faith corroborates and is corroborated by that of the rest of the assembly, and ultimately by the universal church through an authoritative celebration of the church's liturgy, what each one receives back—the full actual presence of Christ in the consecrated bread and wine—is infinitely greater than what each one had originally offered in the first place: their own individual appropriation of the faith of Christ.[69] And so, as was noted earlier, "The sacrifice of Christ becomes sacramentally present insofar and only insofar as it is also the sacrifice of the [*whole*] church."[70]

Because the consecrated bread and wine are the full presence of Christ, it is also true that no one in this life is fully able at any one time to take in all that is being offered. In the words of St. Ephrem the Deacon, "Be glad that you were fed, not sad that there was too much too eat! A thirsty man is glad to drink, not sad that he cannot drink the fountain dry. . . .

What you cannot receive at one time because of your limitations, you can receive at other times if you persevere."[71] The "communion epiclesis" then follows: "Humbly we pray / that, partaking of the Body and Blood of Christ, / we may be gathered into one [1 Cor 10:17] by the Holy Spirit." Thus, in response to the memorial spoken over the bread and wine, the memorial of Christ's Last Supper, death, and resurrection wherein he united all to himself in his self-offering to the Father, the assembly asks to be taken up by the Spirit into the mystery of Christ's all-inclusive love through its participation in those same sacraments. And so it goes on to pray,

> Remember, Lord, your Church,
> spread throughout the world,
> and bring her to *the fullness of charity* [1 John 4:18],
> together with N. our Pope and N. our Bishop
> and all the clergy.

> Remember also our brothers and sisters
> who have *fallen asleep* [1 Cor 15:6] in the *hope* of *the resurrection* [1 Pet 1:3],
> and all who have died in your mercy:
> welcome them *into the light of your face* [Ps 89:16]. (emphases added)

By the power of the Spirit, then, the assembly enters more deeply into Christ's all-inclusive love manifested in his paschal mystery by identifying itself through prayer first with the whole church throughout the world sacramentally embodied in the pope and bishops, next with all the members of the church who have died, and finally with all others as well who have died.

In the same spirit of Christ's universal love the prayer goes on to ask,

> Have mercy on us all, we pray,
> that with the Blessed Virgin Mary, Mother of God,
> with the blessed Apostles,
> and all the Saints who have pleased you throughout the ages,
> we may merit to be *coheirs* [Eph 3:6] to eternal life,
> and may praise and glorify you
> through your Son, Jesus Christ. (emphasis added)

The word "coheirs," as a scriptural allusion, is actually another verbal metonymy. It recalls St. Paul's theology of the church as a part of "the mystery of Christ, which was not made known to the sons of men in other generations as it has now been revealed to his holy apostles and prophets by the Spirit; that is, how the Gentiles are fellow heirs [*sugklēronoma*], members of the same body, and partakers of the promise in Christ Jesus through the gospel" (Eph 3:4-6). Thus, the prayer proclaims once again that the Christ made present through the forms of bread and wine on the altar includes the church as well, united in his universal love (the "fullness of charity") by the power of the Holy Spirit. Together, then, with "all the Saints . . . throughout the ages," the church offers praise and glory to the Father through, with, and in Christ in the unity of the Holy Spirit:

> Through him, and with him, and in him,
> O God, almighty Father,
> in the unity of the Holy Spirit,
> all glory and honor is yours,
> for ever and ever.

The people acclaim, "Amen."

By means of the sacramental words and actions of the eucharistic prayer, then, the Father, through Christ and his church, acts to unite the participants more fully to himself by forming and integrating them more deeply by the power of the Holy Spirit into the one Body of Christ. If, as was noted in chapter 3, any given liturgy or liturgical element (*lex orandi*) manifests the church's faith (*lex credendi*) to the degree that it (1) expresses the *universality* of God's salvation accomplished in Jesus Christ; (2) presents Old Testament realities and events *typologically*, that is, as imaging, making present, and being fulfilled in the life, death, and resurrection of Christ; (3) expresses the Christ mystery in the *anamnetic, epicletic, and doxological* (symbolic exchange) structure of the original apostolic faith experience; and (4), while manifesting the first three principles, is composed of elements that have been practiced from the earliest times and throughout the church, then it is clear from our analysis of Eucharistic Prayer II that this prayer is an especially authoritative expression of the fundamental faith of the universal church throughout the centuries.

The eucharistic prayer comes to an end with the final "Amen" said in response by the people. It is this same "Amen" to which St. Justin Martyr makes reference already in the mid-second century: "The president then prays and gives thanks according to his ability, and the people give their assent with an 'Amen!'"[72] According to St. Augustine, to say "Amen" is to "subscribe" to what was said.[73] In regard to the "Amen," St. Paul writes, "The Son of God, Jesus Christ, whom we preached among you, Silvanus and Timothy and I, was not Yes and No; but in him it is always Yes. For all the promises of God find their Yes in him. That is why we utter the

Amen through him, to the glory of God" (2 Cor 1:18-20). Through the "Amen," then, the assembly explicitly joins the presider in the church's expression of faith through which Christ continues to say his Yes to the Father, to all in the assembly, and through them to the rest of the world as well.

The Communion Rite

The Lord's Prayer

As St. Cyprian of Carthage (ca. 210–58) observes, "We do not say, 'My Father, who art in heaven,' nor 'Give me my daily bread.'. . . Our prayer is public and common, and when we pray, we pray not for one, but for the whole people, because as a whole people we are one."[74] Proclaimed in unison by everyone, the Lord's Prayer thus expresses and deepens the unity of all in the one Body of Christ, the "complex person"[75] of the church, by instilling within them "the mind of the Lord" (1 Cor 2:16; Phil 2:5), the "thoughts of his heart" (Ps 33:11).

According to Robert Taft, "We have no sure evidence of the use of the Lord's Prayer in the rite of the eucharist until the 4th century."[76] By that time it had already long been a part of the sacraments of initiation because "for the Fathers, [it] was a 'summary of the whole Gospel'. . . to be 'handed over' to the neophytes as the summary of their heritage."[77] Therefore, it was first introduced into the eucharistic liturgy just prior to Communion (its comparable location within the rites of initiation), right after the breaking of the bread, most probably not because of its reference to "daily bread" but because of its "penultimate prayer for forgiveness, . . . to obtain forgiveness for what Augustine calls our 'everyday sins' (*peccata quotidiana*), run-of-the-mill post-baptismal sins and failings, so that we can approach the sacrament without condemnation."[78] And yet, the fathers of the church do focus on "our daily bread" in their respective commentaries on the Lord's Prayer, seeing in that phrase a direct reference to the Eucharist. Tertullian (fl. ca. 200), for example, writes, "Christ is our bread. . . . When we ask for our daily bread, we ask for the power to live continually in Christ, the power to identify ourselves with his Body."[79] Because it was widely believed that the apostles actually used the Lord's Prayer to consecrate the bread and wine, St. Gregory the Great (+ 604) moved it to its present position just after the eucharistic prayer in order to ratify with the Lord's own words the eucharistic prayer's consecratory power.[80]

The embolism "Deliver us, Lord . . ." following the Lord's Prayer originated around the time of St. Gregory the Great (590–604)[81] and was modified after Vatican II by the addition of a final expression of eschatological yearning taken from Titus 2:13: "as we await the blessed hope and the coming of our Savior, Jesus Christ." Also new to the post–Vatican II liturgy is an ancient doxology, prayed in unison by all, that is found in the Didache and in some Matthean manuscripts and is also in wide use among Protestant Christians: "For the kingdom, / the power and the glory / are yours now and for ever." Hence, by her use of these words, in effect embracing her baptismal unity in Christ with all Christians everywhere, the church prays in accord with the Lord's Prayer petition for mutual forgiveness and reconciliation.

The Peace

In Christian history, the religious practice of exchanging a kiss can be traced back to the New Testament itself.[82] At the end of four of his epistles, for example, St. Paul instructs his readers to greet each other with a "holy kiss" (Rom 16:16; 1 Cor 16:20; 2 Cor 13:12; and 1 Thess 5:26). As members of the same Body of Christ, early Christians saw themselves animated both bodily and spiritually by the one same Spirit of Christ. Together with the fact that a kiss is a universal sign of love and reverence, Christians exchanged the holy kiss directly on the mouth— women separately from men—because of their belief that the physical breath (*spiritus*) they shared in doing so, which gave life to their bodies, was filled with the Holy Spirit who through baptism animated their souls. Whereas in the Eastern church this took place after the intercessory prayers and was later transferred, in compliance with Matthew 5:23, to just before the offering, thereby turning it into an act of reconciliation, by the fifth century in the West it was performed right after the eucharistic prayer as an expression of the universal love of Christ that binds all the members of the church together. There it was seen both as a seal on the eucharistic prayer and as a preparation for Holy Communion.[83] Although stylized in later history and shared only among the clergy, and then only on solemn occasions, according to Rick Hilgartner the rite maintains the same unitive purpose in the Roman Rite today that it had through the centuries: "The sign of peace affords an opportunity to see Christ 'in one's neighbor' as a way of preparing to encounter Christ sacramentally in the Eucharist . . ., [emphasizing] the ecclesial nature of Communion."[84]

The Fermentum *Rite*

The curious action by the priest of breaking off a small fraction of the large host of the Eucharist and dropping it into the chalice of consecrated wine recalls a similar practice by the pope, dating from the early fifth century, of sending out pieces of consecrated bread to parishes under his jurisdiction. In a letter dated March 19, 416, to Decentius, the bishop of Gubbio, Pope Innocent I (401–17) writes:

> But concerning the *fermentum* that we send to the titular churches on Sunday, you have needlessly wanted to consult us, since all our churches are established within the city. And because their priests cannot come together with us on that day on account of the people entrusted to them, they for this reason receive through acolytes the *fermentum* confected by us so that especially on that day they do not judge that they are separated from us. And I do not think that this ought to be done throughout the parishes because the sacraments should not be carried far, nor do we send them to priests established throughout diverse cemeteries—their priests also [*et*] have the right and permission to confect them.[85]

Innocent's observation that priests assigned to cemeteries (hence serving visitors only) "also have the right and permission" to celebrate Mass suggests that a fortiori so do both the priests stationed at titular churches within the city and those assigned to churches in outlying districts—those who in both cases preside over stable congregations. The only difference, then, between these last two sets of priests is that no *fermentum* is brought to those outside the city, because of Innocent's hesitation to have it carried any great distance. And so what the practice entailed was the pope's breaking off separate consecrated pieces, sending them to the titular parishes located within the walled city, where the priests there then dropped them into the chalice during their own eucharistic celebrations, doing so in order to symbolize through Communion their unity with the pope and, through him, with the whole church of Rome.[86] Indeed, the phrase "especially on that day" (Sunday) suggests that priests at titular churches may sometimes have presided over liturgies on other days of the week as well, days on which, however, no *fermentum* was sent. In any case, on given ferial days throughout the year the pope processed to celebrate "stational liturgies" at those titular churches, doing so also in order to express through his person the overall unity of the church of Rome.[87] Thus, the *fermentum* rite remains in the Roman Rite liturgy today as a poetic allusion to an ancient practice, to symbolize sacramentally how Catholic eucharistic assemblies everywhere are realizations of the one universal Body of Christ through their union with the church and bishop of Rome.

The Fraction Rite and Agnus Dei

The ritual "breaking of bread" (*klasis tou artou* = *fractio panis*) that follows the *fermentum* rite is as ancient as the Eucharist itself. As an action originally needed in order for all to share in the one loaf (cf. Didache 9:4; 1 Cor 10:17), its power to symbolize Christian life as one of sharing was already recognized in the New Testament (1 Cor 11:17-29), where it is presented as a metonymy for the Eucharist as a whole (Luke 24:35; Acts 2:46; 20:7, 11). Thus, even when eucharistic bread began to be shaped beforehand into individual portions, this rite was still continued, albeit in its reduced form.[88] Dom Gregory Dix famously includes the breaking of bread as one of the essential elements in the "four-action shape" of the Liturgy of the Eucharist: "taking" (offertory), "blessing" (eucharistic prayer), "breaking" (fraction rite), and "giving" (Communion).[89] After asserting that "the Christ who comes into presence in the Eucharist is the one who presides over the assembly,"[90] Louis-Marie Chauvet adds, "bread never displays its essence as bread as much as it does in the act of its presentation to God in homage and its sharing with others in God's presence. In this perspective, the action of the breaking of bread is a fundamental rite of the Mass. . . . The fundamental *sacramentum* of the presence of Christ in the Eucharist is indeed bread, but only as broken (or destined to be); bread therefore, but in its essential being as bread, that is to say not as something self-contained and compact, but a reality for sharing."[91] In other words, through the church's life of sharing, liturgically symbolized and enacted in the breaking of the bread, it is ultimately Christ himself who is sharing himself with his people.

The *Agnus Dei* chant during the breaking of the bread, "Lamb of God, you take away the sins of the world, / have mercy on us," is clearly a replication of the similar petition found in the Gloria combining two biblical quotations: John the Baptist's announcement, "Behold, the *Lamb of God, who takes away the sin of the world*" (John 1:29; emphasis added), and the cry of the two blind men in Matthew, "*Have mercy on us*, Son of David!" (9:27; emphasis added). The *Agnus Dei* was first introduced into the Mass by Pope Sergius I in 687. Originally sung only once, it began its current triple performance around the year 1000, with the final "have mercy on us" changed to "grant us peace."

As a chant to "cover" a liturgical action, the *Agnus Dei* makes all in the assembly conscious of the awesome nature of the mysteries unfolding in their midst, how their Lord gave himself up for their salvation "like *a lamb* that is led to the slaughter" (Isa 53:7; emphasis added), and so, like those blind beggars in Matthew, they naturally plead in response to be made worthy of so great a gift.

Communion

After praying silently another "apology" prayer, the priest picks up the host, raises it slightly above either the paten or the chalice, and announces, "Behold the Lamb of God, / behold him who takes away the sins of the world. / Blessed are those called to the supper of the Lamb [Rev 19:9]."

By referring to the raised host as "the Lamb of God," the priest echoes the assembly's own *Agnus Dei* profession of faith in Christ's presence in the eucharistic elements. And by his use of the word "Behold" he proclaims in effect that Christ in the consecrated bread has actually become visible in their midst. Just as, according to Jesus in John's gospel, "He who has seen me has seen the Father" (John 14:9), so too can believers now see Christ in his essential reality present in the host held before them, that is, as the "bread of God . . . which comes down from heaven, and gives life to the world" (John 6:33). Finally, the announcement "Blessed are those called to the supper of the Lamb," a biblical allusion to Revelations 19:9, teaches that the Eucharist is both a preparation for and a foretaste of the eternal banquet of the Lamb, the fullness of our future life in heaven.

By responding, "Lord, I am not worthy / that you should enter under my roof, / but only say the word / and my soul shall be healed," the congregation recalls how the Roman centurion, someone also without saving merit before the Lord, was successful by the use of similar words in persuading Jesus to cure his servant (Luke 7:6-7). Whereas the centurion made his plea for someone else, the assembly in pleading for itself poetically does so with a similar kind of objectivity, as if looking down in pity upon its poor soul lying in bed, unable to stir because of its spiritual weakness, that is, its tendency to try to live without Christ.

After receiving Communion, the priest distributes the consecrated bread and wine to the other eucharistic ministers who then, along with him, descend the altar steps and go to their stations. There they administer both the sacred bread and the chalice to the rest of the faithful, who come forward in the fourth procession of the liturgy. During this time psalms or communion hymns are sung.

As noted already, in Holy Communion Christ can be seen as ("Behold"), and also comes to his people as, both food and drink, as one who so offers himself to his people in love that he wishes to be completely absorbed by them, so as to be totally one with them as his own Body in this world: "that they may all be one, even as you Father, are in me, and I in you, that they also may be in us" (John 17:21). And as we have also seen, it is to his people precisely as social beings that Christ administers salvation through the one bread, broken and distributed, sacramentally deepening their union with him through union with one another in his Body, his church.

As biblically connected with joy (cf. Ps 104:15), wine symbolizes how through their sharing in the one chalice the faithful share also in the joy of the Holy Spirit (Gal 5:22). However, it is a joy not completely separate from but rather only fulfilled through some share in the suffering of Christ: "Are you able to drink the chalice that I drink?" (Mark 10:38; cf. Jer 25:15). And so it is a joy of service, a commitment to "bear one another's burdens" (Gal 6:2) and "lay down our lives for the brethren" (1 John 3:16).

Closing Prayer

After Communion the altar is cleared, and just as Jesus told his disciples, "Come away by yourselves to a lonely place, and rest a while" (Mark 6:31), the priest and the whole congregation sit once again in silence for a brief time, to allow their communion with the Lord to reach into their minds and hearts and into all parts of their lives. Then the priest stands up and gives the invitation, "Let us pray." After another brief moment for silent prayer, he continues,

> Govern by your Spirit, we pray, O Lord,
> those you feed with the Body and Blood of your Son,
> that, professing you not just in word or in speech
> but also in works and in truth,
> we may merit to enter the Kingdom of Heaven.
> Through Christ our Lord.

Here we see a further meaning to the rite of Holy Communion. Just as Elijah on his pilgrimage to the holy mountain of Horeb was told by the angel, "Arise and eat, else the journey will be too great for you" (1 Kgs 19:7), so is this sacred meal food for the journey, the journey of our whole life as a passing over to the Lord through Christian living in the world. It is a food to strengthen the faithful—by the power of Christ working within them—to witness in their daily lives what they have heard and celebrated in the sacred liturgy.

Closing Rites

The closing rites begin once again with the presider's address to the congregation, "The Lord be with you." After receiving the response, "And with your spirit," the priest extends his hands over the people while pronouncing the words "May almighty God bless you, / the Father, and the Son, ✠ and the Holy Spirit," and making the sign of the cross over them. All respond, "Amen."

And then the priest gives the dismissal: "Go forth, the Mass is ended." This is the new translation of the ancient Latin, *Ite, missa est*, which literally means, "Go, it is the sending."[92] On the night before he died, Jesus told his disciples, "As the Father sent me, so do I send you" (John 21:20). Just as during his life on earth Jesus yearned to gather the inhabitants of Jerusalem to himself as a hen does her chicks (cf. Luke 13:34) and sent his apostles into the world to unite all with the Father in his name, so now the whole thrust of a true liturgical assembly, animated by the assembling Spirit of Christ, is also toward mission beyond the liturgy, to gather all of God's children into the one flock of the one Shepherd (cf. John 10:16).

The introductory words of the closing rites, "The Lord be with you," is the fourth use of this ancient greeting in the course of the Mass: the first introduces the introductory rites; the second, the gospel; the third, the preface and the whole eucharistic prayer; and the fourth, the closing rites with their dismissal. Corresponding to Thierry Maerten's four essential characteristics of the liturgical assembly, this greeting marks them out as special instances where Christ as presider engages his people: (1) God's call to assembly, (2) the proclamation of God's saving deeds in history, (3) the assembly's commitment to the Word of God it has just heard, and (4) the dismissal into living God's Word in the world. Once again, then, the closing rites of blessing and dismissal are not a mere act of adjournment but one of Christ's sending his assembly out into the world on mission, just as the apostles themselves were sent to witness to the ends of the earth, to gather all of God's children through Word and witness into the one assembly that is Christ.

Conclusions

In response, then, to the third of the three questions posed at the beginning of this study—namely, how Christ in his saving mysteries is present and acting in a typical Sunday celebration of the Roman Rite Eucharist—we can conclude that

1. just as Jesus of Nazareth as Son received the full gift of the Father in the limits of his humanity by fully identifying himself, through his theandric love, with all humankind,

2. so do church members receive themselves as God's self-gift in Christ by their mutual sharing in the church's grateful liturgical remembrance of Christ's saving events, fully realized in their reception of Communion; and

3. configuring participants to Christ in his saving events through the church's typological thanksgiving memorial, the liturgy in effect sends them out into the world as his "sacraments," to continue *by the pattern of their lives* his reconciling work (cf. 2 Cor 5:18-21) of assembling all of humankind into his one perfect worship of the Father.

Notes, Chapter Seven

[1] A tradition that goes back to the very beginnings of Christianity: cf. 1 Cor 16:1-4; 2 Cor 8-9; Gal 2:10; Jas 2:15-16.

[2] *Graduale Sacrosanctae Romanae Ecclesiae de Tempore et de Sanctis* (Sablé sur Sarthe, France: Abbaye Saint-Pierre de Solesmes, 1979), 301.

³ Justin Martyr, *First Apology* 67, in *Ante-Nicene Fathers*, vol. 1, ed. Alexander Roberts and James Donaldson (Buffalo: The Christian Literature Publishing Co., 1885–96), 186. Cf. Niels Krogh Rasmussen, OP, "Les rites de présentation du pain et du vin," *La Maison-Dieu* 100 (1969): 45.

⁴ Joseph A. Jungmann, SJ, *The Mass of the Roman Rite*, vol. 2 (New York: Benziger Bros., 1955), 20n108.

⁵ Ibid., 26n1.

⁶ Tertullian, *De exhortatione castitatis* 11.

⁷ *Apostolic Tradition* 4:2:"And let the deacons offer to [the bishop] the oblations" (Paul F. Bradshaw, Maxwell E. Johnson, and L. Edward Phillips, eds., *The Apostolic Tradition: A Commentary* [Minneapolis: Fortress Press, 2002], 38; hereafter abbreviated AT).

⁸ Cyprian of Carthage, *Liber de opere et elemosynis* 15 (CSEL III, 384).

⁹ Joseph A Jungmann, SJ, The *Mass of the Roman Rite*, vol. 1 (New York: Benziger Bros., 1951), 2–6.

¹⁰ Rasmussen, "Les rites," 48–49 (emphases in original).

¹¹ Ibid., 50. Note how the *offero* of the prayer is still operative in the "extraordinary form" of the Roman Rite: "Suscipe, Sancte Pater, omnipotens aeterne Deus, hanc immaculatam hostiam, quam *ego* indignus famulus tuus *offero tibi* . . ." (emphasis added). For an explanation of the relationship of the priest-presider to the rest of the assembly in the eucharistic sacrifice, see David Coffey, "The Common and the Ordained Priesthood," *Theological Studies* 58 (1997): 209–36.

¹² Rasmussen, "Les rites," 51.

¹³ Cf. Odo Casel, *The Mystery of Christian Worship*, ed. Burkhard Neunheuser (New York: Crossroad, 1999).

¹⁴ Alex Stock, "Gabenbereitung: Zur Logik des Opfers," *Liturgisches Jahrbuch* 53 (2003): 36.

¹⁵ Ibid., 35.

¹⁶ Jozef Lamberts, "Preparation of the Gifts, Offertory or Celebrating Creation?" *Questions liturgiques* 78 (1997): 32.

¹⁷ "Originally at the special anamnesis [of the eucharistic prayer] the bread and wine were still offered as expressing the willingness of the celebrating community to open herself [*sic*] to God. She [*sic*] had begun to express this willingness at what is called now the Preparation of the Gifts, and whose earlier name 'Offertory' may be more appropriate." Cor Traets, SJ, "Sacrificial Event, Meal Rite, Presence: Some Considerations about the Eucharist," *Questions liturgiques* 88 (2007): 275.

¹⁸ Joseph Gelineau, SJ, *Voices and Instruments in Christian Worship: Principles, Laws, Applications*, trans. Clifford Howell, SJ (Collegeville, MN: Liturgical Press, 1964), 189 (emphasis added). The traditional mystagogical interpretation of "The Great Entrance" of the Byzantine liturgy, originating from St. Germanus of Constantinople (+ 730), makes this same proleptic identification of Christ with the bread and wine of the offertory procession. In the bread and wine, worshipers are to see the crucified Christ being brought forward to the altar as to his sepulcher to be raised up by the anaphoral epiclesis of the Holy Spirit. Cf. Robert F. Taft, SJ, "The Liturgy of the Great Church: An Initial Synthesis of Structure and Interpretation on the Eve of Iconoclasm," *Dumbarton Oaks Papers*, vol. 34/35 (1980/1981): 45–75, esp. 54–55.

[19] Adolf Adam, "Eucharistiches Hochgebet und Selbstofer der Christen," in *Gratias Agamus: Studien zum Eucharistischen Hochgebet; Für Balthasar Fischer*, ed. Andreas Heinz and Heinrich Rennings (Freiburg: Herder, 1992), 5: "Insofern und nur insofern wird das sakamental vergegenwärtigte Opfer Christi auch Opfer der Kirche."

[20] *Daily Prayer Book*, trans. Joseph H. Hertz (New York: Bloch Publishing Company, 1948), 409.

[21] Stock, "Gabenbereitung," 37.

[22] Jeremy Driscoll, OSB, writes, "We bring our lives—with all our efforts to produce and to be together in love, with all our desire and our willingness to share—and we place them in the hands of Christ by placing them in the hands of the bishop" ("Eucharist: Source and Summit of the Church's Communion," *Ecclesia Orans* 21 [2004]: 215).

[23] Augustine, *Enarrationes in psalmos* 98.9, in *Corpus Christianorum* 39, ed. Eligius Dekkers and Johannes Fraipoint (Eindhoven: Thesaurus Linguae Augustinianae, 1985), 1385–86.

[24] J. P. de Jong demonstrates in a series of five theses that in essence this same theology can be found already in the *Adversus haereses* of Irenaeus (ca. 185) ("Der ursprüngliche Sinn ver Epiklese und Mischungsritus nach der Eucharistielehre des hl. Irenäus," *Archiv für Liturgiewissenschaft* 9:1 [1965]: 28–47, esp. 31–40, as quoted by Robert F. Taft, SJ, in "Understanding the Byzantine Anaphoral Oblation," in *Rule of Prayer, Rule of Faith: Essays in Honor of Aidan Kavanagh, O.S.B.*, ed. Nathan Mitchell and John F. Baldovin, SJ [Collegeville, MN: Liturgical Press, 1996], 46–47).

[25] Cf. Cyprian of Carthage, *Epistle* 63:13.

[26] Cf. Fernand Cabrol, "Apologies," *Dictionnaire d'archéologie chrétienne et de liturgie*, eds. Fernand Cabrol and Henri Leclercq (Paris: Letouzey et Ané, 1920–53), cols. 2591–601. Over the years much criticism has been made of the continuance in the new liturgy of these particular "apologies." Cf., e.g., Rasmussen, "Les rites," 51–58; Ralph A. Kiefer, "Preparation of the Altar and the Gifts or Offertory?" *Worship* 48, no.10 (1974): 595–600; and Edward Foley, OFM Cap., Kathleen Hughes, RSCJ, and Gilbert Ostdiek, OFM, "The Preparatory Rites: A Case Study in Liturgical Ecology," *Worship* 67, no.1 (1993): 17–38, esp. 29–30.

[27] Cf. Edward J. Kilmartin, SJ, "Sacrificium Laudis: Content and Function of Early Eucharistic Prayers," *Theological Studies* 35 (1974): 268–87.

[28] Cf. 1 Cor 11:23-25; Mark 14:17-26; Matt 26:20-30; Luke 22:14-39.

[29] Paul Bradshaw, *Reconstructing Early Christian Worship* (Collegeville, MN: Liturgical Press, 2010), 3–19 = "Did Jesus Institute the Eucharist at the Last Supper?" in *Issues in Eucharistic Praying in East and West: Essays in Liturgical and Theological Analysis*, ed. Maxwell E. Johnson (Collegeville, MN: Liturgical Press, 2011). Cf. also Paul F. Bradshaw, *Eucharistic Origins* (New York: Oxford University Press, 2004), 1–23.

[30] "'Was it not necessary that the Christ should suffer these things and enter into his glory?' . . . Then they told what had happened on the road, and how he was known to them in the breaking of the bread" (Luke 24:26, 35).

[31] For a 1995 summary of prior scholarship on the question, see Benoît Thivierge, "The Eucharistic Prayer: From Jewish Prayer to Christian Anaphora," *Liturgical Ministry* 4 (Summer 1995): 97–108.

[32] Cesare Giraudo, *La struttura letteraria della preghiera eucaristica* (Rome: Biblical Institute Press, 1981). In addition, either section of the prayer could be fitted with an "embolism" quoting God's own words as divine warrant for the authority and efficacy of the prayer, such as Jesus' Last Supper injunction, "Do this in memory of me." Cf. Cesare Giraudo, SJ, "Le récit de l'institution dans la prière eucharistique: A-t-il de antécédents?" *Nouvelle revue théologique* (1984): 513–36.

[33] *The Origins of the Eucharistic Prayer*, trans. Ronald E. Lane (Collegeville, MN: Liturgical Press, 1995). A summary form of his argument can be found in "The Eucharist in the First Four Centuries," in *Handbook for Liturgical Studies*, vol. 3, *The Eucharist*, ed. Anscar J. Chupungco (Collegeville, MN: Liturgical Press, 1999), 9–60, esp. 9–31.

[34] For a reconstruction of the ancient *Birkat ha-Mazon* text, see Louis Finkelstein, "The Birkat Ha-Mazon," *Jewish Quarterly Review* 19 (1928–29): 211–62. Its English translation is also available in Lucien Deiss, *Springtime of the Liturgy: Liturgical Texts of the First Four Centuries*, trans. Matthew J. O'Connell (Collegeville, MN: Liturgical Press, 1979), 7–9.

[35] Bradshaw, *Reconstructing*, 52.

[36] Paul F. Bradshaw, *The Search for the Origins of Christian Worship: Sources and Methods for the Study of Early Liturgy*, 2nd ed. (New York: Oxford University Press, 2002), 138. David N. Power writes, "In light of the mass of studies that are almost too many to be mastered, one may mention a number of cautions for a study of elements in the eucharistic prayer. Historical study cannot retrieve a single matrix, as GIRM and BEM might have us believe." "A Prayer of Intersecting Parts: Elements of the Eucharistic Prayer," *Liturgical Ministry* 14 (Summer 2005): 121.

[37] Thivierge, "The Eucharistic Prayer," 101.

[38] For scholarly assessment of the origin and nature of this fascinating document, see Paul F. Bradshaw et al., eds., *The Apostolic Tradition*, "Introduction," 1–16; see also Bradshaw, *The Search*, 80–97.

[39] Ibid., 37–48.

[40] If Paul Griffiths's basing the authenticity of scriptural translations on their use in the church's liturgy is valid, a fortiori the same principle would apply to eucharistic prayers in her liturgical use of them: "Which are the Words of Scripture?" *Theological Studies* 72, no. 4 (December 2011): 703–22.

[41] Daniel McCarthy, OSB, "Living Eternally Now," *The Tablet* (January 22, 2011): 14; cf. also Maxwell E. Johnson, "*Tempus per Annum*: Celebrating the Mystery of Christ in All Its Fullness," *Liturgical Ministry* 17 (Fall 2008): 154–56.

[42] "Even greater than the sheer beauty of specific creatures—a rainbow, a sound, a bird in flight—is the sudden sense of the gratuitousness of all things. The wonder of being at all: this is the origin and the ever-refreshing source of gratitude in the human heart. . . . We may regard Christian liturgy and its central prayer forms as an expression of the primordial gratuitousness of being. As communal prayer and ritual action it also forms human capacities to receive the world as gift and to live thankfully within it. To recite the wonders of nature and history to the source of all being, and to invoke the animating power of all life is to learn gratitude as well as to express thanksgiving and praise." Don E. Saliers, *Worship As Theology: Foretaste of Glory Divine* (Nashville: Abington, 1994), 103.

[43] Robert Cabié, *The Eucharist*, ed. Aimé Georges Martimort, trans. Matthew J. O'Connell, The Church at Prayer series (Collegeville, MN: Liturgical Press, 1986), 94–96.

[44] With the addition of the phrase "Heaven and earth . . ."—thus Robert Taft, SJ, "The Interpolation of the Sanctus into the Anaphora: When and Where? A Review of the Dossier," part 1, *Orientalia Christiana Periodica* 57 (1991): 285. Cf. also Maxwell E. Johnson, "The Origins of the Anaphoral Use of the Sanctus and Epiclesis Revisited: The Contribution of Gabriele Winkler and Its Implications," in *Crossroad of Cultures: Studies in Liturgy and Patristics in Honor of Gabriele Winkler*, ed. Hans-Jürgen Feulner et al. (Rome: Pontificio Istituto Orientale, 2000), 405–42.

[45] The opening "Hosanna to the Son of David" becomes "Hosanna in the highest."

[46] Taft, "The Interpolation," part 2, *Orientalia Christiana Periodica* 58 (1992): 120.

[47] "If the allusion to the 'dewfall of the Spirit' is traditional (cf. Postcommunion of Pentecost), the expression seems born from the combination of two texts: *Spiritua Sancti tui rore perfundas* in the *Missale Gothicum* (# 271, ed. Mohlberg) and *caelestis unguneti rore sanctifica* in the Roman Pontifical (ancient consecration prayer of the bishop)." Pierre Jounel, "La composition des nouvelles prières eucharistiques," *La Maison-Dieu* 94 (1968): 49.

[48] E.g., Hans Bernhard, Meyer, SJ, *Eucharistie: Geschichte, Theologie, Pastoral*, Gottesdienst Der Kirche: Handbuch der Liturgiewissenschaft series (Regensburg: Verlag Friedrich Pustet, 1989), 146.

[49] "The hypothetical quality of some conclusions needs to be kept in view, for example, on the role and provenance of the double epiclesis in [the] Alexandrian tradition." Power, "A Prayer of Intersecting Parts," 122.

[50] The *Quam oblationem* and the *Supplices te rogamus*. Cf. Richard Albertine, "The Epiclesis Problem—The Roman Canon (Canon 1) in the Post-Vatican Liturgical Reform," *Ephemerides Liturgicae* 109, nos. 4–5 (1985): 337–48.

[51] Paul De Clerck, "Les épiclèses des nouvelles prières eucharistiques du rite romain: Leur importance théologique," *Ecclesia Orans* 16 (1999): 202.

[52] Traets, "Sacrificial Event," 274. In regard to earlier efforts to determine when the Eucharist bread and wine become Christ's Body and Blood, see Robert F. Taft, SJ, "Ecumenical Scholarship and the Catholic-Orthodox Epiclesis Dispute," *Ostkirchliche Studien* 45 (1996): 201–26, esp. 222–23.

[53] Cf. Louis-Marie Chauvet, *Symbol and Sacrament: A Sacramental Reinterpretation of Christian Existence*, trans. Patrick Madigan, SJ, and Madeleine Beaumont (Collegeville, MN: Liturgical Press, 1995), chap. 1, "Critique of the Onto-Theological Presuppositions of Classical Sacramental Theology," 7–45.

[54] *Sermo.* 74, 2 (PL 54: 398a): "Quod Redemptoris conspicuum fuit in sacramenta transivit."

[55] Edward J. Kilmartin, SJ, "Sacrificium Laudis: Content and Function of Early Eucharistic Prayers," *Theological Studies* 35 (1974): 269. Kilmartin provides a parallel interpretation of the words over the cup on p. 270.

[56] Cf. Edward J. Kilmartin, SJ, "The Catholic Tradition of Eucharistic Theology: Towards the Third Millennium," *Theological Studies* 55 (1994): 405–58.

[57] "By the action of the Holy Spirit in the transformation of the gifts of bread and wine—gifts which represent at one and the same time the specific history of Christ

and the specific history of the community which brings the gifts—the life and death that Christ underwent in history is brought into profound accord with the life in history that I am living. His particular life from a moment in history far different from my own is meant to function as the only norm and the only meaning of my time in history. Only the Spirit could bridge this otherwise impossible gap. Within one same dynamic, the Spirit who raised Jesus from the dead and who forms and fashions the vessels for the liturgy also forms and fashions from the infinite wealth hidden in the life of Christ the wonderful variety of history, giving to the church of every age and to every believer a unique time in which to live which derives from the unique time in which Jesus of Nazareth lived. But not only does it derive from this past. It derives likewise from the future in which Jesus, risen in the Spirit, already stands. It is this already existing future Jesus in whom I too find the destiny toward which my present, whose origins are in his past, is directed. I can only speak in these terms—and survive this paradoxical language—by relying on the cultic celebration which manages successfully to hold in tension the dialectic between history and the eschaton. The cultic celebration is anamnesis and epiclesis inextricably intertwined and overlapping." Jeremy Driscoll, OSB, "Anamnesis, Epiclesis and Fundamental Theology," *Ecclesia Orans* 15 (1998): 230. Cf. also John D. Laurance, SJ, "The Eucharist as the Imitation of Christ," *Theological Studies* 47 (1986): 286–96.

[58] Cf. Mary M. Schaefer, "Heavenly and Earthly Liturgies: Patristic Prototypes, Medieval Perspectives, and a Contemporary Application," *Worship* 70 (November 1996): 482–505, esp. 503–5.

[59] Giraudo, *La struttura*.

[60] Cf. Giraudo, SJ, "Le récit," 513–36; Power, "A Prayer of Intersecting Parts," 127.

[61] Chauvet, *Symbol and Sacrament*, 276 (emphasis in original). And as noted earlier, according to Karl Rahner, "Our whole existence [consists in] *the acceptance or rejection of the mystery which we are*" ("On the Theology of the Incarnation," in *Theological Investigations*, vol. 4, trans. Kevin Smyth [Baltimore: Helicon Press, 1966], 108 [emphasis added]).

[62] "Corpus ergo Christi si vis intelligere, Apostolum audi dicentem fidelibus, 'Vos autem estis corpus Christi, et membra' (I Cor. XII, 27). Si ergo vos estis corpus Christi et membra, mysterium vestrum in mensa Dominica positum est: mysterium vestrum accipitis. Ad id quod estis, Amen respondetis, et respondendo subscribitis. Audis enim, Corpus Christi; et respondes, Amen. Esto membrum corporis Christi, ut verum sit Amen." Augustine, *Sermo* 272, *In die Pentecostes postremus: Ad infantes, de sacramento* (*PL* 38:1247).

[63] Cf. George E. McCracken, ed., *Early Medieval Theology* (Philadelphia: Westminster Press, 1957), 90–147; Gary Macy, *The Theologies of the Eucharist in the Early Scholastic Period* (Oxford: Clarendon Press, 1984), 1–43; Gary Macy, *The Banquet's Wisdom: A Short History of the Theologies of the Lord's Supper* (Mahwah, NJ: Paulist, 1992), 70–73; James T. O'Connor, *The Hidden Manna: A Theology of the Eucharist*, 2nd ed. (San Francisco: Ignatius, 2005), 85–94.

[64] Cf. John D. Laurance, SJ, "The Eucharist and Eucharistic Adoration," *Louvain Studies* 26 (2001): 313–33.

[65] Tertullian, *Against Marcion* (ca. 207–12) (CSEL 47, 36, 29–37, 4).

[66] Cyril of Jerusalem, *Mystagogical catecheses* IV, 3: *En tupô gar artou . . .* (For in the figure of bread . . .).

[67] Ambrose, *De sacramentis* IV, 21, 25 (*quod est figura corporis et sanguinis Domini nostri Iesu Christi*).

[68] *Saint Cyprien: Correspondance*, vol. 2, ed. Louis Bayard (Paris: Société d'Édition "Les Belles Lettres," 1925), 208 (emphasis added).

[69] "Be constant in the assembly of the church . . . so that no one diminishes the church by failing to assemble, thus causing the body of Christ to be short of a member." Sebastian Brock and Michael Vasey, eds., *The Liturgical Portions of the Didascalia*, Grove Liturgical Study 29 (Bramcote Notts.: Grove Books, 1982), 17. The classic example of the strengthening power of this corporate expression of faith is the tenth-century report emissaries brought back to Prince Vladimir of Kiev about the Divine Liturgy at the Church of Hagia Sophia in Constantinople: "We know only that God dwells there among men, and their service is fairer than the ceremonies of other nations. For we cannot forget that beauty" (Quoted in Robert Taft, SJ, "The Spirit of Eastern Christian Worship," *Diakonia* 12 [1977]: 104).

[70] Adam, "Eucharistiches Hochgebet," 5. Recall the observation made in chap. 2 above: "If, according to Colossians, 'all the *fullness* of God was pleased to dwell' in Jesus (1:19; emphasis added), similarly is the church, as Ephesians tells us, 'his body, the *fullness* of him who fills all in all' (1:23; emphasis added)."

[71] Ephrem the Deacon, *Diatessaron* 1:18-19.

[72] Justin Martyr, *Apologia* I, 67; quoted in Lucien Deiss, CSSp, ed., *Springtime of the Liturgy* (Collegeville, MN: Liturgical Press, 1979), 93.

[73] "Ad hoc dicitis Amen. Amen dicere subscribere est" (PL 46:836); quoted in Jungmann, *Mass of the Roman Rite*, vol. 2, 273n78.

[74] Cyprian, *De dominica oratione*, 8 (PL 4:521). Ambroos Verheul, OSB, suggests that the Roman Rite introduction to the Lord's Prayer ("At the Savior's command . . .") was fashioned from wording found in the writings of St. Cyprian ("Le 'Notre Pere' et l'Eucharistie," *Questions liturgiques* 67 [1986]: 162).

[75] Cf. chap. 2 above.

[76] Robert Taft, SJ, "The Lord's Prayer in the Eucharistic Liturgy: When and Why?" *Ecclesia Orans* 14 (1997): 138.

[77] Ibid., 150.

[78] Ibid., 152.

[79] Tertullian, *De oratione* 6:1 (PL 1:1160-61). Similarly Cyprian: "We ask in this prayer 'that we might receive each day our bread, that is, that we might be able to receive Christ, to have the power to remain and live with him and not be separated from his Body and from his grace" (*De dominica oratione* 18; PL 4:531-32). For further patristic examples, see Verheul, "Le 'Notre Pere,'" 163-70. Regarding the difference between "supersubstantial" (*epiousion*: Matt 6:11; Luke 11:3) and "daily" bread, see Ambrose of Milan, *De sacramentis* V:24-26 (PL 16:452-53).

[80] "It seemed exceedingly unsuitable to me that we would say an intercession over the offering which a scholar had composed and that we would not say the very tradition that our Redeemer had composed over his body and blood." Gregory the Great, *Liber* 11, *ep.* 12 (PL 77:956D-57A), quoted in Gary Macy, "Who and How:

Debates about Consecration in the Twelfth Century," a paper presented at the North American Academy of Liturgy annual meeting, January, 2003, Indianapolis, Indiana.

[81] Cabié, *The Eucharist*, 109.

[82] For much of this history, I rely here on L. Edward Phillips, *The Ritual Kiss in Early Christian Worship*, Alcuin/GROW Liturgical Study series (Cambridge, England: Grove Books Ltd., 1996), passim.

[83] Innocent I, *La lettre du Pape Innocent Ier a Decentius de Gubbio*, ed. Robert Cabié (Louvain: Publications Universitaires de Louvain, 1973), lines 37–43, pp. 20, 22.

[84] Rick Hilgartner, "The Sign of Peace," *Liturgical Ministry* 20 (2011): 140.

[85] Innocent I, *La lettre du Pape*, lines 92–101, pp. 26, 28.

[86] This standard interpretation that Innocent sent the *fermentum* to be included in eucharistic liturgies celebrated by titular priests on Sunday has been recently affirmed by Antoine Chavasse, "Le *fermentum* instrument d'unité dans la liturgie de la ville de Rome," *Ecclesia Orans* 13 (1996): 435–38; and Marcel Metzger, "The History of the Eucharistic Liturgy in Rome, in *Handbook for Liturgical Studies*, vol. 3, *The Eucharist*, ed. Anscar J. Chupungco, OSB (Collegeville, MN: Liturgical Press, 1997), 106–9. For a summary of alternative scholarly interpretations, cf. John Baldovin, SJ, who offers a different translation of this passage ("The *Fermentum* at Rome in the Fifth Century: A Reconsideration," *Worship* 79, no. 1 [January 2005]: 38–53).

[87] Cf. Ignatius of Antioch: "Let no one do anything that has to do with the church without the bishop. Only that Eucharist which is under the authority of the bishop (or whomever he himself designates) is to be considered valid." *To the Smyrnaeans* 8:1, in *The Apostolic Fathers*, ed. Michael W. Holmes (Grand Rapids, MI: Baker Books, 1999), 189.

[88] Cf., e.g., Thomas O'Loughlin, "The Praxis and Explanations of Eucharistic Fraction in the Ninth Century: The Insular Evidence," *Archiv für Liturgiewissenschaft* 45 (2003): 1–20.

[89] Gregory Dix, *The Shape of the Liturgy* (London: Dacre, 1945): 49.

[90] Louis-Marie Chauvet, "Le pain rompu comme figure théologique de la présence eucharistique," *Questions liturgiques* 82 (2001): 25.

[91] Ibid., 32.

[92] Cf. Jungmann, *Mass of the Roman Rite*, vol 1, 173; Adrian Nocent, "Storia della celebrazione dell'eucaristia," in *Eucaristia: Teologia e storia della celebrazione*, Anàmnesis series (Genova: Marietti, 1991), 189–90.

Index of Documents

Index of Scripture References

Index of Proper Names

Index of Subjects